Preface

The Companies Act 1985, which is effective from 1st July 1985, comprises 747 sections and 25 schedules and represents the culmination of four years' work in consolidating the requirements of five major Companies Acts (1948, 1967, 1976, 1980 and 1981) and supporting legislation.

This book aims to guide readers through those parts of the 1985 Act (and related ancillary legislation) which are of particular relevance to accountants, whether in public practice or in industry or commerce generally, and to company administrators. The interaction between the statutory provisions and those of relevant Statements of Standard Accounting Practice is also considered.

The statutory provisions described in this book include:

- the choice of accounting periods and rules governing the preparation, audit and publication of accounts;
- the format and content of accounts;
- reregistration of a private company as public;
- share premium and merger relief;
- distribution of profits and assets;
- transactions with directors;
- financial assistance for and purchase and redemption of own shares.

The text is cross-referenced to the appropriate sections and schedules of the legislation.

The views expressed by the authors do not necessarily represent those of Peat Marwick. The legislation itself should be consulted and appropriate professional advice should be obtained before acting in relation to matters of doubt or of a complex nature.

The authors are grateful to Tolley Publishing Company Limited for their agreement to the use in this book of revised material based on *Guide to Directors' Transactions* by Michael Steen and John Aldis and to the Institute of Chartered Accountants in England and Wales to use revised material from *The Companies Act 1981 Handbook* edited by Alan Hardcastle and Michael Renshall.

Finally, the authors wish to acknowledge the assistance given to them by their colleagues in the Professional Practice Department of Peat Marwick.

Michael Renshall
John Aldis

London
June 1985

The Companies Act 1985

A guide to the accounting and reporting requirements

Michael Renshall and John Aldis
PEAT, MARWICK, MITCHELL & Co.

THE INSTITUTE OF CHARTERED ACCOUNTANTS
IN ENGLAND AND WALES
P.O. BOX 433 CHARTERED ACCOUNTANTS' HALL
MOORGATE PLACE, LONDON EC2P 2BJ

1985

The views expressed in this book are those of the authors and are not necessarily those of the Council of the Institute.

No responsibility for loss occasioned to any person acting or refraining from action as a result of any material in this publication can be accepted by the authors or publishers.

Typeset at Hands Fotoset, Leicester.
Printed and bound at The Bath Press, Avon

Distributed by:
VAN NOSTRAND
REINHOLD (U.K.)
MOLLY MILLARS LANE
WOKINGHAM, BERKS.
RG11 2PY, ENGLAND

Contents

Contents

Chapter 3: PROCEDURE ON COMPLETION OF ACCOUNTS
(contd.)

Chapter 4: PRESCRIBED FORMATS FOR THE ACCOUNTS

Chapter 5: ACCOUNTING PRINCIPLES

Contents

Contents

Contents

Contents

Contents

Contents

Abbreviations used in this book

1948 Act	=	Companies Act 1948
1967 Act	=	Companies Act 1967
1980 Act	=	Companies Act 1980
1981 Act	=	Companies Act 1981
1985 Act	=	Companies Act 1985
The Act	=	Companies Act 1985
B.N. Act	=	Business Names Act 1985
ED	=	Exposure Draft
IAS	=	International Accounting Standard
SI	=	Statutory Instrument
SSAP	=	Statement of Standard Accounting Practice
USM	=	Unlisted Securities Market

Table of statutory references

There follows a list of the sections and schedules of the Companies Act 1985 and other legislation which are referred to in the chapters of this book, together with the appropriate paragraph references.

Section	Paragraph(s)	Section	Paragraph(s)
Limited Partnerships Act 1907	25.07	42	20.50
		87	14.02
Registration of Business Names		Part II	12.03,13.02
Act 1916	25.01,25.28		
		Business Names Act 1985	1.04
Companies Act 1948		1 (1)	25.24
19	25.14	(2)	25.25
56	19.02	2 (1)	25.26
161 (1)(b)	15.13	(2)	25.28
190	7.07	(3)	25.28
191 to 194	7.50	(4)	25.36
Schedule 1 – Table A	1.05,12.25,	3	25.26
	20.07,20.08	(1)	25.35
Schedule 8A	1.06,19.26	(2)	25.37
		4	25.34
Restrictive Trade Practices Act 1956		(1)	25.29
15 (3)	30.09	(2)	25.30
		(3)	25.31
Companies Act (Northern Ireland)		(4)	25.32
1960	25.07	(5)	25.29
356	25.07	(6)	25.32
		(7)	25.32
Industrial and Provident Societies		5	25.34
Act 1965	25.07	6 (1)	25.38
		8 (1)	25.28
Companies Act 1967			
13 (1)	15.14	*Companies Act 1985*	
		1 (3)	21.25
Industrial and Provident Societies Act		25 (1)	25.02
(Northern Ireland) 1969	25.07	(2)	25.02
		26	25.09
Interpretation Act 1978		26 (1)	25.03
Schedule 1	6.07	(2)	25.04
		(3)	25.06
Banking Act 1979	12.03,13.02,30.06,31.04	27 (3)	25.21
		(4)	25.02,25.21
Companies Act 1980		28 (1)	25.09
54 (1)(c)	29.22	(2)	25.10
(2)(c)	29.22	(3)	25.11
		(4)	25.10,25.11
Companies Act 1981		(6)	25.09,25.12
38	19.23,19.26	(7)	25.13
		29	25.04
Insurance Companies Act 1982	20.50	(1)	25.35
18	20.50	(2)	25.36

Table of Statutory Instruments

The Statutory Instruments referred to in this book are noted below together with the appropriate paragraph references.

CHAPTER 1

Introduction

1.01 "There is now a 1985 Companies Act. The consolidation of company law which will be of direct benefit to every company, every shareholder and every company adviser in the country and which has been so eagerly awaited has now taken place". These enthusiastic words were used by the corporate and consumer affairs minister when announcing that the Companies Act 1985 and related Acts had received Royal Assent on 11th March 1985.

1.02 The Companies Act 1985 ("The Act") is one of the largest enactments on the statute book and comprises 747 sections and 25 schedules and came into force on 1st July 1985. The process of consolidation was authorised by the Companies Act 1981 and took four years to complete. It resulted in the consolidation of five major Companies Acts (1948, 1967, 1976, 1980 and 1981) as well as other minor Acts, parts of Acts and statutory instruments. Apart from some technical amendments, the substance of the law has not changed. The Act applies to Great Britain only (not Northern Ireland).

1.03 One practical consequence of the consolidation is that all the "prescribed forms" for filing with the registrar of companies have had to be revised. The opportunity has been taken to renumber the forms, generally corresponding to the section of the Act to which they relate. References in this book to the number of a particular form are to its new number. Transitionally, until 30th June 1986, companies are permitted to use both the new and the old forms.

1.04 As well as the Companies Act 1985, the consolidation also comprises a few ancillary Acts: the "Business Names Act 1985", "Company Securities (Insider Dealing) Act 1985", and the "Companies Consolidation (Consequential Provisions) Act 1985". In order to assist practitioners familiar with the previous legislation, tables of derivations and destinations are available. The tables of derivations are bound in at the back of each of the consolidating Acts; they start from the sections in the 1985 legislation and refer to the sections in the previous legislation from which the new sections are derived. Conversely, the table of destinations, which is published separately by HMSO, starts from the sections in the old legislation and sets out how each section has been dealt with, either in the 1985 consolidation or by previous repeal.

1.05 The previous "model" form of articles and memorandum (Tables A to F of Schedule 1 to the 1948 Act) have not been consolidated but have been revised and reissued in Statutory Instrument 1985 No. 805. The revised versions apply to companies incorporated on or after 1st July 1985. A few statutory instruments made under the authority of the old legislation are to be remade; they are referred to in this book where appropriate.

1.06 The detailed accounting disclosure requirements for banks, insurance and shipping companies which prepare their accounts under Schedule 9 of the 1985 Act (previously Schedule 8A of the Companies Act 1948) are not included in this book. The basic structure under which such companies report is, however, described in Chapter 13.

1.07 This book aims to guide readers through those parts of the Acts which are of particular relevance to accountants, whether in public practice or in industry or commerce generally, and to company administrators. However, two important areas are not dealt with in this book as there are likely to be major changes to the law in the near future. These are (1) liquidations and receiverships, which are the subject of the Insolvency Bill currently going through parliament, and (2) prospectuses and related requirements, which are likely to change when the planned Financial Services or Investor Protection Act is passed in the 1985/86 session of parliament.

1.08 The Acts themselves should also be consulted and appropriate professional advice should be obtained before acting in relation to matters of doubt or of a complex nature.

CHAPTER 2

Accounting periods and requirement to prepare accounts

2.01 The Act requires companies to prepare annual accounts which cover an "accounting reference period". Group accounts are generally also required where a company has subsidiaries, unless the company is itself a wholly-owned subsidiary of another British company. A company's accounting reference period is determined by the company's choice of "accounting reference date". Once chosen, an accounting reference date may be altered only in defined circumstances and by following the procedure set out in the Act. The Secretary of State has wide powers to amend by statutory instrument the information to be included in accounts and the documents to be comprised in a company's accounts [s256].

Selection of accounting reference date

2.02 Within six months of its date of incorporation, a company should give notice, in the prescribed form (form number 224), to the registrar of companies of its intended accounting reference date; that is, the date (day and month) on which in each successive calendar year an accounting reference period of the company is to end. Failure to give such notice within the time limit will result in the company automatically being allocated 31st March as its accounting reference date [s224(2),(3)]. Provided it follows the prescribed procedures within the time limit allowed, a company which has been allocated 31st March may alter it to a date which is more suitable for its purposes (see below) [s224(5)].

2.03 A company's first accounting reference period runs from its date of incorporation to its accounting reference date so as to result in a period which exceeds six months but does not exceed eighteen months. Subsequent accounting reference periods will be for twelve months unless the accounting reference date is altered (see below) [s224(4)]. It is possible that, by following the procedure for altering an accounting

3

reference date, a company may (if it wishes) have a first accounting reference period of six months or less (see also example (3) below).

Examples:

(1) A Ltd was incorporated on 1st May 1985 and did not notify an accounting reference date within the period allowed. Its first accounting reference period is from 1st May 1985 to 31st March 1986, a period of eleven months.

(2) B Ltd was incorporated on 1st April 1985 and, within the time allowed, notified 30th September as its accounting reference date. Its first accounting reference period is 1st April 1985 to 30th September 1986 (that is, a period which *exceeds* six months but does not exceed eighteen months).

(3) C Ltd was incorporated on 1st July 1985. For commercial reasons it wishes to have a first accounting reference period of two months (that is, up to 31st August 1985). If it nominates 31st August as its accounting reference date, the normal operation of the rules will result in its first accounting reference period being for the fourteen months from 1st July 1985 to 31st August 1986. It appears that a two month accounting reference period from 1st July 1985 to 31st August 1985 can be achieved by initially notifying another date, say 30th September, as its accounting reference date and subsequently changing it to 31st August, so that it results in a *shortened* period ending on 31st August 1985.

Alteration of accounting reference date

2.04 Section 225 of the Act provides the means by which an accounting reference date (and period) may be altered, either during the course of a current period or subsequently where the alteration is to bring that company's reference date into line with that of its holding or subsidiary company.

2.05 Where a company operates 52/53 week accounting periods, it is not necessary for it to change its accounting reference date for this purpose, because the Act allows accounts to be prepared as at a date which is up to seven days before or after its accounting reference date [s227(2)].

Alteration of current period

2.06 At any time during the course of an accounting reference period a company may give notice in the prescribed form (form 225(1)) to the registrar of companies specifying a date (the new accounting reference date) on which that accounting reference period (and each subsequent period) is to end or is to be treated as having come to an end [s225(1)].

The current period can thus be shortened or lengthened, but may not be for a period in excess of eighteen months [s225(4),(5)]. There are, however, restrictions on a company's ability to *extend* an accounting reference period and these are set out in para 2.11.

Example:

X plc has an accounting reference date of 31st December. On 1st October 1985 it notifies the registrar of companies that it wishes to change this to 30th June. Its previous accounts were made up to 31st December 1984. X plc has the choice of having an accounting reference period which runs:

(1) from 1st January 1985 to 30th June 1985 thereby shortening its current period so that it is to be treated as having ended on 30th June 1985, or

(2) from 1st January 1985 to 30th June 1986, thereby extending the current period to one of eighteen months.

Alteration of previous period

2.07 In the limited circumstances set out in the following paragraph, a company may, at any time after the end of an accounting reference period, give notice in the prescribed form (form 225(2)) to the registrar of companies specifying a (revised) date on which that (previous) period is to be regarded as having ended. Unless a further alteration is made, subsequent periods would also end on the revised date [s225(2)].

2.08 This facility is available only if the following conditions are satisfied:

(1) the company is a subsidiary or holding company of another British "company" (see below) and the new accounting reference date coincides with the accounting reference date of that other company, and

(2) the period allowed for laying and delivering accounts (see para 3.20) for its previous accounting reference period (as calculated before the alteration of that period) has not already expired when the notice is given.

[s225(3)]

"Company" means a company formed *and* registered under the 1985 Act or one of the earlier Companies Acts, and would thus not include a body corporate incorporated outside Great Britain, even if that body corporate was registered under the Companies Acts as an "oversea company" [s735(1)].

5

2.09 Alteration under this provision may result in a period which is shortened or which is extended [s225(4)], but no period may exceed eighteen months [s225(5)].

2.10 A company which wishes to take advantage of this facility to alter a previous accounting reference period but which does not have a holding or subsidiary company with the desired accounting reference date, may still be able to take advantage of the facility by acquiring an "off the shelf" company which has the required accounting reference date.

Extension of accounting reference period

2.11 Unless the Secretary of State otherwise allows [s225(7)], a notice which, in either of the above-mentioned cases, states that the current or previous accounting reference period is to be extended (whether or not that extended period is to be for longer than twelve months) will not be effective unless:

(1) no earlier period has been extended; or

(2) the notice is given not less than five years after the end of any earlier period which was extended; or

(3) the company is a subsidiary or holding company of another company and the new accounting reference date coincides with the accounting reference date of that other company.

[s225(6)]

Annual accounts of a company

Duty to prepare

2.12 The directors of a company are required to prepare a profit and loss account (or, if the company does not trade for profit, an income and expenditure account) in respect of every accounting reference period of the company [s227(1)] and a balance sheet as at the end of the "financial year" [s227(3)]. A financial year is the period covered by the profit and loss account. A company's first financial year begins on its date of incorporation (even though it may have commenced trading at a later date) and ends on the last day of its first accounting reference period or, if the directors so wish, on a day which is not more than seven days before or after the end of that period [s224(4), 227(2)]. Each successive financial year begins on the day after the date to which the preceding profit and loss account was made up and ends as just described [s227(2)].

2.13 Unless in their opinion there are good reasons against it, the directors of any holding company must ensure that the financial year of all its subsidiaries coincides with that of the company [s227(4)]. If they do not coincide, the holding company must have regard to the matters set out in paras 2.30 and 2.31.

Form and content of individual annual accounts

2.14 A company's individual accounts must comply with the requirements of Schedule 4 with respect to the form and content of the balance sheet and profit and loss account and also any additional information which has to be given in notes to the accounts [s228(1)]. Other sections and schedules of the Act prescribe further disclosures. The Secretary of State may, by statutory instrument, alter or add to the matters to be included in the accounts or directors' report [s256].

2.15 The balance sheet must give a true and fair view of the company's state of affairs as at the end of its financial year, and the profit and loss account must give a true and fair view of the company's profit or loss for the financial year [s228(2)]. This requirement to give a true and fair view is expressly stated as overriding Schedule 4, and all other requirements of the Act as to the matters to be included in the accounts or notes to the accounts [s228(3)]. Where mere compliance with those requirements would not provide sufficient information to give the required true and fair view, any necessary additional information must be given in the accounts or the notes to the accounts [s228(4)]. Exceptionally, where compliance with any such requirement of the Act would result in the accounts failing to give a true and fair view (even if additional information were given), the company must depart from that requirement so far as necessary to give a true and fair view [s228(5)]. Particulars of any such departure, the reasons for it and its effect must be given in a note to the accounts [s228(6)]. Where monetary amounts are involved, giving the effect of any departure would usually involve quantification.

2.16 A separate profit and loss account, dealing only with the results of a holding company, need not be prepared where the holding company's profit and loss account is framed as a consolidated profit and loss account dealing with all or any of its subsidiaries, provided that the consolidated profit and loss account:

(1) complies with the requirements of the Act, and

(2) shows how much of the consolidated profit or loss for the financial year is dealt with in the individual accounts of the company.

Furthermore, if group accounts are prepared and (as is normal practice) advantage is taken of this provision, that fact must be disclosed in a note to the group accounts [s228(7)].

The true and fair view

2.17 The requirement for individual company accounts and group accounts to give a true and fair view is stated to override, if necessary, the other provisions of the Act (see paras 2.15 and 2.29). The concept of true and fair presentation involves questions of judgement which cannot be prescribed in law, but which are frequently governed by generally accepted accounting practices. An authoritative source of such generally accepted practices is found in Statements of Standard Accounting Practice (SSAPs) issued under the auspices of the main UK accounting bodies. The SSAPs describe methods of accounting approved by those bodies for application (unless otherwise stated in an SSAP) to all financial statements intended to give a true and fair view of financial position and profit or loss. The statements have no statutory authority but the accounting bodies expect their members to observe them. As authoritative statements of accounting practice, SSAPs illuminate and elaborate on the requirements of the Act and, for this reason, they are frequently referred to in this book.

Group accounts

Requirement to prepare

2.18 Where at the end of its financial year a company has subsidiaries, the directors are required also to prepare group accounts; that is, accounts or statements which deal with the state of affairs and profit or loss of the company and its subsidiaries [s229(1)].

Exemption
2.19 Group accounts are not required where the company is at the end of the financial year the wholly-owned subsidiary of another body corporate incorporated in Great Britain [s229(2)]: A company is regarded as being the wholly-owned subsidiary of another body corporate only if the company has no members except that other body corporate and its wholly-owned subsidiaries and its or their nominees [s736(5)]. Thus if, for example, preference shares in a company are beneficially held by a third party, the company would not be wholly-owned.

Exclusions
2.20 Group accounts need not deal with a subsidiary if the company's directors are of the opinion that:

(1) it is impracticable, or would be of no real value to the company's members, in view of the insignificant amounts involved, or

(2) it would involve expense or delay out of proportion to the value to members, or

(3) the result would be misleading, or harmful to the business of the company or any of its subsidiaries, or

(4) the business of the holding company and that of the subsidiary are so different that they cannot reasonably be treated as a single undertaking;

and, if the directors are of that opinion about each of the company's subsidiaries, group accounts are not required [s229(3)].

2.21 However, the approval of the Secretary of State is required for not dealing in group accounts with a subsidiary on the grounds that the result would be harmful or on the grounds of difference between the business of the holding company and that of the subsidiary [s229(4)].

Manner of preparation

2.22 Subject to the following paragraph, group accounts must be in the form of consolidated accounts comprising:

(1) a consolidated balance sheet dealing with the state of affairs of the company and all of the subsidiaries to be dealt with in the group accounts, and

(2) a consolidated profit and loss account dealing with the profit or loss of the company and those subsidiaries.

[s229(5)]

2.23 However, if the directors are of the opinion that it is better for the purpose of presenting the *same or equivalent* information about the state of affairs and profit or loss of the company and those subsidiaries, *and* of so presenting it that it may be readily appreciated by the company's members, the group accounts may be prepared other than in consolidated form, and in particular may consist:

(1) of more than one set of consolidated accounts dealing respectively with the company and one group of subsidiaries and with other groups of subsidiaries, or

(2) of separate accounts dealing with each of the subsidiaries, or

(3) of statements in the company's individual accounts expanding the information about the subsidiaries.

or of any combination of those forms.
[s229(6)]

2.24 The group accounts may be wholly or partly incorporated in the holding company's individual balance sheet and profit and loss account [s229(7)]. The intention of this provision is unclear and would appear to be little (if ever) used in practice, particularly in view of the requirements of SSAP 14.

Statement of Standard Accounting Practice No. 14

2.25 SSAP 14 also envisages that consolidated accounts will be the normal form of group accounts and therefore requires that, except as indicated below, group accounts should be "in the form of a single set of consolidated financial statements covering the holding company and its subsidiary companies, at home and overseas". Paragraph 22 of SSAP 14 states "if a group prepares group accounts in a form other than consolidated financial statements [for example, in the manner set out in paras 2.23 and 2.24] in circumstances different from those set out in paragraph 21 [see 2.27 below], the onus is on the directors to justify and state the reasons for reaching the conclusion that the resulting group accounts give a fairer view of the financial position of the group as a whole. Similar considerations apply where consolidated financial statements are prepared dealing with a subsidiary which comes within the scope of the circumstances set out in paragraph 21".

2.26 Paragraph 20 states that where a company does not prepare group accounts dealing with *all* its subsidiaries for any of the reasons set out in section 229(3) of the Act (see para 2.20), the reasons for the exclusion of any subsidiary must be stated and, furthermore, that consideration will need to be given to whether the resulting financial statements give a true and fair view of the position of the group as a whole.

2.27 Under SSAP 14 (paragraph 21), a subsidiary should be excluded from consolidation (but *not* from group accounts) if:

(1) its activities are so dissimilar from those of other companies within the group that consolidated financial statements would be misleading and that information for the holding company's shareholders and other users of the statements would be better provided by presenting separate financial statements for such a subsidiary, or

(2) the holding company, although owning directly or through other subsidiaries more than half the equity share capital of the subsidiary, either:
  (a) does not own share capital carrying more than half the votes, or
  (b) has contractual or other restrictions imposed on its ability to appoint the majority of the board of directors, or

(3) the subsidiary operates under severe restrictions which significantly impair control by the holding company over the subsidiary's assets and operations for the foreseeable future, or

(4) control is intended to be temporary.

Paragraphs 23 to 27 of SSAP 14 specify the accounting treatment to be followed where subsidiaries are excluded from consolidation in the above circumstances.

Form and content of group accounts

2.28 Group accounts prepared by a holding company must comply with the requirements of Schedule 4 with respect to their form and content and also any additional information to be provided by way of notes to those accounts [s230(1)]. Other sections and schedules of the Act prescribe further disclosures. Group accounts (together with any related notes) must give, in relation to the company and the subsidiaries dealt with in those accounts as a whole, a true and fair view of the state of affairs and profit or loss, so far as concerns members of the company [s230(2)].

2.29 The requirement for the group accounts to give a true and fair view overrides the statutory requirements in the same manner as it does for individual accounts [s230(3)]. Consequently, where necessary for this purpose, additional information must be provided and, in exceptional circumstances (where the accounts fail to give a true and fair view even if additional information is given), the provisions *must* be departed from [s230(4),(5)]. Particulars of any departure, the reasons for it and its effect must be given in a note to the accounts [s230(6)].

Subsidiary with a different financial year end
2.30 The Act specifies which accounts of a subsidiary should be used as the basis for incorporating the results and assets and liabilities of the subsidiary, where the financial year of that subsidiary does not coincide with the financial year of the holding company. Unless the Secretary of State permits otherwise, the accounts to be used are:

(1) where the subsidiary's financial year ends with that of the holding company, the accounts for that financial year, and

(2) if the financial years do not end on the same day, the accounts for the subsidiary's financial year ending last before that of the holding company.

[s230(7)]

2.31 SSAP 14 (para 18) specifies the circumstances in which special (interim) accounts for a subsidiary should be drawn up to the holding company's accounting date and, in such cases, the approval of the Secretary of State will have to be sought.

Modification of the requirements of Schedule 4
2.32 A company may apply to the Secretary of State to have the requirements of Schedule 4, as they apply to group accounts, modified to suit the circumstances of the company [s230(8)]. However, there is no similar provision in section 228 in relation to a company's own accounts, as such discretion is not permitted by the EEC Fourth Directive. When the EEC Seventh Directive on group accounts is implemented, this discretion in relation to group accounts is expected to cease to be available.

CHAPTER 3

Procedure on completion of accounts

3.01 This chapter sets out the procedure which has to be followed when a set of accounts has been approved by the board and audited, including the period within which the accounts must be laid before the members and delivered to the registrar of companies.

Signing of balance sheet

3.02 The balance sheet of a company, as well as every copy thereof which is laid before the company in general meeting or delivered to the registrar of companies, must be signed on behalf of the board by two directors of the company or, if there is only one director, by that director [s238(1)]. It follows that the signature on these copies of the balance sheet must be in manuscript; facsimiles are not acceptable. Furthermore, it is a company's individual balance sheet which has to be signed. Although the consolidated balance sheet is often also signed, it is not a requirement to do so and does not relieve the directors from the obligation to sign the company's individual balance sheet. There are penalties for non-compliance [s238(2)].

3.03 On the copies which are distributed to the shareholders and others, it is likely that the names of the directors who signed the balance sheet will be printed or typewritten (or will, possibly, be facsimile signatures); they should be spelt out in exactly the same form as the manuscript versions.

3.04 The following must be approved by the board of directors before the balance sheet is signed on their behalf and must be annexed to the company's balance sheet:

(1) its profit and loss account [where prepared, see para 2.16], and

(2) any group accounts [s238(3),(4)].

The report of the auditors must be attached [s238(3)].

3.05 SSAP 17 (para 26) requires accounts to include a statement as to the date on which they were approved by the board of directors. It is normal practice for this to be made above the directors' signatures on the balance sheet, although it is sometimes given in a note to the accounts.

Definition of "accounts"

3.06 For the remainder of this chapter, a reference to "a company's accounts" is to be taken as comprising all of the following:

(1) the company's balance sheet and, where prepared (see para 2.16), its profit and loss account,

(2) the directors' report,

(3) the auditors' report and,

(4) where the company has subsidiaries and is required to prepare group accounts, the group accounts.

[s239]

The Secretary of State has the power to add to or reduce the classes of documents required to be comprised in a company's accounts [s256].

Entitlement to receive accounts

As of right

3.07 Subject to the exceptions set out below, not less than 21 days before the general meeting at which the accounts are to be laid (see para 3.14), a copy of the accounts must be sent to:

(1) every member of the company (whether or not entitled to receive notice of general meetings),

(2) every holder of the company's debentures (whether or not so entitled), and

(3) all persons, other than members or debenture holders, who are entitled to receive notice of general meetings.

[s240(1)]

There are penalties for failure to comply with this requirement [s240(5)].

3.08 Where a company does not have a share capital, it is not required by section 240 to send a copy of the accounts to any member or debenture

13

holder who is not entitled to receive notices of general meetings of the company [s240(2)]. There are further exceptions. Copies of the accounts are not required to be sent:

(1) to a member or debenture holder who is not entitled to receive notices of general meetings and of whose address the company is unaware, or

(2) to more than one of the joint holders of any shares or debentures where none of those holders is entitled to receive notices of general meetings, or

(3) where there are joint holders of shares or debentures some of whom are, and some not, entitled to receive notices of general meetings, to those who are not so entitled.

[s240(3)]

3.09 It is presumably open to a company's articles of association to require copies of the accounts to be sent in such cases.

3.10 If copies of the accounts are sent less than 21 days before the date of the general meeting at which they are to be laid, they are deemed to have been properly sent if this is agreed to by all the members entitled to attend and vote at the meeting [s240(4)]. Consent of the debenture holders is thus not required.

On demand

3.11 In addition to the above rights, any member or debenture holder is entitled to be given, without charge and within seven days of his request, a copy of the company's most recent accounts [s246(1),(2)].

3.12 A company is not obliged to comply with a demand made under section 246 if the member concerned has already made a demand for and been given a copy of the most recent accounts [s246(2)].

3.13 There are penalties for non-compliance with these requirements [s246(2)].

Duty to lay and deliver accounts

3.14 In respect of each financial year, the directors must lay accounts (including any group accounts) for that year before the company in general meeting [s241(1), 742(1)(b)]. Common practice is for a company's accounts to be laid at the Annual General Meeting and some companies' articles actually specify that the accounts must be presented at the AGM.

3.15 The auditors' report must be read out at the general meeting (but not necessarily by the auditors) and be open to the inspection of any member of the company [s241(2)].

3.16 The directors must send to the registrar of companies a copy of the accounts for each financial year. If any of the documents comprised in the accounts is not in English, a copy of a translation thereof into English, certified in the prescribed manner to be a correct translation, must also be filed [s241(3)].

Exception for unlimited companies

3.17 The directors of an unlimited company are not required to send to the registrar of companies a copy of the accounts of the company in respect of a financial year, if all of the following conditions are satisfied throughout the accounting reference period to which the accounts relate:

(1) (a) The company was not, to its knowledge, the subsidiary of a company that was then limited, and
   (b) to the company's knowledge, there have not been held or been exercisable, by or on behalf of two or more companies that were then limited, shares or powers which, if held or exercisable by one of them, would have made the company its subsidiary.

(2) The company did not have a subsidiary company which was then limited.

(3) The company was not carrying on business as the promoter of a trading stamp scheme within the Trading Stamps Act 1964.

[s241(4)]

3.18 References above to a company that was limited at a particular time, are to a body corporate (under whatever law incorporated) the liability of whose members was at that time limited [s241(4)].

3.19 This exception for unlimited companies, which is given in return for their members having unlimited liability, is in respect *only* of the filing of their accounts with the registrar of companies. It does not override the normal rules relating to the preparation, audit and laying of accounts before members.

Period allowed for laying and delivery of accounts

3.20 The period allowed for laying accounts before the company in general meeting and for delivering them to the registrar of companies is ten months for a private company and seven months for a public company. This period is determined by reference to the end of the accounting reference period to which the accounts relate [s242(1),(2)].

3.21 An extra three months in which to lay and deliver accounts may be claimed from the registrar of companies where the company carries on business, or has interests, outside the UK, the Channel Islands and the Isle of Man. The claim must be made on the prescribed form (form 242) in respect of each financial year for which the extension is required, and must reach the registrar of companies before the end of the seven or ten month period described above [s242(3)].

Special cases

First accounting reference period
3.22 Where a company's first accounting reference period is a period of more than twelve months, the period which would otherwise be allowed for laying and delivering its accounts is reduced by the number of days by which the accounting reference period exceeds twelve months. However, this rule will not reduce the period allowed to less than three months from the end of the first accounting reference period [s242(4)].

Shortened accounting reference period
3.23 Where a company has shortened its accounting reference period, the period allowed for laying and delivering its accounts prepared in relation to that new accounting reference period is:

(1) the normal period allowed calculated as from the new accounting reference date, or

(2) the period of three months beginning with the date of the notice of alteration,

whichever of those periods last expires [s242(5)].

Example:

X plc gives notice on 15th December 1985 altering its accounting reference date from 31st December to 30th June, so as to have a six month period ending on 30th June 1985. Its accounts to 30th June 1985 will have to be filed by 15th March 1986, which is the later date of 31st January 1986 (being seven months from 30th June 1985) and 15th March 1986 (being three months from the giving of the notice).

Extended period granted by registrar
3.24 If for any reason the Secretary of State thinks fit to do so, he may by written notice (from the registrar of companies) extend, for any financial year of a company, the period within which it is required to lay and deliver its accounts [s242(6)].

3.25 Where a company wishes to benefit from this discretionary power, it would be for the company to approach the registrar of companies outlining the exceptional circumstances which support its application.

Penalties

3.26 The Act provides for penalties and the making of a default order where a company does not comply with the requirements for laying and delivering accounts [s243, 244]. There are also penalties for laying or delivering accounts which do not comply with the requirements of the Act [s245].

CHAPTER 4

Prescribed formats for the accounts

General provisions

4.01 The Act prescribes specific formats which apply to both individual company accounts and group accounts [Sch 4 para 8]. The formats are reproduced in Appendix 3. The balance sheet and profit and loss account formats incorporate a hierarchy of letters, Roman numerals and Arabic numerals although, in drawing up accounts, the distinguishing letters and numbers do not have to be reproduced [Sch 4 para 1(2)]. Once having adopted a particular format for the balance sheet or profit and loss account, the same format must be used in subsequent years unless, in the opinion of the directors, there are special reasons for adopting one of the alternative prescribed formats [Sch 4 para 2(1)]. In such cases, particulars of the change and the reasons for it must be disclosed and explained in a note to the accounts for the year in which the new format is first adopted [Sch 4 para 2(2)].

4.02 The order, headings and sub-headings in the formats must be adhered to but the items identified by an Arabic numeral must be rearranged or adapted where the special nature of the business requires such a rearrangement or adaptation [Sch 4 para 1(1), 3(3)]. Items to which Arabic numerals are assigned may be combined if they are not material, or if the combination facilitates an assessment of the company's state of affairs or profit or loss but, in the latter case, the individual amounts must be disclosed in the notes to the accounts [Sch 4 para 3(4)]. This enables a company to show much of the detail in the notes to its accounts (rather than on the face of the accounts) where it considers that such a presentation facilitates such an assessment. The Act cross-refers some items in the formats to notes which follow the formats. Where these notes require further information in respect of the items to which they relate or require the total amount disclosed under the item to be analysed, this further information or analysis may be given on the face of the accounts or in the notes to the accounts, according as to whether the items to which they relate are shown on the face of the accounts or in the notes [Sch 4 para 6, 7]. Items for which there is no amount for both the current year and the immediately preceding year must be omitted [Sch 4 para 3(5), 4(3)].

4.03 Any balance sheet or profit and loss account item may be shown in more detail than required by the Act [Sch 4 para 3(1)]. Additional items may be added to the balance sheet or profit and loss account but only where the amounts involved are not already covered by any of the items in the format adopted [Sch 4 para 3(2)].

4.04 There is also a general proviso that any amounts which are not material in the context of any requirement of Schedule 4 to the Act may be disregarded for the purposes of that requirement [Sch 4 para 86]. This appears to refer to the materiality of an amount judged against the total amount which is disclosable under the particular requirement of Schedule 4, rather than materiality in the context of, say, shareholders' funds or the accounts as a whole. The concept of materiality is not defined in the Act.

4.05 The corresponding amount for the previous financial year in respect of each item in the balance sheet and profit and loss account must be disclosed [Sch 4 para 4(1)]. Where the corresponding amount is not comparable, it must be adjusted and particulars of the adjustment and the reasons for it must be disclosed in a note to the accounts [Sch 4 para 4(2)]. This latter provision allows for prior year adjustments to be made on the basis required by SSAP 6 (Extraordinary items and prior year adjustments).

Balance sheet

4.06 There are two formats prescribed for the balance sheet [Sch 4 para 8]. Format 1 is a continuous "vertical" format, while Format 2 sets out firstly all assets, followed by all liabilities, which would allow for presentation on facing pages (that is, a "horizontal" format). Both formats require the same basic disclosure but Format 1 requires, in addition, disclosure of the amount of net current assets or liabilities. The formats do not allow for assets to be classified as being neither fixed nor current (that is, so-called "in between" assets) as is permitted under Schedule 9 to the Act for "special category companies" (see Chapter 13) [Sch 9 para 4(2)].

Fixed assets

4.07 Fixed assets are defined as assets which are "intended for use on a continuing basis in the company's activities, and any assets not intended for such use shall be taken to be current assets" [Sch 4 para 77]. This raises the question of how assets should be presented in the accounts when there is an intention to dispose of them, perhaps shortly after the balance sheet date.

4.08 An intention or decision to dispose of a fixed asset should not of itself automatically result in the asset being reclassified as a current asset. If a company intends to continue to use such as asset subsequent to the balance sheet date, the asset would still appear to meet the statutory definition of a fixed asset (quoted above) and there would be no need to reclassify assets which, for example, are due to be replaced in the normal course of business during the coming year. Similarly, standby equipment which is not in use but which is intended for use in the future as and when necessary, should also come within the statutory definition of a fixed asset.

4.09 On the other hand where assets have been taken out of use by the balance sheet date and there is no intention to use them again in the company's activities, they would not come within the statutory definition of a fixed asset and would need to be reclassified as current assets.

4.10 In most cases, amounts realisable after more than one year (in respect of assets not in use at the balance sheet date) will not be particularly material. In some cases, though, there may be significant properties not in use which the company is unlikely to be able to sell for a considerable period due to depressed market conditions, and it could be considered misleading to include these in current assets. If this is the case it may be necessary to invoke the true and fair view override (see paras 2.15 and 2.29) and for the assets to continue to be shown as "land and buildings", under fixed assets, possibly being described as "awaiting disposal".

Items which may not be treated as assets

4.11 The following may not be treated as assets:

(1) preliminary expenses,

(2) expenses of and commission on any issue of shares or debentures, and

(3) costs of research (but this does not include development costs, which may be treated as an asset – see para 5.20).

[Sch 4 para 3(2)]

Preliminary expenses and share and debenture issue expenses may be written off to the share premium account to the extent available (see para 19.07).

Profit and loss account

4.12 There are four formats prescribed for the profit and loss account; they are based either on the type of expenditure (for example, raw materials, staff costs, etc.), which is akin to a value added statement, or on the function or purpose of the expenditure (for example, cost of sales, distribution costs and administrative expenses), which is similar to many internal management accounts, and, in both cases, there is a "horizontal" and "vertical" format [Sch 4 para 8]. Although not listed in the prescribed formats, the amount of the company's profit or loss on ordinary activities before taxation must be shown on the face of every profit and loss account [Sch 4 para 3(6)]. This applies also to the following items:

(1) any amount set aside or proposed to be set aside to, or withdrawn or proposed to be withdrawn from, reserves (that is, any transfer to or from reserves and the profit and loss account) and,

(2) the aggregate amount of any dividends paid and proposed.

[Sch 4 para 3(7)]

4.13 The information required by Formats 1 and 3 is not equivalent to that required by Formats 2 and 4. For example, the former require "gross profit or loss", "distribution costs" and "administrative expenses" to be stated, whereas the latter do not. Companies for which distribution expenses, for example, are of special competitive significance may therefore prefer to choose either Format 2 or Format 4.

Interpretation of statutory terms

4.14 Apart from "turnover" and "staff costs", the terms used in the prescribed profit and loss account formats are not defined by the Act. In view of this and the general nature of many of the terms, a variety of interpretation has become apparent in practice. Most difficulties appear to arise in respect of format 1 and it has become essential for groups to formulate internal definitions of statutory terms (such as "cost of sales", "distribution costs" and "administrative expenses") in order to ensure consistency within the group, particularly where material overseas operations are involved. Furthermore, format 1 does not contain an item which is specifically designated for selling and marketing expenses but, in practice, most companies appear to be including such costs under the item "distribution costs".

4.15 In format 2, a difficulty has arisen in distinguishing between those costs which fall under "other external charges" (item 5(b)) and "other operating charges" (item 8). The former is linked to "raw materials and consumables" (item 5(a)) and it thus appears that the intention was for "other external charges" to include items such as carriage inwards and direct production costs other than "staff costs" (for example, sub-

4.15   *Prescribed formats for the accounts*

contractors' charges, fuel costs and hire of plant), leaving "other operating charges" for more general overhead items. It appears that many companies are not attempting to make a distinction between the two and use only one item or the other.

CHAPTER 5

Accounting principles

Basic accounting principles

5.01 The Act requires companies (other than special category companies – see Chapter 13) to follow prescribed accounting principles in preparing financial statements. These principles derive from the EEC Fourth Directive and were included in the 1981 Act. Many of the accounting principles are also embodied in SSAPs.

5.02 The following basic accounting principles are stated in the Act:

(1) a company is presumed to be carrying on business as a going concern [Sch 4 para 10],

(2) accounting policies must be applied consistently from one financial year to the next [Sch 4 para 11],

(3) prudent bases must be used and, in particular, only realised profits are permitted to be included in the profit and loss account. All liabilities and losses which have arisen or are likely to arise in respect of the financial year to which the accounts relate, or a previous financial year, must be taken into account, including those which become apparent after the balance sheet date and before the balance sheet is signed on behalf of the board of directors [Sch 4 para 12],

(4) the accruals concept – all income and charges for the financial year to which the accounts relate must be taken into account, without regard to the date of receipt of payment [Sch 4 para 13],

(5) in determining the aggregate amount to be shown in respect of any item in the accounts, the amount of each individual component asset or liability must be determined separately [Sch 4 para 14].

5.03 Additionally, but not expressed by the Act as an accounting principle, amounts in respect of items representing assets or income may not be set off against amounts in respect of items representing liabilities or expenditure (as the case may be), or vice versa [Sch 4 para 5].

5.04   *Accounting principles*

5.04 With the possible exception of 5.02(5) and 5.03, these rules were normally followed prior to the 1981 Act's coming into force. SSAP 2 (Disclosure of accounting policies) recognises as fundamental accounting concepts (that is, broad basic assumptions which underlie the financial accounts) those of "going concern", "accruals", "consistency" and "prudence". Under the prudence concept, SSAP 2 requires that revenue and profits should not be anticipated but be recognised by inclusion in the profit and loss account only when realised in the form either of cash or of assets, the ultimate cash realisation of which can be assessed with reasonable certainty; also, provision should be made for all known liabilities (expenses and losses). The latter point is amplified by SSAP 17 (Accounting for post balance sheet events) which requires the accounts to be adjusted for events which occur between the balance sheet date and the date on which the financial statements are approved by the board of directors, in so far as they provide additional evidence of conditions existing at the balance sheet date.

Departures from basic accounting principles

5.05 If it appears to the directors that there are special reasons for departing from any of the principles stated in 5.02 above, they may do so but particulars of the departure, the reasons for it and its effect must be given in a note to the accounts [Sch 4 para 15]. Any such departures must not result in the accounts failing to give a true and fair view.

5.06 If a company wishes to depart from the no set-off rule, the departure would have to be made on the basis of the overriding requirement for the accounts to give a true and fair view (see paras 2.15 and 2.29).

5.07 The most common departures from the fundamental accounting policies are likely in practice to be:

(1) a change in accounting policy (that is, a departure from the consistency concept), which is covered by SSAP 6, although SSAP 6 does not require disclosure of the reasons for the change,

(2) the inclusion in the profit and loss account of unrealised exchange translation profits in accordance with SSAP 20, and

(3) the going concern concept being inappropriate; in such cases, the accounts would, presumably, be prepared on a break-up basis.

In (1) above, the corresponding amounts for the preceding financial year would be appropriately adjusted, thereby resulting in the amounts for that year and the current year being stated on a comparable basis [Sch 4 para 4(2)].

24

Individual assessment

5.08 The requirement to determine separately the amount of each individual component asset and liability when computing the aggregate amount to be shown in respect of any item in the accounts [Sch 4 para 14] has the effect of prohibiting the use of the "portfolio" method of valuation which was sometimes used before the 1981 Act came into force, particularly when valuing investments.

Realised profits

5.09 Schedule 4 para 12(a) states that only profits realised at the balance sheet date may be included in the profit and loss account. "Realised profits" in this context means those which are regarded as realised profits for the purposes of the accounts, in accordance with accounting principles which are generally accepted when those accounts are prepared [Sch 4 para 91].

5.10 In September 1982, the accountancy bodies gave guidance on the meaning of realised profits (CCAB Technical Release Nos. 481 and 482). One matter not dealt with in that guidance but which was later covered by SSAP 20, is foreign currency translation. The legal section of SSAP 20 states that for companies other than banks and insurance companies, "all exchange gains taken through the profit and loss account, other than those arising on unsettled long-term monetary items, are realised". Long-term is defined as due in over one year from the balance sheet date. The application of the SSAP may therefore result in unrealised exchange gains on unsettled long-term monetary items being taken to the profit and loss account. The SSAP states that the need to show a true and fair view is considered to constitute a special reason for departure from the general principle under paragraph 15 of Schedule 4.

Historical cost accounting rules

5.11 The Act provides two sets of accounting rules: historical cost accounting rules and alternative accounting rules. The latter allow for occasional and selective revaluations of fixed and other assets (which are common in the U.K., particularly in respect of property assets) as well as for full current cost accounting in a company's primary accounts. The two sets of rules are given equal status in the Act and it is entirely optional as to which set any particular company follows but where the alternative rules are applied, corresponding historical cost information must be disclosed. The historical cost rules are considered first.

Fixed assets

5.12 Fixed assets are to be stated at their purchase price or production cost, less any provision for depreciation or diminution in value where required [Sch 4 para 17]. The terms "purchase price" and "production cost" are defined in paras 5.33 and 5.34.

5.13 The purchase price or production cost less any estimated residual value of all fixed assets which have a limited useful economic life must be systematically written off by provisions for depreciation made over their estimated useful economic life [Sch 4 para 18].

5.14 Where a fixed asset investment (including a loan – see item BIII in the prescribed balance sheet formats) has diminished in value, a provision for the diminution in its value *may* be made [Sch 4 para 19(1)]. However, where the reduction in value of *any* fixed asset (including investments) is expected to be permanent, a provision for diminution in value *must* be made [Sch 4 para 19(2)]. Where the reasons for any provision for diminution in value no longer apply, the provision must be written back to the extent that it is no longer required [Sch 4 para 19(3)]. This is in order to prohibit the creation of "hidden reserves". In each case where provisions for diminution in value and amounts written back are not shown (that is, disclosed separately) on the face of the profit and loss account, they are required to be disclosed, either separately or in aggregate with other similar provisions made or amounts written back, in a note to the accounts. In any case, amounts provided must be separately disclosed from amounts written back [Sch 4 para 19 (2),(3)].

5.15 The optional provisions under Sch 4 para 19(1) are designed to allow companies to recognise short term downward fluctuations in the value of their fixed asset investments if they so wish, while Sch 4 para 19(2) requires provisions against permanent diminutions in value. This latter provision is akin to SSAP 12 (Accounting for depreciation) para 18, which states, "if at any time the unamortised cost of an asset is seen to be irrecoverable in full, it should be written down immediately to the estimated recoverable amount which should be charged over the remaining useful life".

Fixed assets shown at a fixed amount

5.16 Where tangible fixed assets are constantly being replaced and their overall value is not material to assessing the company's state of affairs and their quantity, value and composition are not subject to material variation, they may be included at a fixed quantity and value [Sch 4 para 25]. Where this practice is adopted (for example, for loose tools), purchases of such assets would be charged to the profit and loss account.

Investment properties

5.17 There is no exception to the rule that depreciation must be provided on a systematic basis for all fixed assets which have a limited useful economic life. The requirement to depreciate investment properties over their useful economic life is regarded as inappropriate by SSAP 19 (Accounting for investment properties), which defines investment properties and requires that, in order for the accounts to give a true and fair view, investment properties should not be depreciated on a systematic basis over their useful economic lives but should be included in the balance sheet at their open market value, with changes in such values being shown as a movement on an investment revaluation reserve (that is, using the Act's "alternative accounting rules"); where the total of the investment revaluation reserve is insufficient to cover a deficit, the amount by which the deficit exceeds the amount in the investment revaluation reserve should be charged to the profit and loss account. Such a departure from the requirements of the Act is justified in SSAP 19 by the overriding requirement for the accounts to show a true and fair view.

5.18 In practice, most companies following SSAP 19 have failed to quantify the effect of the departure from the Act, and give instead an accounting policy note on the lines suggested in May 1983 by the British Property Federation, which reads:

> "Depreciation
>
> In accordance with SSAP 19, (i) investment properties are revalued annually and the aggregate surplus or deficit is transferred to a revaluation reserve, and (ii) no depreciation or amortisation is provided in respect of freehold investment properties and leasehold investment properties with over twenty years to run. The directors consider that this accounting policy results in the accounts giving a true and fair view. Depreciation or amortisation is only one of the factors reflected in the annual valuation, and the amount which might otherwise have been shown cannot be separately identified or quantified.
>
> Depreciation is provided on other tangible fixed assets at rates calculated to write off the cost or valuation, less estimated residual value, evenly over its expected life as follows: . . ."

5.19 Although this form of note does not state that the accounts would have failed to give a true and fair view had the departure from the statutory requirement not been made, SSAP 19 (para 17) states that application of SSAP 19 "will usually be a departure, for the overriding purpose of giving a true and fair view, from the otherwise specific requirement of the law to provide depreciation on any fixed asset which has a limited useful economic life". The Department of Trade and Industry has indicated that this kind of note is acceptable *only* on the basis that the life of the investment properties is indeterminate, and that if the directors are able to estimate the useful economic life of an investment property, the law requires them to show the effect, in quantified form, of not providing for depreciation.

Research and development costs

5.20 Costs of research must not be treated as an asset but development costs may be capitalised in "special circumstances", which are not defined in the Act [Sch 4 para 20(1)]. Where development costs are capitalised they must be amortised; the reasons for capitalisation and the period over which they are being written off, or are to be written off, must be disclosed in a note to the accounts [Sch 4 para 20(2)]. The terms "cost of research" and "development costs" are not defined in the Act.

5.21 Guidance on the definition and accounting treatment of research and development costs is found in SSAP 13. This defines two categories of expenditure on research:

(1) Pure (or basic) research – original investigation undertaken in order to gain new scientific or technical knowledge and understanding. It is not primarily directed towards any specific practical aim or application.

(2) Applied research – original investigation undertaken in order to gain new scientific or technical knowledge and directed towards a specific practical aim or objective.

5.22 SSAP 13 defines development as "the use of scientific or technical knowledge in order to produce new or substantially improved materials, devices, products, processes, systems or services prior to the commencement of commercial production".

5.23 SSAP 13 requires expenditure on pure and applied research (other than on fixed assets) to be written off in the year of expenditure but permits development costs to be deferred in defined circumstances (SSAP 13 para 21). Such costs must then be amortised on a systematic basis by reference to the sale or use of the product or process or period over which it is expected to be sold or used. The provisions of SSAP 13 are considered to be compatible with those of the Act and compliance with SSAP 13 should ensure compliance with the Act on these matters.

Goodwill

5.24 Only goodwill which was acquired for valuable consideration (that is, purchased rather than internally generated) may be carried as an asset [note 3 to the balance sheet formats]. Goodwill may not be stated at an amount in excess of its historical cost [Sch 4 para 31]. Where goodwill (but not goodwill arising on consolidation – see below) is shown as an asset, it must be systematically written off through the profit and loss account over a period which does not exceed (but may be less than) its useful economic life; the period over which it is being written off and the reasons for choosing that period must be disclosed in a note to the accounts [Sch 4 para 21(1) to (4)]. The Act does not prescribe a maximum number of years over which goodwill (or any other fixed asset) must be written off. As noted in para 5.26 below, SSAP 22 expresses a preference for the immediate elimination of goodwill against reserves.

5.25 The Act states specifically that goodwill arising on consolidation is not required to be written off [Sch 4 para 66]. The reason for this is thought to be that in 1981 when these provisions were originally enacted, an accounting standard on goodwill was only in the early stages of development and the government did not want to prejudge the issue (particularly as the Fourth Directive, on which this part of the legislation is based, deals only with a company's individual accounts). The balance sheet formats, which segregate assets (including goodwill) from liabilities and the rule which prohibits assets from being set-off against liabilities effectively prohibit goodwill from being shown as a "dangling debit" (that is, the deduction of unamortised goodwill – that is, an asset – from total shareholders' funds in the balance sheet).

5.26 The EEC Seventh Directive, which was adopted in 1983 and which member states are required to implement by 1990, requires goodwill arising on consolidation to be accounted for either by amortisation in the consolidated profit and loss account over a period not exceeding its useful economic life or as an immediate deduction from consolidated reserves (article 30). SSAP 22 (Accounting for goodwill) adopts the same approach as the Seventh Directive, although it expresses a preference for immediate write-off on acquisition against reserves and envisages that this will be the normal practice.

5.27 SSAP 22 itself does not specify the particular reserve against which consolidation goodwill should be eliminated when it is immediately written off against reserves. Appendix 2 (which deals with the effect on a company's distributable profits) suggests that where this treatment is adopted in respect of positive goodwill in a company's *individual* accounts, the write off should be made initially against the company's unrealised reserves (for example, negative goodwill) with a subsequent transfer to realised reserves, so as to reduce those reserves on a systematic basis in the same way as if the goodwill had been amortised.

5.28 It is generally considered that the rules governing the revaluation reserve which arises under the alternative accounting rules (which do not permit the revaluation of goodwill), do not allow the immediate or systematic write-off of goodwill (whether in a company's individual accounts or goodwill arising on consolidation) to be charged against the revaluation reserve [Sch 4 para 34]. This view is supported by article 33 of the Fourth Directive on which the present law (which governs the re-valuation reserve in both individual and group accounts) is based. The Seventh Directive applies, without amendment, the rules relating to the revaluation reserve to group accounts.

5.29 It has been suggested that (in the absence of any other available reserve) a separate reserve for the writing off of goodwill could be created. This would start off at nil and the goodwill written off would then produce a so-called "negative reserve", shown separately and grouped with other reserves. The existence of a "negative reserve" is neither specifically envisaged nor prohibited by Schedule 4, though its creation in this context may be thought to be contrived.

Current assets

5.30 Current assets are to be stated at the lower of their net realisable value and their purchase price or production cost [Sch 4 para 22,23]. The term "purchase price" includes a reference to any consideration (cash or otherwise) given for an asset [Sch 4 para 90]. Trade debtors should *not* be stated net of any profit element. The consideration given by a company for a trade debtor is represented by the goods and services supplied at the price charged and, consequently, the amount to be included in respect of a trade debtor is the amount due to the company, unless the net realisable value is less, when suitable provision should be made. The problems in relation to the statement of long-term contract work in progress at cost plus attributable profit are considered in para 5.43.

5.31 Where current assets have been written down and the reasons for the write-down no longer apply either in full or in part, the provision must be written back to the extent that it is no longer necessary [Sch 4 para 23(2)].

Discount and premium on debts

5.32 Where the amount repayable on any debt owed by the company exceeds the value of the consideration received in respect of the trans-action (for example, where debentures are issued at a discount or are redeemable at a premium), the difference may be treated as an asset

[Sch 4 para 24(1)]. Where any such amount is shown as an asset, it must be written off by "reasonable" annual instalments and be completely written off before the debt is repaid. Where the unamortised amount is not shown separately in the balance sheet, it must be disclosed in the notes to the accounts [Sch 4 para 24(2)]. The basis of write-off is not specified; the Act merely requires it to be "reasonable".

Determination of purchase price or production cost of fixed and current assets

5.33 The purchase price of an asset is to be taken as the actual price paid plus any expenses incidental to its acquisition [Sch 4 para 26(1)].

5.34 The production cost of an asset (fixed or current) is to be determined by adding to the purchase price of the constituent raw materials and consumables, the direct costs of production [Sch 4 para 26(2)]. In addition, a reasonable proportion of indirect production costs and the interest on capital borrowed to finance the production of that asset may be added, but only in so far as they relate to the period of production. If interest is included, that fact and the amount must be disclosed in a note [Sch 4 para 26(3)].

5.35 Distribution costs may not be included in the production cost of current assets [Sch 4 para 26(4)]. The implications of this for stocks are discussed in para 5.46.

5.36 Where there is no record of the purchase price or production cost or of any other relevant amounts, or any such records cannot be obtained without unreasonable expense or delay, the purchase price or production cost of any asset shall be taken as the value ascribed to it in the earliest available record of its value made on or after its acquisition or production by the company [Sch 4 para 28]. Particulars of any such cases when advantage is first taken of this provision must be given in the notes to the accounts [Sch 4 para 51(1)].

Stocks and fungible assets (including investments)

5.37 Instead of having to determine the actual purchase price of production cost of individual items included in stock or of any fungible assets (including investments), a company may use one of the following methods:

(1) First in, first out (FIFO).

(2) Last in, first out (LIFO).

(3) Weighted average price.

(4) Any other similar method (for example, standard cost).

5.38   *Accounting principles*

The method chosen must, however, be one which appears to the directors to be appropriate in the circumstances of the company [Sch 4 para 27(1),(2)]. Fungible assets are those which are substantially indistinguishable one from another; for example, nuts and bolts, or crops held in storage, with the result that they are freely interchangeable [Sch 4 para 27(6)].

5.38 Whichever method is used, if the balance sheet amount of stocks or fungible assets differs materially from their replacement cost at the balance sheet date, the amount of the difference must be disclosed in a note to the accounts [Sch 4 para 27(3),(4)]. The comparison may be made by reference to the most recent actual purchase price or production cost before the balance sheet date, where this appears to the directors to be the more appropriate standard of comparison [Sch 4 para 27(5)].

5.39 It would appear that this disclosure is not required where one of the above cost formula methods (such as FIFO or weighted average price) is not used. For example, the aggregate balance sheet amount of the trading properties held as stock by a property company would normally be determined on an individual property basis, rather than by means of a cost formula and, consequently, where this is the case, the above disclosure would not be required. As properties may remain in stock for a considerable period, this could be a significant exception in a time of rapid price changes.

5.40 Where stocks etc. are turned over quickly, the difference may, in practice, not be material. However, where significant amounts of stock are held for relatively long periods (for example, maturing spirits), and the cost prices relating thereto have changed materially, this requirement is likely to be applicable and could result in significant accounting work. Where a company's accounting system does not provide such information, appropriate methods might include the use of the latest invoice prices, current price lists or appropriate indices.

5.41 Raw materials and consumables may be included at a fixed quantity and value (that is, the base stock method) but only where they are constantly being replaced and their overall value is not material to assessing the company's state of affairs and their quantity, value and composition are not subject to material variation [Sch 4 para 25].

5.42 SSAP 9 (Stock and work in progress) Appendix 1 paragraph 12, regards methods of costing such as base stock and LIFO to be generally unsuitable as they do not usually bear a reasonable relationship to actual costs obtaining during the period. Although LIFO is permitted under the Act, its use is regarded by SSAP 9 as not normally being appropriate. Its adoption would therefore be acceptable only if it appears to the directors to be appropriate in the circumstances of the company and if its use is nevertheless considered to give a true and fair view. The Explanatory Foreword to SSAPs requires that any significant departure from an SSAP must be disclosed and explained.

Long-term contract work in progress

5.43 SSAP 9 (paragraph 27) requires long term contract work in progress to be stated at cost plus any attributable profit, reflecting the proportion of the work carried out at the accounting date. Schedule 4 para 12 states that only realised profits may be included in the profit and loss account. In paragraph 91 it defines such profits as those which are regarded as realised under generally accepted accounting principles. Paragraph 3 of the CCAB Technical Release No. 481 states that any profit on long-term contract work in progress which is included in the profit and loss account in accordance with SSAP 9 is to be regarded as a realised profit. A difficulty arises, however, in relation to the balance sheet because of the rule (in Sch 4 paras 22 and 23) that current assets must be shown at the lower of their cost and net realisable value. The overriding requirement for the accounts to show a true and fair view is used to justify the inclusion of attributable profit in the amount at which long-term contract work in progress is stated in the balance sheet. The requirement to give the "effect" of any such departure from the requirements of the Act has proved controversial in this case because some companies have been reluctant to disclose the amount of the attributable profit. There seems little doubt that disclosure of the "effect" means quantification but there is a dispute as to whether the effect has to be given in relation to the "gross" work in progress (that is, before deduction of progress payments received and receivable) or in relation to "net" work in progress (that is, after such deductions), with some arguing that in the latter case it is not possible to give a meaningful quantification.

5.44 In a news release dated 27th March 1985, the Accounting Standards Committee announced that it has embarked on a review of all SSAPs in the light of the statutory requirements introduced into law by the 1980 and 1981 Acts. Such a review would include consideration of the problems relating to long-term contract work in progress which are described above. Attached to the news release is a copy of a letter dated 30th October 1984 from the Department of Trade and Industry which states that the Department's view is that "'effect' demands some quantification" and that "the departure which has to be justified is the inclusion [of attributable profit] in the gross figure". The Department notes further that where quantification is possible, the law requires it.

5.45 If the format item concerned, "Work in progress", is a net figure (note 8 to the prescribed balance sheet formats states that payments received on account may be deducted from stock) there appear to be reasonable grounds for the "net" view but, in the absence of any definitive ruling clarifying the law, it seems that either interpretation is supportable and acceptable but quantification of the effect is clearly required unless it is genuinely impossible to do so.

Distribution costs

5.46 As stated in paragraph 5.35, the Act does not permit the inclusion of "distribution costs" (a term which is not defined) in the production cost of current assets [Sch 4 para 26(4)]. SSAP 9(17) defines "cost" as being "that expenditure which has been incurred in the normal course of business in bringing the product or service into its present location and condition", and identifies "cost of purchase" and "cost of conversion" as components of cost. Cost of conversion includes overheads attributable to bringing a product to its present location and condition. It is common practice, on the basis of SSAP 9, to include in the cost of stock, costs incurred in transporting goods from the factory to distribution centres or to retail shops run by the company to sell its products. It is not entirely clear whether by following SSAP 9 a company would be departing from the rule in Schedule 4 of the Act. In practice, some companies have noted this as a departure.

Alternative accounting rules

5.47 The Act is drawn up on the basis that a company will prepare its accounts according to the historical cost accounting rules unless it adopts any of the alternative accounting rules which allow for certain assets to be revalued or included at their current cost. The alternative accounting rules are:

(1) Intangible fixed assets, other than goodwill (which must be included at no more than its historical cost – see also para 5.24), may be included at their current cost.

(2) Tangible fixed assets may be included either at their market value as at the date of their last valuation or at their current cost.

(3) Investments shown under fixed assets may be included either:
   (a) at their market value as at the date of their last valuation, or
   (b) at a value determined on any basis which the directors consider to be appropriate in the circumstances,
   but, in the latter case, particulars of the method of valuation adopted and of the reasons for adopting it must be disclosed in a note to the accounts.

(4) Investments shown under current assets may be included at their current cost.

(5) Stocks may be included at their current cost.

[Sch 4 para 31]

The term "current cost" is not defined in the Act but may be assumed to have the meaning given to it in the pronouncements on Current Cost Accounting by the accounting bodies. The Act does not use the term "replacement cost" in the context of the alternative accounting rules, but does so under the historical cost accounting rules in relation to information to be given where the balance sheet amount of stock differs materially from its replacement cost (see para 5.38).

Calculation of depreciation

5.48 Where the value of any asset is determined on the basis of one of the alternative accounting rules mentioned above, that value is the starting point for determining the amount to be included in respect of that asset, and the depreciation rules referred to above (see paras 5.13, 5.14 and 5.30) apply accordingly [Sch 4 para 32(1)]. Where any fixed asset is valued under the alternative accounting rules, the amount to be shown in the profit and loss account in respect of depreciation of that asset may be the historical cost amount instead of the amount based on the alternative accounting rules, provided that the amount of the difference between the two is separately shown in the profit and loss account or in a note to the accounts [Sch 4 para 32(3)]. This provision might appear at first sight to allow additional depreciation required on the revaluation surplus element of a fixed asset not to be charged to the profit and loss account but to be charged directly against the revaluation reserve. SSAP 12(21) requires the provision for depreciation to be based on the revalued amount but does not state explicitly that the full amount must be charged in the profit and loss account. Paragraph 16 of ED 37 (which is a proposed revised version of SSAP 12) makes it clear that not only should the depreciation charge be based on the carrying value of the asset in the balance sheet but that the whole of the depreciation charge should be reflected in the profit and loss account. When a revalued asset is depreciated, the transfer (within reserves) of an amount equal to the depreciation on the revaluation surplus, from the revaluation reserve to the profit and loss account, would be in order, thus recognising the reduction in or realisation of that reserve.

5.49 It could also be argued with justification that paragraph 32(3) is concerned with the presentation of the depreciation charge rather than allowing it to be charged elsewhere than to the profit and loss account. This interpretation is supported by the Fourth Directive (on which the provision in the Act is based) which, in article 33(3), refers to the additional depreciation being "shown separately in the layouts" and, in article 35(1)(c)(cc), states that depreciation "must be charged to the profit and loss account and disclosed separately in the notes on the accounts if [it has] not been shown separately in the profit and loss account".

Comparable historical cost information

5.50 Whenever an alternative accounting rule is followed, there must be stated in the notes to the accounts separately for each item affected (that is, aggregate amounts to which a letter or Roman numeral is ascribed in the formats as well as individual items to which an Arabic numeral is ascribed):

(1) the item and the basis of the valuation adopted in determining the amounts of the component assets, and

(2) except for stocks, the amount at which the item would have been stated according to the historical cost accounting rules and the amount of the cumulative provisions for depreciation or diminution in value which would have been made under the historical cost rules, or the differences between these amounts and the corresponding amounts actually shown in the accounts.

[Sch 4 para 33]

Revaluation reserve

5.51 Where any asset is revalued under any of the alternative accounting rules, any difference between the revalued amount and the previous book amount must be credited or debited to a revaluation reserve [Sch 4 para 34(1)]. The revaluation reserve must be shown separately in the balance sheet, in the prescribed position, but need not be called by that name [Sch 4 para 34(2)].

5.52 The revaluation reserve must be reduced to the extent that the amounts standing to the credit of the reserve are, in the opinion of the directors, no longer necessary for the purpose of the accounting policies adopted by the company (for example, where a company disposes of an asset which has been revalued). Any amount may be transferred from the reserve to the profit and loss account only if either:

(a) the amount in question was previously charged to the profit and loss account, or

(b) it represents realised profit (for example, on the sale of a revalued asset).

[Sch 4 para 34(3)]

5.53 The treatment for taxation purposes of amounts credited or debited to the revaluation reserve must be disclosed in a note to the accounts [Sch 4 para 34(4)].

5.54 As noted earlier, paragraph 19(2) of Schedule 4 requires a company to make a provision (which is chargeable to the profit and loss account) where a fixed asset suffers a permanent diminution in its value. By virtue of paragraph 32 of that Schedule, this rule applies also under the alternative accounting rules. The interaction between this requirement and paragraph 34 which refers to a loss on revaluation (that is, a revaluation deficit) being debited to the revaluation reserve, is complex and would appear to be contradictory. The difference between a revaluation deficit and a permanent diminution in value is not readily apparent but is reconcilable by the interpretation that only temporary deficits may be debited directly to the revaluation reserve. The amount of a temporary deficit which may be debited to the revaluation reserve is not limited to the reversal of a credit included in that reserve which arises from an earlier revaluation of the same asset. However, paragraph 41 of ED 36 (a proposed revised version of SSAP 6 "Extraordinary items and prior year adjustments") proposes that "deficits on the revaluation of fixed assets should be debited to the profit and loss account . . . . . to the extent that they exceed any surplus held in the reserves and identified as relating to previous revaluations of the same assets".

CHAPTER 6

Notes to the accounts

6.01 The Act sets out minimum information which must be given either in the notes to the accounts or on the face of the balance sheet or profit and loss account [Sch 4 paras 35,87]. Amounts which are not material in the particular context of any requirement may be disregarded for that purpose [Sch 4 para 86].

6.02 Where items to which Arabic numerals are assigned in the prescribed formats are combined because the combination facilitates an assessment of the company's state of affairs or profit or loss, as allowed by Schedule 4 para 3(4)(b), the information required by the Act to be given in the notes must still be given in respect of the individual items which are combined. The reference to a combination of items means the combination of items listed in the formats, say "trade debtors" combined with "other debtors", to be shown as one item on the face of the balance sheet. It does not refer to the normal aggregation of individual component assets or liabilities which make up an item.

6.03 The Act deals firstly with a statement of accounting policies followed by the company and then with information supplementing the balance sheet. This is followed by information supplementing the profit and loss account.

Accounting policies

6.04 The accounting policies followed by a company in determining the amounts of balance sheet items and the profit or loss of the company must be stated. In particular, details are required of the policies adopted with respect to the depreciation and diminution in value of assets [Sch 4 para 36]. SSAP 2 requires disclosure of the accounting policies followed for dealing with items which are judged material or critical in determining profit or loss for the year and in stating the financial position of the company. In view of the immateriality exemption [Sch 4 para 86], the Act should normally not require greater disclosure of accounting policies than is required by SSAP 2.

Information supplementing the balance sheet

Share capital

6.05 The following is required to be stated:

(1) (a) the authorised share capital,
   (b) where more than one class of shares has been allotted, the number and aggregate nominal value of each class of shares allotted.
   [Sch 4 para 38(1)]

(2) In respect of redeemable shares:
   (a) the earliest and latest dates on which the company has power to redeem those shares,
   (b) whether they must be redeemed in any event or are liable to be redeemed at the option of the company, and
   (c) whether and (and, if so, what) premium is payable on their redemption.
   [Sch 4 para 38(2)]

(3) Where the company has allotted any shares during the financial year:
   (a) the reason for the allotment,
   (b) the classes of shares allotted, and
   (c) for each class of shares, the number allotted, their aggregate nominal value, and the consideration received by the company.
   [Sch 4 para 39]

(4) Where there is any contingent right to the allotment of shares in the company (that is, any option to subscribe for shares and any other right to require shares to be allotted to any person whether on the conversion into shares of any other securities or otherwise):
   (a) the number, description and amount of the shares in question,
   (b) the period during which the right is exercisable, and
   (c) the price to be paid for the shares allotted.
   [Sch 4 para 40]

Debentures

6.06 The following is required to be stated:

(1) Where the company has issued any debentures during the financial year:
   (a) the reason for the issue,
   (b) the classes of debentures issued, and
   (c) in respect of each class, the amount issued and the consideration received.
   [Sch 4 para 41(1)]

(2) Particulars of any redeemed debentures which the company has power to reissue [Sch 4 para 41(2)].

(3) The nominal amount and book value of any debentures of the company held by a nominee or trustee of the company [Sch 4 para 41(3)].

Fixed assets

6.07 Except where stated, the following disclosures apply to all categories of fixed asset (that is, every fixed asset item prefixed by an Arabic numeral under intangible assets, tangible assets and investments) [Sch 4 para 42(1)].

(1) Their aggregate purchase price or production cost, or valuation determined under one of the alternative accounting rules, as at the beginning and end of the financial year [Sch 4 para 42(1),(2)].

(2) In respect of provisions for depreciation or diminution in value:
(a) the cumulative amount of such provisions as at the beginning and end of the year,
(b) the amount provided during the year,
(c) the amount of any adjustments made during the year in consequence of the disposal of any asset, and
(d) the amount of any other adjustments (for example, exchange translation differences) made during the year.
[Sch 4 para 42(3)]

(3) The effect on any amount shown in the balance sheet in respect of each fixed asset item as a result of:
(a) any revaluation made in accordance with the alternative accounting rules, and
(b) any acquisitions, disposals or transfers during the year.
[Sch 4 para 42(1)]

(4) Where the amount of any fixed asset (other than listed investments) is arrived at on the basis of any of the alternative accounting rules:
(a) the years (so far as they are known to the directors) in which the assets were severally valued and the several values, and
(b) where assets have been valued during the year, the names of the valuers or particulars of their qualifications for so doing and (whichever is stated) the basis of valuation used.
[Sch 4 para 43]

(5) In respect of any amount included under land and buildings, there must be stated separately:
(a) the amount of freehold land, and
(b) the amounts of both long leasehold and short leasehold land.
[Sch 4 para 44]

The term "land" includes buildings [Interpretation Act 1978 Sch 1]. The term "lease" includes an agreement for a lease. "Long lease" means a lease which has at least fifty years to run from the end of the current financial year and "short lease" means any other lease [Sch 4 para 83].

Investments

6.08 For each fixed or current asset item shown under the general heading of "investments", there must be disclosed how much of the amount relates to listed investments [Sch 4 para 45(1)]. The amount for listed investments must be analysed between those which are listed on The Stock Exchange and those which are listed on a stock exchange of repute outside Great Britain [Sch 4 para 84, s744]. Securities traded on the Unlisted Securities Market would not be regarded as listed investments.

6.09 Additionally, for each item which includes listed investments, disclosure is required of:

(1) the aggregate market value of the listed investments where it differs from their balance sheet amount, and

(2) both the market value and the stock exchange value, where the market value is taken as being higher than the stock exchange value.

[Sch 4 para 45(2)]

6.10 The above disclosure is required in respect of each balance sheet item which includes listed investments and not just an overall aggregate. This includes investments in associated companies which are considered further in Chapter 11.

Reserves and provisions

6.11 Where there is any movement on the amount of any item shown under reserves or provisions, disclosure of the following must be made:

(1) the amount of the reserves or provisions as at the beginning and end of the financial year,

(2) any amount transferred to or from the reserves or provisions during the year, and

(3) the source and application respectively of any amounts transferred.

A provision is defined as any amount retained as reasonably necessary for the purpose of providing for any liability or loss which is either likely to be incurred, or certain to be incurred but uncertain as to amount or as to the date on which it will arise [Sch 4 para 89].

6.12 This information is not required where the movement consists of the application of a provision for the purpose for which it was established [Sch 4 para 46(1),(2)].

6.13 Particulars must be given of each material provision included under the item "other provisions" in the prescribed layouts [Sch 4 para 46(3)]. In practice, this requirement is interpreted as permitting the aggregation of individual provisions which are of a similar kind (for example, warranty provisions) and as requiring separate disclosure of the aggregate amounts (if material) for different kinds of provisions (for example, provisions for warranties, self-insurance or for rationalisation).

6.14 The amount required to be shown separately under "Provision for Taxation" in the balance sheet formats (item I2 in Format 1 and item B2 under liabilities in Format 2) must be analysed between the amount provided for deferred taxation and other provisions for taxation [Sch 4 para 47]. In practice, this item should normally include only deferred tax, as all other taxation liabilities (unless there is any particular uncertainty as to their amount), whether payable in less than or more than one year, will be shown under creditors in the balance sheet formats.

Details of indebtedness

6.15 The Act requires a considerable amount of detail to be disclosed in respect of indebtedness. For each of the nine items shown under creditors falling due after more than one year, there must be stated:

(1) the aggregate amount of any debts included under that item which are payable in whole, otherwise than by instalments, after more than five years from the balance sheet date, and

(2) the aggregate amount of any debts included under that item which are payable by instalments any of which fall due for payment after more than five years from the balance sheet date.

The aggregate amount of the instalments which fall due for payment after more than five years from the balance sheet date must also be stated [Sch 4 para 48(1),(5),85].

6.16 In relation to each amount owed by a company (as distinct from balance sheet format item) which falls due after more than one year, the terms of payment or repayment and the rate of interest payable on the debt must be stated [Sch 4 para 48(2)]. However, if, in the opinion of the directors, compliance with this latter requirement would result in a statement of excessive length, it is sufficient to give a general indication of the terms of payment or repayment and the rates of interest payable on the debts [Sch 4 para 48(3)].

6.17 Where the company has given security in respect of any of its debts, the aggregate amount of those debts and an indication of the nature of the security (for example, whether the charge is fixed or floating, and the category of assets on which the liabilities are secured) must be given. This information must be given in respect of each item shown under creditors (both those falling due within one year and after more than one year from the balance sheet date) [Sch 4 para 48(4),(5)].

6.18 Where a company includes in its creditors an amount which is secured by a retention of title clause, the CCAB recommends* that the fact be disclosed. It would appear to be in keeping with the requirements of the Act if an indication of the nature of the security is given in such cases, and also in respect of the creditors for goods acquired under hire purchase and leases which are capitalised. Compliance with SSAP 21 should normally ensure compliance in the case of leases and hire purchase agreements.

6.19 The amount of any arrears of fixed cumulative dividends on the company's shares and, for each class of share where there is more than one class, the period for which the dividends are in arrear, must be stated [Sch 4 para 49].

Guarantees and other financial commitments

6.20 The following is required to be given:

(1) Particulars of any charge on the assets of the company to secure the liabilities of any other person, including, where practicable, the amount secured [Sch 4 para 50(1)].

(2) In respect of any other contingent liability not provided for:
  (a) the amount or estimated amount of that liability,
  (b) its legal nature (for example, guarantee or performance bond), and
  (c) whether, and if so what, valuable security has been provided by the company in respect thereof.
  [Sch 4 para 50(2)]

SSAP 18 (Accounting for contingencies) para 14 defines a contingency as a "condition which exists at the balance sheet date, where the outcome will be confirmed only on the occurrence or non-occurrence of one or more uncertain future events". The SSAP requires that a material contingent loss should be accrued where it is

---

* Guidance statement on "Accounting for goods sold subject to reservation of title" – July 1976 (section 2.207 in ICAEW Members' Handbook).

probable that a future event will confirm that loss and it can be estimated with reasonable accuracy. Where a material contingent loss is not accrued, SSAP 18 requires detailed particulars to be disclosed unless the possibility of loss is remote.

(3) Where practicable:
   (a) the aggregate or estimated amount of contracts for capital expenditure in so far as not provided for, and
   (b) the aggregate or estimated amount of capital expenditure authorised by the directors but not contracted for.
   [Sch 4 para 50(3)]

(4) Particulars of any pension commitments:
   (a) included under any provision shown in the company's balance sheet, and
   (b) for which no provision has been made.

Where any pension commitment relates wholly or partly to pensions payable to past directors of the company, separate particulars of the commitment so far as it relates to such pensions must be given [Sch 4 para 50(4)].

In November 1984, the ASC published a Statement of Intent on "Accounting for Pension Costs". The statement deals with the measurement and disclosure of pension costs. The disclosure proposals are substantially the same as those in ED32 ("Disclosure of pension information in company accounts", May 1983), which is not to be converted into a standard at this stage. The eventual standard is expected to provide guidance on the extent of disclosure required in order to comply with the law.

(5) Particulars of any other financial commitments which have not been provided for and which are relevent to assessing the company's state of affairs [Sch 4 para 50(5)]. This requirement refers to significant revenue commitments and one of the most common examples of this is leasing.

Leasing is the subject of SSAP 21 "Accounting for leases and hire purchase contracts", which is effective for accounting periods beginning on or after 1st July 1984. It deals with the disclosure of leasing commitments and compliance with the SSAP would ensure compliance with the above requirements insofar as they relate to leasing commitments.

Examples of other types of commitment which would require disclosure are intra-group letters of support and forward purchases of raw materials.

Commitments on behalf of group companies

6.21 Separate disclosure within the above categories is required of commitments undertaken by the company on behalf of or for the benefit of:

(1) any holding company or fellow subsidiary of the company, or

(2) any subsidiary of the company,

showing (1) and (2) separately [Sch 4 para 50(6)].

Dividends/financial assistance

6.22 The following is required:

(1) The aggregate amount of proposed dividends must be stated (as noted in para 4.12, the aggregate amount of dividends paid and proposed must be shown on the face of the profit and loss account) [Sch 4 para 51(3)].

(2) Particulars must be given of outstanding loans made under section 153(4)(b) or (c) or 155 of the Act (Financial assistance for the acquisition of shares) [Sch 4 para 51(2)].

Information supplementing the profit and loss account

Separate disclosure of certain items of income and expenditure

6.23 Separate disclosure is required of the following:

(1) The amount of the interest on or any similar charges in respect of:
   (a) bank loans and overdrafts, and other loans which are wholly repayable within five years of the balance sheet date, and
   (b) all other loans made to the company.

   Disclosure is required irrespective of whether the loans are secured or not, but it is not required in respect of interest or charges on loans to the company from other members of the group [Sch 4 para 53(2)].

(2) The amount set aside for the redemption of share capital [Sch 4 para 53(3)].

(3) The amount set aside for the redemption of loans [Sch 4 para 53(3)].

(4) The amount of income from listed investments [Sch 4 para 53(4)].

(5) The amount of rents from land and buildings (after deduction of ground rents, rates and other outgoings) where it forms a substantial part of the company's revenue for the financial year [Sch 4 para 53(5)].

(6) The amount charged to revenue in respect of the hire of plant and machinery (which would include the rental expense of related operating leases and, arguably, the depreciation and finance charges for related finance leases capitalised in accordance with SSAP 21) [Sch 4 para 53(6)].

(7) The remuneration of the auditors; this includes any sums paid by the company in respect of the auditors' expenses [Sch 4 para 53(7)].

Particulars of tax

6.24 The following is required to be stated:

(1) The basis on which the charge for UK corporation tax and UK income tax is computed [Sch 4 para 54(1)].

(2) Particulars of any special circumstances which affect the liability to taxation of profits, income or capital gains for the financial year or for succeeding financial years (for example, group relief, utilisation of losses or overseas taxation) [Sch 4 para 54(2)].

(3) (a) The charge for UK corporation tax,
    (b) the amount which the charge for UK corporation tax would have been but for double taxation relief,
    (c) the charge for UK income tax, and
    (d) the charge for taxation imposed outside the UK on profits, income and (so far as charged to revenue) capital gains.
    [Sch 4 para 54(3)]

6.25 The above disclosures must be made separately in respect of the tax on the profit or loss arising on the ordinary activities of the company and the tax on the extraordinary profit or loss [Sch 4 para 54(3)]. SSAP 6 (Extraordinary items and prior year adjustments) makes a similar distinction.

6.26 SSAP 8 ("The treatment of taxation under the imputation system in the accounts of companies") provides for additional disclosures including the amount of any irrecoverable ACT. As previously mentioned (para 6.14), the amount of any provision for deferred taxation included in the balance sheet must, in practice, be disclosed [Sch 4 para 47, balance sheet formats]. The recognition and disclosure in accounts of deferred taxation is also regulated by SSAP 15 ("Accounting for deferred taxation").

Turnover

Definition
6.27 Turnover is defined as the amounts derived from the provision of goods and services falling within the company's ordinary activities, after deduction of trade discounts, value added tax, and other sales based taxes (for example, excise duty) [Sch 4 para 95].

Analysis of turnover and profits by class of business and by geographical market supplied

6.28 Where a company (or group) has, during the financial year, carried on business of different classes which, in the opinion of the directors, differ substantially from each other, the notes to the accounts must include a description of each class of business and the amount of turnover, and what is, in the opinion of the directors, the amount of the profit and loss before taxation attributable to each class of business [Sch 4 para 55(1)].

6.29 An analysis of turnover by geographical area is also required where the company has, during the financial year, *supplied* geographical markets which, in the opinion of the directors, differ substantially from each other [Sch 4 para 55(2)]. The Act does not define "geographical markets" but "differ substantially" may be construed as implying, at the minimum, clear separation by distance (for example, continents) or economic character (for instance, distinct economic zones, such as Western Europe and Eastern Europe). Listed companies are required by The Stock Exchange to give an analysis of profit by geographical area where the contribution to profit from one area is materially disproportionate to the contribution from other areas [Continuing Obligations for Companies, para 21.2].

6.30 Where the directors are of the opinion that any of the above statutory disclosures would be seriously prejudicial to the interests of the company, the information need not be given, but the fact of the omission must be stated [Sch 4 para 55(5)].

6.31 In making the required analyses, the directors are required to have regard to the manner in which the company's activities are organised – for instance, where a company or group is organised into divisions, this may be the appropriate basis for analysis [Sch 4 para 55(3)].

6.32 Where, in the opinion of the directors, classes of business and geographical markets do not differ substantially from each other, they are to be treated as one class or market as the case may be. Where amounts attributable to a class of business or a geographical market are not material, they may be included in the amount stated in respect of another [Sch 4 para 55(4)].

6.33 As noted above, in making the analyses, the directors must have regard to the manner in which the company's (or group's) activities are organised. One of the more important practical problems which has arisen is the treatment of interest. The analysis of profit is required at the pre-tax level (that is, after taking account of interest payable and receivable). Many groups do not allocate interest to specific activities because they manage their finance on a central basis and would regard any allocation as being arbitrary. Where there is a central treasury function of this kind, it would appear reasonable for the directors to regard it as a separate class of business.

6.34 The Stock Exchange requirement for listed companies to give a geographical analysis of turnover and trading results (para 21(c) of "Continuing Obligations for Companies") is worded slightly differently from the Act, in that The Stock Exchange refers to "overseas trading operations", whereas the Act refers to "markets supplied". However, it is understood that The Stock Exchange considers that a geographical analysis by markets supplied would be sufficient for its purposes (and para 21.2 indicates that "overseas operations include direct exports and activities carried out otherwise than in the country where the main place of business of the company (or group) is situated").

Employees

6.35 The notes to the accounts are required to state:

(1) The average number of employees of the company in the financial year and, except insofar as the amounts are stated on the face of the profit and loss account, the aggregate amounts of their:
(a) wages and salaries,
(b) social security costs, and
(c) other pension costs.
[Sch 4 para 56(1),(4)]

(2) The average number of the company's employees by category of employment, as determined by the directors, having regard to the manner in which the company's activities are organised [Sch 4 para 56(1),(5)]. Obvious methods of categorisation include doing so by function or by division.

The information which is required is comprehensive and relates to all the company's (or group's) employees and not only those who work in the UK.

6.36 "Social security costs" means any contribution by the company to any state social security or pension scheme, fund or arrangement. "Pension costs" includes any other contributions by or amounts set aside by, the company for an employee pension scheme, as well as amounts paid by the company in respect of pensions not funded by a scheme [Sch 4 para 94].

6.37 The average number of employees is to be calculated by adding together the number of persons employed under contracts of service by the company in each week of the financial year (whether throughout the week or not) and dividing it by the number of weeks in the financial year. The number of employees by category is to be similarly calculated [Sch 4 para 56(2),(3)].

Extraordinary and prior year items

6.38 In addition to the disclosure of the aggregate amounts of extraordinary income and charges as separate items in the prescribed formats for the profit and loss account, the notes to the accounts must give particulars of any extraordinary income or charges arising in the financial year [Sch 4 para 57(2)]. The effect of any transactions which fall within the ordinary activities of the company but which are exceptional by virtue of size or incidence must also be stated [Sch 4 para 57(3)]. These provisions are similar to those of SSAP 6, which also defines extraordinary items. Formats 2 and 4 also require the disclosure of "exceptional amounts written off current assets", such amounts being taken into account in determining profit or loss on ordinary activities.

6.39 Where any amount relating to any preceding financial year is included in any item in the profit and loss account (that is, not treated as a prior year adjustment), the effect must be stated [Sch 4 para 57(1)]. SSAP 6 sets out the circumstances in which it is appropriate to make a prior year adjustment by restating the prior year amounts and giving, immediately after the profit and loss account, a statement of retained profits/reserves showing the prior year adjustments. SSAP 6 considers it appropriate for the effects of a change in accounting policy and for the correction of a fundamental error to be dealt with in this way, but requires all other prior year items to be dealt with in the profit and loss account for the year in which they are recognised and to be shown separately if material.

Foreign currencies

6.40 The notes to the accounts must state the basis on which sums originally denominated in foreign currencies have been translated into sterling in respect of both balance sheet and profit and loss account items [Sch 4 para 58(1)].

Particulars of investments in subsidiaries and other bodies corporate

6.41 The Act requires the notes to the accounts to contain specified particulars of the company's subsidiaries and other bodies corporate in which it holds more than 10% [Sch 5 Parts I, II and III]. In exceptional cases, it is possible to obtain from the Secretary of State exemption from some of the disclosures in relation to a body corporate which carries on business outside the UK, where in the opinion of the directors disclosure would be harmful.

Identification of ultimate holding company

6.42 If at the end of its financial year the company is a subsidiary of another body corporate, the notes to the accounts must state the name of the body corporate regarded by the directors as being the company's ultimate holding company and, if known to them, the country in which it is incorporated [Sch 5 para 20]. This disclosure is not required by a company which carries on business outside the UK if, in the opinion of the directors, disclosure would be harmful to the business of the company or of that holding company (or any of its other subsidiaries) and approval is obtained from the Secretary of State [Sch 5 para 21].

Corresponding amounts

6.43 Except as noted below, the corresponding amount for the immediately preceding financial year in respect of all note disclosures must also be stated. Where the corresponding amount is not comparable, it must be adjusted and particulars of the adjustment and the reasons for it given (for example, as a result of a change in accounting policy or the correction of a fundamental error in accordance with SSAP 6) [Sch 4 para 58(2)].

6.44 The corresponding amount is *not* required in respect of disclosures under the following provisions: Parts I and II of Schedule 5 (Particulars of investments in subsidiaries and other bodies corporate), Sections 232 to 234 and Schedule 6 (Particulars of transactions with directors and other officers) and Schedule 4 para 42 (fixed assets) and para 46 (reserves and provisions) [Sch 4 para 58(3)].

CHAPTER 7

Disclosure of directors' and higher paid employees' remuneration

7.01 The accounts of a company are required to disclose comprehensive particulars of the remuneration of persons who were directors of the company at any time during the period covered by the accounts. The aggregate amounts of their "emoluments", "pensions" and "compensation for loss of office" must be disclosed and must include all amounts received in respect of their services to the company *and* its subsidiaries.

7.02 For a company which is a member of a group or whose aggregate directors' "emoluments" exceed a prescribed amount, currently £60,000, separate disclosure is required of the amount of the emoluments of the chairman and those of the highest paid director if greater than those of the chairman. Additionally, the emoluments of all the directors must be given in bands of £5,000, stating the number of directors whose emoluments fall within each band. There is an exception for those who perform their duties as chairman or director wholly or mainly abroad.

7.03 The emoluments of employees *of the company* earning in excess of a prescribed amount, currently £30,000, in respect of their services to the company and its subsidiaries must also be given in bands of £5,000.

Requirement to disclose aggregate directors' remuneration by category

7.04 Companies are required to disclose in the notes to their accounts the aggregate amounts for each of the following:

(1) directors' emoluments,

(2) directors' or past directors' pensions, and

(3) any compensation to directors or past directors in respect of loss of office.

[s231(1),(2)(d), Sch 5 paras 22(1), 28(1), 29(1)]

This requirement is described in detail in the paragraphs which follow.

51

Amounts to be included under all categories

7.05 In ascertaining the aggregate amounts to be disclosed under the headings in 7.04 above, the amounts to be taken into account are not limited to those payments made by (or charged to) the company or, where remuneration in respect of services to a subsidiary of the company also has to be included, by that subsidiary. There must be taken into account all relevant sums paid by or receivable from:

(1) the company,

(2) the company's subsidiaries, and

(3) any other person (which would, for example, include any holding company of the company but only in respect of services given by the director to the company and not to the holding company),

except for sums to be accounted for to the company or any of its subsidiaries, which are to be excluded [Sch 5 para 30(1),(2)].

7.06 An example of such an exclusion would be where a director of a holding company is also a director of its subsidiary but is required to pay over to the holding company any emoluments he receives from the subsidiary. In such a case, the director's emoluments from the subsidiary would be disclosable in the subsidiary's accounts (because it would not be accountable for to that subsidiary or any of its own subsidiaries) but would not be included in the disclosure of the directors' emoluments in the holding company's accounts.

Example:
Mr X is a director of both M Ltd and its subsidiary N Ltd. M Ltd is, in turn, a subsidiary of H Ltd (of which Mr X is not a director). Mr X receives £25,000 from M Ltd and £10,000 from N Ltd in respect of his services to those companies and a further £6,000 from H Ltd as additional remuneration in respect of his services to N Ltd, but this amount is not charged to N Ltd. The amounts to be included in respect of Mr X in the aggregate directors' emoluments disclosed by M Ltd and N Ltd are £41,000 and £16,000 respectively. No amount is disclosable in the accounts of H Ltd.

7.07 Disclosure is unlikely to be avoided by routeing the payment of emoluments through an intermediary. Firstly, it could be argued that the amounts were in fact "receivable" by the director (see 7.09(1) below) but that he chose an indirect method of payment. Secondly, it could be argued that where the payment is made to a company owned by a director, that company would be "the creature of the director – his puppet" and the payment should therefore be treated as a payment to him; this view was expressed by Lord Denning in *Wallersteiner v Moir* *[1974] 1 WLR 991* in connection with the previously repealed section 190 of the 1948 Act which, prior to the introduction of the rules in the 1980 Act, regulated loans to directors, but the view would appear to be equally valid in the case of emoluments. Furthermore, any onward payment by (or entitlement to payment from) such a third party is likely to be regarded as a payment within 7.05(3) above.

7.08 The amounts to be shown for any financial year are, generally, those sums receivable in respect of that year, whenever paid, or for sums not receivable in respect of a period, the sums paid during that year [Sch 5 para 31(1)].

Emoluments

7.09 The amount shown under "directors' emoluments" must:

(1) include emoluments gaid to or receivable by any person in respect of his services as director of the company or in respect of his services, while director of the company, as director of any subsidiary thereof or otherwise in connection with the management of the affairs of the company or any subsidiary thereof, and

(2) distinguish between emoluments in respect of:
   (a) services as director, whether or the company or its subsidiary, and
   (b) other emoluments.

[Sch 5 para 22(2)]

Amounts to be shown under (2)(a) would include directors' fees and other amounts received which relate to the directorship, while (2)(b) would include executive and managerial remuneration.

7.10 Disclosable emoluments therefore include all amounts receivable in respect of a director's services as director and in a managerial capacity for both the company and its own subsidiaries, but not for its holding company or fellow subsidiaries.

Example:
A Ltd has a wholly-owned subsidiary B Ltd, which in turn has a wholly-owned subsidiary C Ltd. Mr X is a director of both A Ltd and B Ltd and a manager of C Ltd. His emoluments in respect of his services to A Ltd, B Ltd and C Ltd were £35,000, £25,000 and £12,000 respectively. The amounts to be disclosed as part of directors' emoluments in the accounts of A Ltd and B Ltd are respectively £72,000 and £37,000.

Definition of "emoluments"

7.11 The scope of the term "emoluments" is broad and specifically includes, but is not limited to:

(1) fees and percentages,

(2) any expense allowance in so far as it is charged to UK income tax,

(3) any contribution paid in respect of the director under any pension scheme, and

(4) the estimated money value of any other benefits received by the director otherwise than in cash (that is, benefits in kind).

[Sch 5 para 22(3)]

7.12 A director's "gross" salary or any other managerial remuneration would, of course, form part of directors' emoluments. No deduction would therefore be made for the employees' pension or state social security contributions. It is generally accepted that the employers' state social security contribution does not form part of emoluments.

7.13 Where a person is a director of the company (whose accounts are being prepared) for only part of the financial year, the only amounts to be disclosed under directors' emoluments are those which relate to that period during which he was a director [Sch 5 para 22(2)].

7.14 There is no requirement to adjust or authority for adjusting emoluments to an annual rate where a financial year is for a period of greater or less than twelve months. In such cases, where companies wish to give an annual rate, it should be given in addition to the statutory disclosures.

7.15 The requirement to include in emoluments the estimated money value of benefits in kind may sometimes present a problem of measurement. The Act does not define what is meant by a benefit; in particular, whether it should be measured in terms of the benefit (or saving) to the director or in terms of the cost to the company. It is necessary for a realistic amount to be attributed to the benefit and the taxable amount, if any, is not necessarily appropriate for this purpose but is frequently used in practice where the "estimated money value" cannot be ascertained. For example, it is commonly recognised that the car scale benefit does not represent the real value of the benefit. Examples of circumstances which are likely to give rise to a disclosable benefit in kind are the provision of a company car, free or subsidised housing, and loans at less than an arm's length rate of interest. The possibility of such arrangements falling under the prohibitions and disclosure provisions of Chapters 27 and 29 should also not be overlooked.

Pensions

7.16 The amount to be shown under 7.04(2) above should *not* include any pension paid or receivable under a pension scheme if the "contributions" to that scheme are substantially adequate for its maintenance [Sch 5 para 28(2)]. The reason for this exclusion is that the contributions would have been included under "emoluments" at the time they were made (see 7.11(3) above).

7.17 With this exception, the amount to be disclosed must include any pension paid or receivable in respect of the services (whether as director or in a managerial capacity, for the company or for any of its subsidiaries) of a director or past director of the company, irrespective of whether paid to or receivable by the director or past director or any other person (on his nomination or by virtue of dependence on or other connection with him) [Sch 5 para 28(2)].

7.18 The amount disclosed must distinguish between pensions in respect of services as director, whether of the company or a subsidiary, and other pensions [Sch 5 para 28(3)].

Definitions

7.19 The Act defines the terms "pension", "pension scheme" and "contribution" as follows:

"pension" includes any superannuation allowance, superannuation gratuity or similar payment.

"pension scheme" means a scheme for the provision of pensions in respect of services as director or otherwise, which is maintained in whole or in part by means of contributions.

"contribution" in relation to a pension scheme means any payment, including an insurance premium, paid for the purposes of the scheme by or in respect of persons rendering services in respect of which pensions will or may become payable under the scheme, except that it does not include any payment in respect of two or more persons if the amount in respect of each of them is not ascertainable.
[Sch 5 para 33(3)]

In most instances, the individual contributions should be ascertainable and would therefore fall to be disclosed as part of directors' emoluments (see 7.11(3) above).

Compensation for loss of office

7.20 The scope of the term "compensation for loss of office" is widely drawn and includes all "sums paid as consideration for or in connection with a person's retirement from office" [Sch 5 para 29(3)].

7.21 The amount to be shown under compensation for loss of office:

(1) must include any sums paid to or receivable by a director or past director by way of compensation for loss of office as director of the company or for the loss, while director of the company or on or in connection with his ceasing to be director of the company, of any other office in connection with the management of the company's affairs or of any office as director or otherwise in connection with the management of the affairs of any subsidiary of the company, and

(2) must distinguish between compensation in respect of the office of director, whether of the company or its subsidiary, and compensation in respect of other offices.

[Sch 5 para 29(2)]

Examples of payments which would fall under this heading are damages for breach of contract where a director is dismissed before his service contract expires and ex gratia payments on a director's resignation.

Apportionment

7.22 There may be occasions where a single payment is made for more than one purpose and, for one reason or another, it is not clear how much of the payment relates to each purpose. In such cases, the directors may apportion any payments between the three categories of disclosure (see para 7.04) in such a manner as they think appropriate [Sch 5 para 32].

Subsidiaries and associates

7.23 Where a director of a company is or was while being director of the company also, by virtue of the company's direct or indirect nomination, a director of another body corporate, that body corporate is to be regarded as being a subsidiary of the company (where it would not otherwise be) for the purposes of the disclosure rules and, thus, the remuneration which the director receives from that other company would be included in the directors' remuneration disclosed by the investing company (see para 7.04), unless it has to be accounted for to the company or any of its subsidiaries (see para 7.05) [Sch 5 para 33(2)(a)]. This could be the case where a director of an investing company is also a director of one of its "associated companies" (within the meaning of SSAP 1).

7.24 References to a subsidiary are to be taken as referring to a subsidiary at the time the services are rendered (for "emoluments" and "pensions") or to a subsidiary immediately before the loss of office as director of the company (for "compensation for loss of office") [Sch 5 para 33(2)(b)].

Further disclosures

7.25 In addition to the disclosures described in the preceding paragraphs, the Act requires disclosure of particulars of emoluments waived (subject to the exception in para 7.34 below), the amount of the chairman's and highest paid director's emoluments as well as those of all the directors in bands of £5,000 (all of which are subject to the exceptions described in paras 7.33 and 7.34).

Waiver of emoluments

7.26 The number of directors who have waived their rights to receive emoluments in respect of the financial year and the aggregate amount waived must be disclosed [Sch 5 para 27]. This is subject to the exception described in para 7.34 below.

7.27 For listed companies, The Stock Exchange Continuing Obligations for Companies (paragraph 21(n)) requires particulars also of any waiver of future emoluments. USM companies are required to give particulars of any arrangement under which a director has waived or agreed to waive any emoluments (General Undertaking paragraph 10(k)).

Chairman's and highest paid director's emoluments

7.28 If there was one person who acted as chairman (that is, at directors' meetings) throughout the financial year, the amount of his "emoluments" must be stated. If this was not the case, for each person who was chairman during the period the amount of the emoluments attributable to the period during which he was chairman must be stated [Sch 5 para 24(1),(2),(3)].

7.29 The "emoluments" of the highest paid director must be stated if his emoluments exceeded the amount disclosed as the emoluments of the chairman or chairmen (that is, where there was more than one chairman during the year); the comparison should be made with the aggregate of the amounts disclosed as chairmen's emoluments [Sch 5 para 25(3),(4),(5)].

7.30 For the purposes of the above disclosures and those which follow in 7.31 and 7.32 below, the term "emoluments" has the same meaning as that set out in para 7.11 above, *except* that any contributions paid in respect of the director under any pension scheme are disregarded for these purposes [Sch 5 paras 22(3),26]. A director's emoluments would, however, not be reduced for those purposes by the amount of any contribution he makes to a pension scheme by way of a deduction from his salary.

Example:
Mr A, who is a director of X Ltd, receives directors' fees of £1,000 and an annual salary of £25,000. In addition, the company pays £3,000 to a pension scheme in respect of Mr A. The amount to be taken into account in respect of Mr A for the disclosure of directors' emoluments in bands is £26,000.

Banding of directors' emoluments

7.31 In respect of all the directors (that is, including the chairman and highest paid director) the notes to the accounts must show the number of directors whose "emoluments" (see 7.30 above) fell within bands of £5,000. The first band is for those whose emoluments were nil or did not exceed £5,000. The remaining bands are in successive multiples of £5,000 (for example, £5,001 to £10,000 etc) [Sch 5 para 25(2)]. It is not uncommon practice for the first band to be split into those whose emoluments were nil and those who received emoluments which did not exceed £5,000.

7.32 Whilst the requirement to give emoluments in bands applies to all directors, as a matter of presentation many companies may prefer not to include the chairman or highest paid director under more than one heading. This should be acceptable if it is made clear which directors have been included or excluded; for example, by the use of the words "all directors" or "other directors" when giving the bands.

Exception for service abroad

7.33 Separate disclosure of the chairman's and highest paid director's emoluments and inclusion in the bands is *not* required for persons whose services were performed wholly or mainly outside the United Kingdom [Sch 5 paras 24(2),(3),25(2),(3),(4)]. This exception is, however, not without qualification. In the case of the chairman, his duties "as chairman" must be wholly or mainly discharged outside the UK; for exclusion from disclosure as the highest paid director and from the bands of directors' emoluments, the directors' duties "as such" must have been discharged wholly or mainly outside the UK. Unless the majority of board meetings are held abroad it is difficult to see how disclosure of the chairman's emoluments can be avoided. For the other provisions, the reference to "as such" appears to mean, although it may not have been the intention, that their services as *director*, as distinct from any executive or managerial function, must be performed wholly or mainly abroad in order to qualify for the exception. Although it is difficult to discern any general practice in this regard, it appears that many companies have interpreted the exception fairly widely to exclude any director who, on company affairs, actually spends all or most of his time abroad.

There is, however, *no* exception in relation to the disclosure of aggregate directors' remuneration (see 7.04 above).

Exception where emoluments do not exceed £60,000

7.34 The requirements set out in paras 7.26 and 7.28 to 7.32 above, do not apply to a company which is neither a holding company nor a subsidiary company (whether the parent or the subsidiary is incorporated in Great Britain or elsewhere) for any financial year in which its aggregate directors' "emoluments" (as defined in para 7.11 above) does not exceed £60,000 [Sch 5 para 23]. There is no authority for adjusting the limit where the financial year is for a period which is more or less than twelve months.

Modified accounts of small companies

7.35 Small companies, as defined (see para 12.06), which are entitled to file modified accounts with the registrar of companies are exempt from the requirement to include particulars of their directors' remuneration in those filed accounts. This exemption covers the aggregate disclosures required (see para 7.04), the waiver of emoluments and the chairman's/highest paid director's remuneration and banding of emoluments but is available *only* in respect of the accounts filed with the registrar of companies. The normal rules apply to the accounts which must nevertheless still be prepared by such companies for circulation to their members.

Employees' emoluments

7.36 Where a company has employees, other than directors, whose emoluments, as defined in para 7.38 below, exceed £30,000 for the financial year (that is, the period covered by the accounts irrespective of its length), the notes to the accounts must show the number of employees whose emoluments fell within successive bands of £5,000. The first band is from £30,001 to £35,000 [Sch 5 para 35(1),(2)]. Disclosure is required only for persons who were in the employment of the company itself [Sch 4 para 63(a), Sch 9 para 23]. Where a holding company wishes to give the information in respect of the group's employees (whether by way of note to its individual accounts or its group accounts), it must do so in such a way that the information in relation to the company's own employees is also stated.

7.37 The foregoing does not apply in respect of employees who, when in the company's employment during the financial year, worked wholly or mainly outside the United Kingdom [Sch 5 para 35(2)].

7.38 "Emoluments" for these purposes includes fees and percentages, any sums paid by way of expenses allowance in so far as those sums are charged to United Kingdom income tax, and the estimated money value of any other benefits received by a person otherwise than in cash [Sch 5 para 36(2)].

7.39 The emoluments to be included in respect of any person are those paid by or receivable from the company, its subsidiaries and any other person, in respect of his services as an employee of the company or as a director or employee of any subsidiary of the company, except for sums to be accounted for to the company or any of its subsidiaries [Sch 5 para 36(1)]. References to a subsidiary are to be taken as referring to a subsidiary at the time the services were rendered [Sch 5 para 37(b)].

7.40 The amounts to be brought into account for a financial year are the sums receivable in respect of that year, whenever paid [Sch 5 para 36(3),(4)].

7.41 Where an employee of a company is a director of another body corporate (for example, an "associated company") by virtue of the company's nomination (direct or indirect), that body corporate is deemed to be a subsidiary of the company for the purposes of the above disclosures [Sch 5 para 37(a)].

7.42 Where an employee is appointed as a director during the course of a financial year, that person's emoluments receivable before the appointment fall under "employees' emoluments" while those receivable after that date fall under "directors' emoluments".

> **Example:**
> A person with an annual salary of £50,000 is promoted from employee to director half-way through a twelve month financial year. No amount would be included under the bands of "employees' emoluments" (because in the first six months his emoluments would not have exceeded £30,000) and £25,000 would be included under "directors' emoluments" (in the aggregate amount and in the bands).

Corresponding amounts

7.43 The corresponding amounts for the previous financial year must be given in respect of all amounts disclosed under the requirements described in this chapter [s260(2), Sch 4 para 58(2)].

Consolidated accounts

7.44 The disclosure of directors' and higher paid employees' emoluments in the accounts of individual members of a group should not be aggregated when preparing consolidated accounts (or any other form of group accounts) [Sch 4 para 63(a), Sch 9 para 23(a)]. The disclosures apply in all cases, including intermediate holding companies, to persons who are (or were) directors or employees of the company whose accounts (or group accounts) are being prepared, in the manner set out in the preceding paragraphs. Thus, for example, the remuneration of a person who is a director of a subsidiary, but not of its parent, is not included under directors' remuneration in the accounts or group accounts of that parent. It may be that, in such cases, the person concerned will be an employee of the parent; if so, his remuneration from the subsidiary must still be taken into account for the purposes of the banding of the parent's higher paid employees' emoluments.

7.45 It is, however, not uncommon for group accounts, in giving the bands for higher paid employees' emoluments, not to limit disclosure to employees of the holding company, but to include also the employees of the subsidiaries. Where this is the case, the group accounts should also disclose separately the information in relation to employees, if any, of the holding company, in order to comply with the statutory requirements (see 7.36 above).

Disclosure of an annual rate

7.46 Where an accounting period is for more or less than twelve months,

61

companies sometimes wish to express directors' and employees' emoluments at an annual rate. This is permissible, provided the information for the actual period covered by the accounts is also given, in order to comply with the statutory requirements (see 7.14 and 7.34).

General duty of disclosure to company

7.47 Directors have a statutory duty to make such disclosures to a company as are necessary to enable the company to make proper disclosure of directors' remuneration [s231(4)].

Duty of auditors

7.48 If the statutory requirements described in this chapter are not complied with, the auditors are required insofar as they are able to do so, to give the relevant particulars in their audit report [s237(5)].

Authority for payment

7.49 The authority for the payment of directors' remuneration (including compensation for loss of office) is the subject of both legislation and case law. The matter is complex, partly due to the distinction which has been drawn between the office of director and any other (executive) office which a person who is a director may also hold. This subject is beyond the scope of this book.

7.50 The White Paper ("Financial services in the United Kingdom" – Cmnd 9432, January 1985) indicates that the government expects to introduce in the 1985/86 session of parliament legislation which will extend and amend sections 191 to 194 of the 1948 Act [now sections 312 to 316] "which deal with payments to directors in connection with loss of office resulting from a take-over or transfer of shares. This will be designed to prevent abuse of these provisions".

CHAPTER 8

Disclosure of directors' share and debenture interests

8.01 The directors' report or, at the option of the company the notes to the accounts, is required to give, individually for all persons who were directors of the company at the end of its financial year, prescribed particulars of their interests (which are deemed to include those of their spouse, children and stepchildren under eighteen) in the shares and debentures of the company and of other members of the group. Where a director has no disclosable interests, a statement to that effect is required [s235(3), Sch 7 para 2]. The provisions relating to dealing in share options are described in paragraphs 8.25 and 8.26.

Interests in shares and debentures

Disclosure in directors' report or in notes to the accounts

8.02 The directors' report, or notes to the accounts, is required to state, in respect of each person who was a director of the company at the end of the financial year, prescribed particulars of that person's disclosable "interests" (see paras 8.09 to 8.14) as recorded in the register of interests, as at the beginning and end of the financial year, in shares and debentures of the company, its subsidiaries and any body corporate (whether or not incorporated in Great Britain) which is its holding company or which is a subsidiary of that holding company [s235(3), Sch 7 para 2]. If a person becomes a director during the financial year, his interests are to be stated as at the date of his appointment and at the end of that financial year. The particulars to be disclosed with respect to each director, which would be extracted from the register, are:

(1) whether or not the director was interested in group shares and debentures at those dates and, if so:

(2) the name of the body corporate in whose shares or debentures the director has an interest, and

63

(3) the number and amount of shares and debentures in which the director is interested.

[Sch 7 para 2(1)]

Where a person became a director on more than one occasion during the year, his date of appointment is taken to be the first such occasion [Sch 7 para 2(2)].

8.03 Where a company has a different holding company at the beginning and end of its financial year, the information to be given in relation to interests in its holding company will relate to the original holding company at the beginning of the financial year and to the new holding company at the end of the financial year. This is because the register will contain information on this basis.

8.04 Listed companies and companies traded on the Unlisted Securities Market are required additionally:

(1) in respect of year-end interests in the capital of any members of the group, to distinguish between beneficial interests and non-beneficial interests, and

(2) to note any change in those interests which has occurred between the end of the financial year and a date (of the company's choosing) not more than one month prior to the date of the notice of the general meeting at which the accounts are to be laid. If there has been no such change, a statement to that effect should be included.

In addition, for listed companies, equivalent information is required in respect of directors' interests in *options* in such capital.

[Continuing Obligations for Companies, para 21(h); General Undertaking paragraph 10(h)].

8.05 For these purposes, an interest should be shown as non-beneficial only if neither the director nor his spouse nor any of his infant children has any beneficial interest in the shares concerned. Particulars should also be given of the extent of any duplication which occurs, for example, where two directors are jointly interested in shares [Continuing Obligations for Companies, para 21.5]. The term "beneficial" is not defined but its ordinary dictionary meaning is "of, or having, the use or benefit of property etc". Thus, for example, the interest of a beneficiary under a non-discretionary trust would be a beneficial interest, whereas the interest of the trustee may well be non-beneficial (see also 8.15 below).

Obligation to notify a company

8.06 Directors are under an obligation to notify the company within five working days of the particulars which require inclusion in the register of directors' share and debenture interests [s324(3), Sch 13 paras 14,15 and 16]. A director is not required to notify a company of any event of which he becomes aware after he has ceased to be a director [s324(4)]. The provisions apply to shadow directors as they do to directors [s324(6)].

Exceptions

8.07 Notification, and hence disclosure in the directors' report or notes to the accounts, is not required in respect of an interest in the *shares* of a body corporate which is a wholly-owned subsidiary [s324(6)]. A subsidiary is regarded as wholly-owned if it has no members other than its holding company and any wholly-owned subsidiary of that holding company (and its or their nominees) [s736(5)].

8.08 Statutory instrument 1985 No. 802 made under the authority of section 324(3) of the Act, provides exemption from the requirement to notify (and hence disclose) interests in the following cases.

(1) A director of a company which is a wholly-owned subsidiary of a company incorporated in Great Britain need not notify the company of his interests in the shares and debentures of group companies, provided he is also a director of the parent; in such a case, his interests will be notifiable to, and hence disclosable by, the parent.

(2) Where the company is a wholly-owned subsidiary of a body corporate incorporated outside Great Britain, the directors do not have to notify interests in shares or debentures of that overseas body corporate or of any other overseas body corporate.

"Wholly-owned" has the same meaning as in 8.07.

(3) Other interests which do not require notification include those of a person in his capacity as a trustee of, or as a beneficiary under, a trust relating exclusively to an approved superannuation fund or scheme or a retirement benefits scheme.

Meaning of "interest"

8.09 Schedule 13 of the Act defines the meaning of an interest in shares or debentures for the purpose of the maintenance of the register and hence disclosure in the directors' report [s324(3), Sch 7 para 2]. The definition, which is very broad, is described in the paragraphs which follow.

8.10 The general rule is that any interest of any kind whatsoever in shares or debentures of the company or any other group company constitutes a notifiable interest and, accordingly, any restraints or restrictions to which the exercise of any rights attached to the interest are or may be subject are to be disregarded [Sch 13 para 1]. Persons having a joint interest are each separately regarded as being interested in all the shares or debentures in question [Sch 13 para 7]. Where this is the case, that fact is normally indicated in the disclosures. It is immaterial that shares or debentures in which a person has an interest are unidentifiable [Sch 13 para 8].

8.11 An interest of a director's spouse, infant child or stepchild in the shares or debentures of group companies is treated as being an interest of the director, except where the spouse, child or stepchild is also a director of the company [s328(1),(8)].

8.12 For the purposes of these rules, a person is regarded as being "interested" in shares or debentures in the following instances:

(1) Where he enters into a contract for their purchase by him [Sch 13 para 3(1)(a)].

(2) Where, if not being the registered holder, he is entitled to exercise, or control the exercise of, any right conferred by holding the shares or debentures [Sch 13 para 3(1)(b)]. This applies also where a person has a right the exercise of which, or an obligation the fulfilment of which, would make him so entitled [Sch 13 para 3(2)]. However, a person appointed to act as proxy at a specified meeting, or appointed by a corporation to act as its representative at any meeting, is not taken to be interested in the shares or debentures by virtue *only* of that appointment [Sch 13 para 3(3)].

(3) Where a body corporate is interested in them and either that body corporate or its directors are accustomed to act in accordance with that person's directions or instructions, or that person is entitled to exercise, or control the exercise of, one-third or more of the voting power in general meeting of that body corporate [Sch 13 para 4]. Paragraph 8.14 explains the operation of this provision where an interest arises through an intermediate company.

(4) Where otherwise than by virtue of having an interest under a trust, he has a right to call for delivery of the shares or debentures to himself or to his order, or he has a right to acquire, or an obligation to take, an interest in the shares or debentures. However, a right or obligation to *subscribe* for shares or debentures is not taken as being a right to acquire or an obligation to take an interest in shares or debentures; this is expressed as being "without prejudice to" the general definition of an interest set out in 8.10 above [Sch 13 para 6].

8.13 The intention and impact of the words "without prejudice to" is unclear. The reason for the exclusion of rights to subscribe is not obvious but the exclusion may have been made in view of the obligation on a company to record in the register, without waiting for notification by the director, particulars of any option it grants to the director to subscribe for its shares or debentures. There is also an obligation on the director to notify the company where another group company grants similar options to him. An effect of excluding options to subscribe for shares and debentures from the definition of "interests" is that they are not therefore required to be included in the directors' share and debenture interests required by the Act to be disclosed in the directors' report. Listed companies are required to disclose particulars of options (see para 8.04). Furthermore, the following information relating to options to subscribe for shares must be given in aggregate in the notes to the accounts:

(1) the number, description and amount of the shares in question,

(2) the period during which the right is exercisable, and

(3) the price to be paid for the shares allotted.

[Sch 4 para 40, Sch 9 para 13(2)]

This disclosure relates to all options to subscribe for shares and is not limited to options granted to directors, which may also require disclosure in the notes to the accounts as an arrangement in which the director has a "material interest" (see Chapter 29).

8.14 For the purpose of determining the proportion of the voting power exercisable by a person, any voting power in one body corporate which is exercisable by a second body corporate is regarded as being exercisable by a person if that person is entitled to exercise or control the exercise of one-third or more of the voting power of the second body corporate [Sch 13 para 5].

Example:	Mr X	Mr Y
	|	|
	30%	40%
	↓	↓
	A Ltd	A Ltd
	|	|
	80%	80%
	↓	↓
	B Ltd	B Ltd

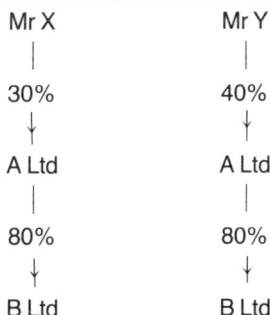

Mr X is not regarded as being interested in A Ltd's 80% holding in B Ltd, whereas Mr Y, who controls more than one-third of the voting power of A Ltd, is deemed to be interested in that holding.

Interests under a trust

8.15 Where property is held on trust and part of that property comprises an interest in shares or debentures, any beneficiary of the trust is regarded as having an interest in those shares or debentures [Sch 13 para 2]. However, where a person is entitled to receive (during his lifetime or that of another) income from trust property, comprising the shares or debentures, any other person who merely has an interest in reversion or remainder is not regarded as being interested in those shares or debentures [Sch 13 para 9]. Where shares or debentures are held by a person as a bare trustee or as a custodian trustee under English Law, or as a simple trustee under Scots Law, that person is to be treated as not having an interest in those shares or debentures [Sch 13 para 10].

8.16 As noted in 8.08(3) above, there is an exception from the requirement to *notify* interests which arise under trusts relating exclusively to a superannuation fund or scheme. Thus, in most cases where shares or debentures are held by a nominee, the nominee would be regarded as not having an interest (or notifiable interest) in those shares or debentures.

Register or directors' share and debenture interests

8.17 Every company is required to keep a register of its directors' interests in the shares and debentures of group companies; the register must be available for inspection by members and the public generally [s325(1),(5), Sch 13 para 25]. The information that has to be included in this register is divided into that which must be notified by the directors and that which must be included without any notification. The exceptions to the notification requirements are set out in 8.07 and 8.08 above.

Information to be notified by directors

8.18 The information to be notified by the directors and which the company must enter in the register is set out below. In each case the director must notify the class and number of shares and the class and amount of debentures.

(1) On appointment as a director, particulars of the director's interests in the shares and debentures of the company or any other body corporate being its subsidiary, its holding company or any subsidiary of its holding company (referred to below as "group companies") [s324(1)].

(2) During the period of the directorship, the occurrence of any of the following events:
   (a) Any event in consequence of which the director becomes or ceases to be interested in shares in, or debentures of, any group company.
   (b) The entering into by the director of a contract to sell any such shares or debentures.

(c) The assignment by the director of a right granted to him by the company to subscribe for shares in, or debentures of, the company.

(d) The grant to the director by another group company of a right to subscribe for its shares or debentures and the exercise or assignment of such a right.

(e) The grant to the director's spouse, infant children or stepchildren of a right to subscribe for shares in, or debentures of, the company and the exercise of any such right.

[s324(2), 328(3),(8)]

8.19 In addition, the following must be notified to the company:

(1) In the event of a director becoming or ceasing to be interested in shares or debentures, by way of entering into a contract for their purchase or sale, the director must notify the price to be paid under the contract [Sch 13 para 17].

(2) The consideration for the assignment, where a director assigns a right to subscribe for shares or debentures in the company or other group companies or, where there is no consideration, a statement of this fact [Sch 13 para 18].

(3) Where a director is granted a right to subscribe for shares or debentures in *other* group companies:
(a) the date on which the right was granted,
(b) the period during which, or the time at which, the right is exercisable,
(c) the consideration for the grant (or, if there is no consideration, the fact), and
(d) the price to be paid for the shares or debentures.
[Sch 13 para 19(1)]

(4) Where a director exercises a right to subscribe for shares or debentures in *other* group companies:
(a) the number of shares or debentures in respect of which the right was exercised, and
(b) if they were registered in the director's name, the fact and, if not, the name or names of the person or persons who are the registered holders and, if the shares or debentures were registered in the names of two or more persons, the number or amount thereof registered in the name of each of them.
[Sch 13 para 19(2)]

References to the price paid or received include any consideration other than money [Sch 13 para 20].

Information to be recorded by the company without notification

8.20 A company must also enter the following information in the register, without any notification by the directors:

(1) On the grant to a director of a right to subscribe for shares in, or debentures of, the company:
  (a) the date on which the right is granted,
  (b) the period during which, or the time at which, it is exercisable,
  (c) the consideration for the grant (or, if there is no consideration, that fact),
  (d) the description of shares or debentures involved and the number or amount thereof, and
  (e) the price to be paid (or the consideration, if otherwise than in money).
  [s325(3)]

(2) When a director exercises a right to subscribe for shares in, or debentures of, the company:
  (a) the fact of the exercise of the right,
  (b) the number or amount of shares or debentures in respect of which it is exercised, and
  (c) if they were registered in his name, that fact and, if not, the name or names of the person or persons who are the registered holders and, if the shares or debentures were registered in the names of two persons or more, the number or amount thereof registered in the name of each person.
  [s325(4)]

For the purpose of the above requirements, a shadow director is deemed to be a director [s325(6)].

Form of register

8.21 Part IV of Schedule 13 prescribes regulations regarding the form, content and inspection of the register of directors' interests.

Removal of entries from the register

8.22 The Act does not appear to permit the removal of entries from the register either on a director's ceasing to have an interest or on his ceasing to hold office.

Notification to The Stock Exchange

8.23 Where a company, any shares or debentures of which are listed on The Stock Exchange, receives a notification from a director in pursuance of the notification requirements of sections 324 or 328 of the Act, and that notification relates to shares or debentures (of group companies) which are listed on The Stock Exchange, the Act requires the company to notify The Stock Exchange thereof by the following working day [s329(1),(2)].

The Stock Exchange, however, requires this notification to be made immediately in conformity with the normal practice for the communication of announcements (Admission of Securities to Listing, Section 5 chapter 2 paragraph 16(b)). The Unlisted Securities Market imposes a similar obligation on USM companies (General Undertaking paragraph 5(g)).

8.24 The Stock Exchange is empowered to publish any such information which it receives [s329(1)].

Dealing in options

8.25 The directors of a company are prohibited from buying options to purchase or sell listed shares or debentures of the company, its subsidiaries, its holding company or any subsidiary of its holding company [s323(1),(3)]. Failure to comply with this prohibition carries a penalty [s323(2)]. The prohibition does not extend to the purchase of a right to subscribe for shares or debentures or to the purchase of debentures which are convertible into shares; thus share option schemes under which directors subscribe for shares are permitted.

8.26 The prohibition extends to the spouse, infant children and step-children of the director, as well as to shadow directors [s323(4), 327].

CHAPTER 9

Directors' report

Requirement to prepare

9.01 All companies are required to prepare a directors' report in respect of each financial year of the company [s235(1)]. The prescribed contents of the report vary according to whether:

(1) the company's individual accounts are prepared in compliance with Schedule 4 of the Act, or

(2) the company's individual accounts are prepared in compliance with Schedule 4 but are accompanied by group accounts which are "special category" (and therefore prepared under Schedule 9 – see Chapter 13) (such a reporting package is sometimes referred to as a "hybrid" set of accounts), or

(3) the company's individual accounts are special category.

9.02 This chapter deals only with the first two cases; the rules which apply where a company's individual accounts are special category are set out in Chapter 13.

Contents

9.03 Section 235 specifies some disclosures but the majority are contained in Schedule 7. For "hybrids", Schedule 10 requires additional disclosures. The disclosure requirements for the directors' report for both Schedule 4 and hybrid accounts are set out below:

(1) A fair review of the development of the business of the company and its subsidiaries during the financial year and of their position at the end of it [s235(1)].

(2) The amount (if any) which the directors:
   (a) recommend should be paid as dividend, and
   (b) propose to carry to reserves.
   [s235(1)]

(3) Names of the persons who were directors at any time in the financial year [s235(2)].

(4) Principal activities of the company and of its subsidiaries during the financial year and any significant changes therein during the year [s235(2)].

(5) Significant changes in fixed assets of the company, or any of its subsidiaries, during the financial year [s235(3), Sch 7 para 1].

(6) An indication (with such degree of precision as is practicable) of the difference between the book value and market value (as at the end of the financial year) of land and buildings of the company, and any of its subsidiaries, if significant to members or debenture holders [s235(3), Sch 7 para 1].

(7) In relation to the company and its subsidiaries:
   (a) particulars of any important events which have occurred since the end of the financial year,
   (b) an indication of likely future developments in the business, and
   (c) an indication of any activities in the field of research and development.
   [s235(3), Sch 7 para 6]

Directors' interests in shares and debentures
(8) Prescribed particulars of interests in shares or debentures of group companies (negative statement where applicable) as recorded in the register of directors' interests at:
   (a) the beginning of the period (or later date of appointment as director), and
   (b) the end of the period,
   to be given in respect of each person who was a director of *the company* at the end of the financial year. This disclosure may be given, instead, in the notes to the accounts. The particulars to be disclosed are:
   (a) the name of the director with the interest,
   (b) the name of the body corporate in whose shares or debentures the director has an interest, and
   (c) the number, amount and class of shares and debentures in which the director is interested.
   For the purpose of the above, the interests of a director's spouse and minor children, which are treated as being an interest of the director (see para 8.11), are to be included. Furthermore, where a person became a director on more than one occasion during the financial year the particulars to be given in respect of the date of appointment as director are those as at the first such occasion.
   [s235(3), Sch 7 para 2]

Political and charitable contributions

(9) If a company, which is not the wholly-owned subsidiary of another British company, has on its own (or, if at the end of the financial year it has subsidiaries, the company and those subsidiaries between them have) in the financial year given, for political purposes or for charitable purposes or both, in aggregate more than £200, there must be disclosed:

(a) the total amounts given for both:
  (i) political purposes, and
  (ii) charitable purposes.
(b) in the case of payments for political purposes, the following particulars (so far as applicable):
  (i) the name of each person to whom money exceeding £200 in amount has been given for those purposes and the amount given,
  (ii) if money exceeding £200 in amount has been given by way of donation or subscription to a political party, the identity of the party and the amount given.
[s235(3), Sch 7 para 3,4]

The following applies for the interpretation of the above requirements:

(a) A company is regarded as giving money for political purposes if, directly or indirectly:
  (i) it gives a donation or subscription to a political party of the United Kingdom, or any part of it, or
  (ii) it gives a donation or subscription to a person who, to the company's knowledge, is carrying on, or proposing to carry on, any activities which can, at the time at which the donation or subscription was given, reasonably be regarded as likely to affect public support for such a political party.
  The Act does not define "political party".
(b) Money given for charitable purposes to a person who, when it was given, was ordinarily resident outside the United Kingdom is to be left out of account.
(c) "Charitable purposes" means purposes which are exclusively charitable.
[s235(3), Sch 7 para 5]

Acquisition of own shares

(10) Where shares in a company are:

(a) purchased by the company, or
(b) acquired by the company by forfeiture or surrender in lieu of forfeiture, or
(c) acquired by the company otherwise than for valuable consideration or in a reduction of capital (under section 143(3) of the Act), or

(d) acquired from a third party by a nominee of the company *without* direct or indirect financial assistance from the company, or are acquired by any person *with* direct or indirect financial assistance from the company and, in both cases, the company has a beneficial interest in the shares, or

(e) made subject to a lien or charge under section 150 of the Act or section 6(3) of the Consequential Provisions Act,

the directors' report must disclose with respect to a financial year:

(i) number* and nominal value of shares so purchased, aggregate consideration paid by the company and the reasons for the purchase,

(ii) number* and nominal value of, respectively, shares so acquired by the company, acquired by another person in such circumstances and so charged during the financial year,

(iii) maximum number* and nominal value of shares which having been so acquired by the company, acquired by another person in such circumstances or so charged (whether or not during that year) are held at any time by the company or that other person during that year,

(iv) number* and nominal value of such shares so acquired by the company or by another person or so charged (whether or not during the year) which are disposed of by the company or that other person or cancelled by the company during the year,

(v) where any of the shares were disposed of for money or money's worth, the amount or value of the consideration in each case,

(vi) the amount of the charge in each case where shares have been so charged.

* in each case, state the percentage of the called-up share capital which the shares represent.
[s235(4), Sch 7 paras 7,8]

Disabled persons

(11) Where the average number† (see footnote over) of persons employed by the company (under contracts of service but excluding those employed to work wholly or mainly outside the UK) over the financial year exceeded 250, the directors' report must contain a statement describing such policy as the company has applied during the financial year:

(a) for giving full and fair consideration to applications for employment by the company made by disabled persons, having regard to their particular aptitudes and abilities,

(b) for continuing the employment of, and for arranging appropriate training for, employees of the company who have become disabled persons during the period when they were employed by the company, and

(c) otherwise for the training, career development and promotion of disabled persons employed by the company.
[s235(5), Sch 7 para 9]

Employee involvement

(12) Where the average number† of persons employed by the company (under contracts of service but excluding those employed to work wholly or mainly outside the UK) over the financial year exceeded 250, the directors' report must contain a statement describing the action taken during the financial year to introduce, maintain or develop arrangements aimed at:

(a) providing employees systematically with information on matters of concern to them as employees,

(b) consulting employees or their representatives on a regular basis so that the views of employees can be taken into account in making decisions which are likely to affect their interests,

(c) encouraging the involvement of employees in the company's performance through an employees' share scheme or by some other means,

(d) achieving a common awareness on the part of all employees of the financial and economic factors affecting the performance of the company.
[s235(5), Sch 7 para 11]

---

†The average number of employees is to be derived by dividing by the number of weeks in the financial year the number derived by ascertaining, in relation to each of those weeks, the number of persons who, under contracts of service, were employed in the week (whether throughout it or not) by the company and adding up the numbers ascertained. [Sch 7 paras 9(2), 11(2)]

The provisions are formulated to apply to individual companies, not groups, so that a company is subject to these requirements only where it (on its own) has more than 250 employees. Thus, where, for example, a holding company has 200 employees and its subsidiary has 100 employees, *neither* company would be subject to the requirements. If the holding company had 100 employees and the subsidiary had 300 employees, *only* the subsidiary company would have to make the disclosures.

Having established that a company is required to make disclosures, the Act does not state explicitly whether this disclosure has to be made only in respect of the action taken by the company itself or whether, in the case of a holding company, the particulars given have to be extended to embrace the action taken by its subsidiaries. It appears, however, that the requirement relates only to the action taken by the company itself. There is no requirement for the directors' report which accompanies group accounts to "consolidate" the information contained in the directors' reports of individual group companies. Generally in UK company law, where information on a group basis is required, that is specifically stated.

Thus, where a company to which the disclosure provisions apply voluntarily gives the above information on a group basis or gives information relating to its subsidiaries, it should be careful to ensure that the correct information relating to the company itself, is also given in order to comply with the statutory requirements.

Employees' health, safety and welfare at work
(13) The Secretary of State has the power to make regulations pre-
scribing disclosures to be made about the arrangements in force in
the financial year for securing the health, safety and welfare at work
of employees of the company and its subsidiaries, and for protecting
other persons against risks to health or safety arising out of or in
connection with the activities at work of those employees.

This power was introduced by the Health and Safety at Work etc.
Act 1974 but, to date, no regulations have been made.
[s235(5), Sch 7 para 10]

Hybrids

9.04 If a company's individual accounts are accompanied by group
accounts which are "special category" (see Chapter 13), the directors'
report must, in addition to complying with the requirements set out
above, also give the information required by Schedule 10 paras 2 to 6
(turnover and profitability; size of labour force and wages paid) (see para
13.17) [s235(6)].

Penalties

9.05 There are penalties for non-compliance with the statutory requirements relating to the directors' report [s235(7)].

CHAPTER 10

Groups

10.01 The requirement for the preparation of group accounts which give a true and fair view and other related provisions have been discussed in Chapter 2. Schedule 4 Part IV contains additional provisions which apply where a company is a holding or subsidiary company. The provisions include modifications to a holding company's individual accounts, consolidation adjustments and special requirements where group accounts are not prepared.

Company's Own Accounts

10.02 Where the prescribed balance sheet layouts require disclosure of the amounts attributable to dealings with or interests in group companies (for example, shares in group companies, amounts owed by or to group companies), separate disclosure is required of the aggregate amounts in respect of:

(1) any holding or fellow subsidiary company, and

(2) any subsidiary company.

[Sch 4 para 59]

10.03 Where the company is a holding company, the number, description and amount of the shares in and debentures of the company held by its subsidiaries or their nominees must be disclosed in a note to the company's accounts [Sch 4 para 60(1)]. This requirement does not apply where the subsidiary is concerned as personal representative or as trustee, provided that, in the latter case, neither the company nor any subsidiary of the company is beneficially interested under the trust, otherwise than by way of security only, for a transaction entered into by it in the ordinary course of a business which includes the lending of money [Sch 4 para 60(2)].

Consolidated accounts

10.04 Section 229 of the Act establishes the requirement for a holding company to prepare group accounts except where it is a wholly-owned subsidiary of another British company (see para 2.19). The form of group accounts and the exclusion of individual subsidiaries therefrom is considered in Chapter 2. Where group accounts are prepared in the form if a single set of consolidated accounts of the holding company and its subsidiaries (as required by SSAP 14 "Group accounts", except in defined circumstances), the consolidated balance sheet and profit and loss account are to be prepared by combining the information contained in the separate balance sheets and profit and loss accounts of the holding company and of its subsidiaries dealt with by the consolidated accounts, but with any adjustments as the directors of the holding company think necessary [Sch 4 para 61]. These adjustments would normally include the elimination of intra-group transactions including related profit and dividends, and intra-group balances. In giving the required information, the consolidated accounts must comply, so far as practicable, with the requirements of Schedule 4 and any other requirements of the Act, as if they were the accounts of an actual company [Sch 4 paras 62,64]. Paragraph 16 of SSAP 14 requires that uniform group accounting policies should normally be followed in preparing consolidated accounts, with any necessary adjustments being made where a subsidiary does not adopt these policies in its own accounts.

10.05 In combining the information given in the individual accounts of the group companies which are to be consolidated, the following disclosures are *not* to be aggregated:

(1) Financial information about subsidiaries and particulars of other holdings in excess of 10% [Schedule 5 Parts II and III of the Act].

(2) The remuneration of directors and the emoluments of directors and employees by reference to bands of £5,000 [Schedule 5 Parts V and VI].

(3) Transactions with directors and other officers, except insofar as the requirements relate to group accounts [Sections 232 to 234 and Schedule 6].

[Sch 4 para 63]

The information disclosed by a holding company in respect of these matters would be that which is contained in its own individual accounts.

10.06 These exemptions are designed to prevent unnecessary or misleading duplication of information and to restrict disclosure of information on directors and employees to those of the holding company only. The extent of the disclosure required in respect of the remuneration of and transactions with such persons is set out in Chapters 7 and 29 to 31.

10.07 Where any subsidiaries are not included in the consolidated accounts, the consolidated accounts must give the information in respect of those subsidiaries required by Schedule 4 paras 59 and 60 (intra-group balances and holdings, and holdings of shares and debentures of the company by its subsidiaries – see paras 10.02 and 10.03 above) [Sch 4 para 67].

10.08 Goodwill arising on consolidation is not subject to compulsory writing off [Sch 4 para 66]. Accounting for goodwill is considered in paragraphs 5.24 to 5.29.

Group accounts not prepared as consolidated accounts

10.09 Where group accounts are prepared otherwise than as consolidated accounts, they are required to give the same or equivalent information as that set out in paras 10.04 to 10.08 above [Sch 4 para 68].

Provisions of general application

Subsidiaries excluded from group accounts

10.10 Where a holding company does not prepare group accounts, or prepares group accounts which do not deal with one or more of its subsidiaries, the following provisions apply [Sch 4 para 69(1),(7)]. The notes to the company's accounts (or, where appropriate, the consolidated or group accounts) must give in respect of the subsidiaries which are excluded from group accounts:

(1) the reasons why the subsidiaries are not dealt with in group accounts [Sch 4 para 69(2)(a)],

(2) a statement of any qualifications in the reports of the auditors on the accounts of the subsidiaries for their financial years ending with or during that of the holding company and any note or saving made in those accounts to draw attention to a matter which, apart from the note or saving, would have been the subject of qualification (for example, disclosure in the notes of a departure from the accounting provisions of the Act made in order for the accounts to give a true and fair view and which, if not explained in the notes, would result in a qualified audit report), insofar as they are not covered by the holding company's own accounts and are material from the point of view of its members [Sch 4 para 69(2)(b)], and

(3) the aggregate investment of the holding company in the shares of the subsidiaries calculated by way of the equity method of accounting [Sch 4 para 69(3)]. This is not required where the company is a

wholly-owned subsidiary of another body corporate incorporated in Great Britain and if there is included in a note to the company's accounts (or, where appropriate, the consolidated accounts) a statement that, in the opinion of the directors of the company, the aggregate value of the assets of the company consisting of shares in, or amounts owing from the company's subsidiaries (whether on account of loan or otherwise) is not less than the aggregate of the amounts at which those assets are stated or included in the company's (or, where appropriate, the consolidated) balance sheet [Sch 4 para 69(4),(7)].

10.11 The above information is not required where:

(1) it is unobtainable, provided that a statement to this effect is given in a note to the accounts [Sch 4 para 69(5)], or

(2) to the extent that the Secretary of State may, on the application or with the consent of the company's directors, so direct [Sch 4 para 69(6)].

Non-coterminous financial years

10.12 If the financial years of any subsidiaries are not coterminous with that of the holding company, the notes to the accounts (or where group accounts are prepared, the group accounts) must give for each subsidiary:

(1) the reasons why the holding company's directors consider that the financial years should not be coterminous, and

(2) the subsidiaries' latest accounting dates before that of the holding company (or the earliest and latest of those dates). [Sch 4 para 70]

EEC Seventh Directive

10.13 The EEC Seventh Company Law Directive was adopted in 1983 and is required to be enacted by the end of 1987 and implemented by 1990. The Department of Trade and Industry is expected to set out its proposals in a consultative paper. The impact of the directive on UK company law can be summarised as follows:

– A broadening of the definition of a subsidiary to include companies in which a parent holds a majority of its voting rights, and companies in which a minority shareholder has control pursuant to an agreement with other shareholders.

– The exemption from the requirement for an intermediate parent to prepare consolidated accounts where it is a wholly-owned subsidiary of another British company must be extended to those intermediate parents which themselves have a parent situated in *any* member state (not just Great Britain) and which either holds all of their shares or holds at least ninety per cent and the remaining shareholders have approved the exemption.

– Statutory rules governing the accounting treatment of goodwill arising on consolidation, the optional use of merger accounting, and accounting for joint ventures.

In addition, the directive permits member states to exempt small groups from the requirement to prepare consolidated accounts, and it is conceivable that the UK government might grant such an exemption.

CHAPTER 11

Related and associated companies

Related company

11.01 The concept of a "related company" was introduced into UK company law by the 1981 Act. The prescribed formats for the accounts require disclosure of shares in, loans to, and amounts owed to and by related companies, and also of income from shares in related companies.

11.02 A related company is any body corporate (other than a group company) in which the investing company holds, on a long-term basis, a "qualifying capital interest", for the purpose of securing a contribution to the investing company's own activities by the exercise of any control or influence arising from that interest [Sch 4 para 92(1)].

11.03 A qualifying capital interest is one comprised of equity share capital carrying the right to vote in all circumstances at general meetings [Sch 4 para 92(2)].

11.04 Where a company holds a qualifying capital interest equal to twenty per cent or more of the nominal value of all such capital in another body corporate, the latter is presumed to be a related company, unless the contrary is shown [Sch 4 para 92(3)].

11.05 There are close similarities between the definition of a related company and the definition in SSAP 1 of an associated company. In the latter case, the interest of the investing group as a whole is taken into account, but in the definition of a related company only shares held by the investing company may be taken into account in determining whether another body corporate is a related company. Because the Act does not state any minimum percentage of the equity share capital which must be held in order for a company to be regarded as a related company (merely a rebuttable presumption that a twenty per cent holding constitutes such a relationship), in practice, most associated companies will fall within the definition of a related company.

Associated company

11.06 The Act provides that an investment (of the company or any other member of the group) in the shares of any other body corporate may be accounted for in the consolidated accounts by way of the equity method of accounting in any case where it appears to the directors (of the holding company) that the other body corporate is so closely associated with any member of the group as to justify that treatment [Sch 4 para 65]. The equity method is not defined, nor is any minimum percentage holding prescribed. It would thus be up to the directors to justify the use of the equity method of accounting for investments in non-subsidiaries in the light of accepted accounting practice (particularly SSAP 1 – "Associated companies").

11.07 SSAP 1 requires a policy of equity accounting for interests in associated companies to be followed in an investing company's consolidated accounts. Paragraphs 24 and 35 of SSAP 1 state that where an investing company (other than one which is a wholly-owned subsidiary) does not prepare consolidated accounts, it should show the information required to be disclosed by the SSAP, by preparing a separate (extra-statutory) profit and loss account and balance sheet or by adding the information in supplementary form to its own balance sheet and profit and loss account. In so doing, the share of the profits of the associated companies should not be treated in such a manner as to give the impression that it is a realised profit as far as the reporting company is concerned.

11.08 Where a company has no subsidiaries or does not otherwise prepare consolidated accounts, equity accounting in the investing company's balance sheet for investments in associates would be permitted only as a revaluation under one of the alternative accounting rules (see para 5.47) and the amount of the revaluation would be subject to the constraints placed on the revaluation reserve.

11.09 The prescribed layouts for the balance sheet and profit and loss account do not refer to associated companies. Amounts in respect of an associated company which comes within the definition of a related company should normally be shown under the relevant item for a related company.

CHAPTER 12

Small, medium and dormant companies

12.01 This chapter outlines the provisions which allow the filing, by small and medium companies, of modified accounts with the registrar of companies, and the exemption of dormant companies from the requirement to have their accounts audited. These provisions are not available in respect of special category accounts (see Chapter 13).

Entitlement to file modified accounts

12.02 The Act allows small and medium companies (as defined – see below), if they wish, to file abridged accounts (referred to as "modified accounts") with the registrar of companies [s247(1)]. They are, however, still required to send full audited accounts to their members who have no authority to dispense with this requirement. Provided the conditions are met, the option for small and medium companies to prepare modified accounts for filing with the registrar of companies, is available both in respect of individual company accounts and group accounts.

Restriction

12.03 Modified accounts for a financial year may *not* be filed with the registrar of companies in respect of a company which is (at the time of filing), or was at any time during that financial year:

(1) a public company,

(2) a "special category company" (that is, broadly, a banking, insurance or "exempt" shipping company – see para 13.02), or

(3) a member of a group which is "ineligible" (see below) for this purpose.

[s247(2)]

"Group" means a holding company and its subsidiaries together. A group is "ineligible" if any of its members is:

(1) a public company or a special category company, or

(2) a body corporate (other than a "company") which has power under its constitution to offer its shares or debentures to the public and may lawfully exercise that power, or

(3) a body corporate (other than a "company") which is either a recognised bank or licensed institution within the Banking Act 1979, or which is an "insurance company" to which Part II of the Insurance Companies Act 1982 applies.

[s247(3)]

A "company" means a company formed and registered under the 1985 Act or under an earlier Companies Act [s735(1)]. The term "body corporate (other than a *company*)" is intended primarily to cover foreign bodies corporate which meet the criteria but would also cover any which are British.

12.04 The effect of the above restrictions is that only independent private companies or "private" groups may qualify for the exemptions.

12.05 The special position of dormant companies is discussed in para 12.30.

Qualification as a small or medium company

12.06 A company qualifies as small or medium in a financial year if for that year it is, on its own (that is, excluding any other member of a group), within the limits of at least two of the following three criteria:

CRITERIA	SIZE	
	Small	Medium
Balance sheet total (that is, total assets)	£700,000 (£900,000)	£2,800,000 (£3,500,000)
Turnover	£1,400,000 (£1,850,000)	£5,750,000 (£7,300,000)
Average number of employees	50	250

[s248(1) to (4)]

12.07 Where the financial year of a company is shorter or longer than twelve months, the maximum amounts for turnover in the above table must be proportionately adjusted [s248(5)].

12.08 The above limits are as set by the 1981 Act. The amounts shown in parentheses are the approximate revised maximum monetary limits as set by the Council of the EEC in 1984 but which have not yet been incorporated into UK legislation (see para 12.16).

12.09 A company's turnover and balance sheet total are to be ascertained by reference to accounts prepared in accordance with Schedule 4 of the Act. Furthermore, the exemptions are also based only on Schedule 4. The concession to file modified accounts is thus not available where the company's accounts are "special category" (see Chapter 13).

When modified individual accounts may be delivered

12.10 Modified individual accounts, complying with Part I of Schedule 8, may be delivered to the registrar of companies by small and medium companies in the circumstances set out below [s249(1)]. There are additional provisions for holding companies which are required to prepare group accounts (see para 12.13) [s250].

12.11 In respect of a company's *first* financial year it may:

(1) deliver modified accounts for a small company if it qualifies as small in that first financial year,

(2) deliver modified accounts for a medium-sized company if it qualifies as medium in that first financial year.

[s249(2)]

12.12 In respect of a company's financial year other than its first financial year, in order to be entitled to file modified accounts a company must satisfy the relevant criteria for two consecutive financial years [s249(4)]. However, once it has satisfied these criteria for two consecutive financial years and thus become entitled to file modified accounts, it does not lose this entitlement unless it subsequently fails to satisfy the criteria for two consecutive financial years, in which case it loses the entitlement in the second such year [s249(3) to (6)].

12.13 *Small, medium and dormant companies*

Example: X Ltd was incorporated in 1970.

Financial year ending 30th June	Criteria satisfied		Entitlement to Modified accounts	
1985	(1) Small	(2) Small	(1) Small*	(2) Small*
1986	Small	Small	Small	Small
1987	Medium	Medium	Small	Small
1988	Small	Medium	Small	Medium
1989	Medium	Neither	Small	Medium
1990	Medium	Neither	Medium	No entitlement
1991	Small	Medium	Medium	No entitlement
*assumed for the purpose of this example.				

Note: Where a company is entitled to file modified accounts for a small company, it may, if it wishes, file modified accounts for a medium-sized company or not take advantage of the position at all and file full accounts.

Groups

12.13 Where a company is a holding company which is required to prepare group accounts, an additional condition has to be fulfilled before it is entitled to deliver to the registrar of companies modified *individual* accounts in respect of a financial year. Not only must the conditions set out in paras 12.11 or 12.12 be fulfilled, but the group (consisting of that holding company and its subsidiaries), taken as a whole, must satisfy the criteria, set out in section 248, for a small or medium company in that financial year. Furthermore, the modified individual accounts to which such a holding company would be entitled would be based on the size of the group taken as a whole [s250(1),(2)]. Thus, if the group taken as a whole would qualify as a medium company, the holding company will be treated as a medium company notwithstanding that, if taken on its own, it might otherwise qualify as a small company. It follows that where an intermediate holding company is not required to prepare group accounts (for example, where it is a wholly-owned subsidiary of another company incorporated in Great Britain), it would be considered on an individual company basis and could qualify as small or medium based on its individual size alone.

12.14 Where a holding company is entitled to file modified individual accounts with the registrar of companies, the company may also deliver modified *group* accounts to the registrar of companies. The extent to which the group accounts may be modified, depends upon whether the group, taken as a whole, qualifies to be treated as small or medium [s250(6), Sch 8].

Application of size criteria to groups

12.15 In determining whether a group, taken as a whole, is small or medium-sized the following rules apply. The figures to be taken into account for turnover, balance sheet total and numbers employed are those in the consolidated accounts or, where the group accounts are not in the form of consolidated accounts, the corresponding figures in the group accounts with such adjustment as would have been made if the accounts had been prepared in consolidated form. In either case there must be added the relevant figures for any subsidiaries omitted from the group accounts, except those omitted on the grounds of impracticability [s250(3)]. The relevant figures for any subsidiary which is omitted from the group accounts must be after such adjustment as would have been made had they been included in consolidated accounts, and must be extracted from the subsidiary's annual accounts for its financial year which ends with that of the holding company or, if it does not, with its financial year ending last before that of the holding company [s250(4),(5)].

Amendment by the Secretary of State

12.16 The Secretary of State for Trade may, by statutory instrument, amend the accounting exemption provisions, both in relation to the criteria to be met in order to be classified as small or medium, and also the modifications available to such companies and groups [s251(1) to (3)]. It is possible that this facility may be used in order to raise the monetary limits for qualification (see para 12.08).

Modifications available

12.17 The modifications which are available for individual accounts and group accounts in the circumstances described above are set out in Schedule 8 of the Act. The modifications available to small companies and groups are far more extensive than those available to medium companies and groups. In taking advantage of the modifications, companies will be able to retain some confidentiality of information, but will have to prepare two sets of accounts (one for their members and one for filing with the registrar of companies).

Small companies and groups

12.18 The modifications available are:

(1) There is no requirement for a profit and loss account or directors' report [paras 3,14].

(2) A modified balance sheet showing only those items to which a letter or Roman numeral is assigned (that is, only the main headings) need be given (for example, the aggregate amount of current assets and the individual aggregate amounts of stocks, debtors, investments, and cash at bank and in hand). It is, however, still necessary to analyse the aggregate amounts shown for debtors and creditors into the amounts which fall due within one year and after more than one year from the balance sheet date [paras 2,6,13,16]. The modified balance sheet must be signed by the directors in the manner required by section 238 (see para 3.02) [para 2].

(3) The information required by Schedule 4 of the Act to be given in the notes to the accounts need not be given, with the exception of that relating to the following which must still be given:

(a) accounting policies,

(b) share capital,

(c) particulars of shares allotted,

(d) particulars of indebtedness (amounts repayable in excess of five years and details of secured liabilities),

(e) basis of translation of foreign currency amounts into sterling, and

(f) corresponding amounts for the previous financial year.

[paras 5,15]

(4) The information required by Parts V and VI of Schedule 5 of the Act (particulars of directors' and higher-paid employees' remuneration) need not be given [paras 4,17].

Medium companies and groups

12.19 The modifications available to medium companies are:

(1) A modified profit and loss account commencing with an item "gross profit or loss" which combines those items in the prescribed formats which would otherwise require the disclosure of turnover and cost of sales information [paras 7,18]. For a company adopting format 2, the term "gross profit" may not represent what is normally understood by that term, because it is before taking account of staff costs and depreciation.

(2) The analysis of turnover and profit normally required by Schedule 4 para 55 to be given in the notes to the accounts (see paras 6.28 to 6.32) need not be given [paras 8,19].

The modifications are summarised in the table on the next page.

Modifications available to small and medium companies for their accounts filed with the registrar of companies		
	SMALL	MEDIUM
Directors' report	not required	required in full
Profit and loss account	not required	modified – may commence with "gross profit or loss"
Balance sheet	modified – only main headings and amounts required	required in full
Notes to the accounts	Modified – only limited information required. Particulars of directors' and higher paid employees' emoluments not required	analyses of turnover and profit need not be given
Auditors' report	special report required	special report required

Statement by directors

12.20 Where modified individual accounts are filed by small or medium companies with the registrar of companies they must include a statement by the directors, immediately above their signatures (on the balance sheet), that they rely on sections 247 to 249 of the Act as entitling them to deliver modified accounts and that they do so on the ground that the company is entitled to the benefit of those sections as a small or medium-sized company, as the case may be [Sch 8 para 9]. Where modified group accounts are filed, the directors' statement must include a statement that the documents delivered include modified group accounts, in reliance on section 250 of the Act [Sch 8 para 21].

A suitable form of statement by the directors would be:

"We have relied on sections 247 to 249 of the Companies Act 1985 as entitling us to deliver modified accounts and have done so on the basis that the company is entitled to the benefit of those sections as a [small] [medium-sized] company. [The documents delivered include modified group accounts, in reliance on section 250 of that Act.]"

Special report by the auditors

12.21 Where the directors of a company propose to take advantage of the option to file modified accounts (or modified group accounts) it is the duty of the auditors to provide the directors with a report stating whether, in their opinion, the directors are so entitled and whether the documents to be delivered as modified (individual) accounts or modified group accounts are properly prepared in accordance with the Act [Sch 8 paras 10,22]. The purpose of this report would appear to be to confirm to the directors that they are entitled to deliver modified accounts; however, by requiring the auditors to report that the modified accounts are properly prepared, the Act assumes that the modified accounts will already have been prepared. No doubt, in practice, before they prepare modified accounts the directors will approach the auditors for verbal confirmation where they are unsure as to whether they are entitled to deliver modified accounts. Furthermore, it is likely that the auditors' special report on the modified accounts (which is described in the next paragraph) will, in practice, also fulfil the above requirement.

12.22 Where modified accounts or modified group accounts are delivered to the registrar of companies, they must be accompanied by a special auditors' report instead of the normal audit report [Sch 8 paras 10,22]. In this special report, the auditors are required to state that, in their opinion, the directors are entitled to deliver modified (individual) accounts in respect of the financial year (and, where applicable, are entitled to deliver modified group accounts), as claimed in the directors' statement, and that the modified individual accounts (and modified group accounts) are properly prepared in accordance with Schedule 8 of the Act [Sch 8 paras 10,22]. The special report must also reproduce the full text of the auditors' report on the full accounts [Sch 8 paras 10,22].

Dormant companies

12.23 In the circumstances which are described in the following paragraphs, a "dormant" company may, by passing a special resolution, exempt itself from the obligation to appoint auditors, and may thus present to its members and file unaudited accounts [s252(1)].

12.24 A company is regarded as being dormant during any period in which it has no "significant accounting transaction". A significant accounting transaction is any transaction which is required by section 221 of the Act to be entered in the company's accounting records (see Chapter 16), other than the taking of shares in the company by a sub-scriber to the memorandum in pursuance of an undertaking in the memorandum. A company which has been dormant ceases to be so on the occurrence of any such transaction [s252(5)]. Transactions entered into as agent would not fall to be recorded in the agent's statutory accounting records.

12.25 It appears that a dormant company may pass a special resolution excluding the obligation to appoint auditors only if this is not in conflict with the company's articles. When these provisions were brought into force (on 15th June 1982) as part of the 1981 Act, Table A to the 1948 Act (the "model" articles of association) was suitably amended to allow for the passing of such a resolution by a dormant company. However, this amendment was not retrospective and would thus affect only those companies adopting the relevant article of Table A (article 130) on or after that date. The new model articles (as set out in SI 1985 No. 805) which are relevant to companies incorporated on or after 1st July 1985 make no reference to the appointment of auditors, leaving the matter to be regulated by the Act. Many dormant companies therefore are likely to have to amend their articles before they can take advantage of the audit exemption.

12.26 A dormant company may, by special resolution, resolve that auditors shall not be appointed. This resolution must be passed at a general meeting at which audited accounts for a financial year are laid, but the following conditions must be satisfied:

(1) the directors must not be required to lay group accounts for that financial year,

(2) the directors must be entitled to deliver, in respect of that financial year, modified individual accounts available to small companies, or would be so entitled but for the company being, or having at any time in that financial year been, a member of an "ineligible group" (as defined, para 12.03), and

(3) the company must have been dormant since the end of that financial year.

[s252(2)]

12.27 A newly formed company (other than one which is a public company or a "special category company" – see para 13.02) may pass a similar resolution at any time before its first accounts are laid in general meeting, provided that the company has been dormant from the time of its formation until the resolution is passed [s252(3),(4)].

12.28 The exemption relates only to the appointment of auditors. Accounts must still be prepared and filed. A company which has passed a special resolution under this section may, presumably, rescind it at a later date if it so wishes.

12.29 Where a company which has taken advantage of the above provisions ceases to be dormant or, for some other reason, becomes ineligible, it immediately ceases to be exempt from the obligation to appoint an auditor [s252(6)]. An auditor must be appointed by the directors (or, if they do not do so, the shareholders may do so) to hold office until the conclusion of the next general meeting at which accounts are laid [s252(7)].

Filing of modified accounts

12.30 As noted in para 12.03, a company which is a member of an "ineligible group" is not normally entitled to deliver modified accounts to the registrar of companies. However, modified accounts for a financial year may be delivered to the registrar of companies by a company if, under the provisions of section 252 set out above, it is exempt from the obligation to appoint auditors, and either:

(1) was so exempt throughout that financial year, or

(2) became so exempt by virtue of a special resolution passed during that financial year.

[s247(4)]

This provision is designed particularly to help public groups with dormant subsidiaries.

Laying and delivery of unaudited accounts

12.31 The following applies in respect of a company's accounts for a financial year if the company is exempt under section 252 from the obligation to appoint auditors and either:

(1) was so exempt throughout that year, or

(2) became so exempt by virtue of a special resolution passed during that year, and retained the exemption until the end of that year.

[s253(1)]

12.32 Once exempt from the obligation to appoint auditors, a dormant company would obviously take advantage of the position and, consequently, there would not be an audit report to present to the members or file with the registrar of companies [s253(2)]. In such cases:

(1) the balance sheet must contain a statement by the directors (immediately above their signatures on the balance sheet) that the company was dormant throughout the financial year, and

(2) if modified accounts are delivered to the registrar, they need not contain the statement by the directors (see para 12.20), or include the special report of the auditors (see para 12.22).
[s253(3)]

Dormant company profit and loss account

12.33 All companies (including dormant companies) are required to prepare a profit and loss account for presentation to their members [s227]. A dormant company will, of course, have no income or expenditure to be recorded in its pofit and loss account and therefore none of the format items need be reproduced. It will, though, have a "result" for the year which will be nil. Schedule 4 paragraph 3(6) requires disclosure of this fact. It is suggested that the requirement to present a profit and loss account in these circumstances can be satisfied as follows:

> **"Profit and loss account**
> The company has not traded during the financial year and has received no income and incurred no expenditure. Conseqently, during the period the company has made neither a profit or a loss."

If the company is acting solely as an unremunerated agent for another company, the above statement should be read "The company has not traded on its own account during . . ."

CHAPTER 13

Accounts of special category companies

(Banking, Insurance and Exempt Shipping)

13.01 The Act allows special category companies to choose between preparing their individual and group accounts in accordance with Schedule 4 or Schedule 9 of the Act. It also allows the holding company of a special category company to prepare its group accounts in accordance with Schedule 9 (instead of Schedule 4) even if the holding company is not itself a special category company.

Meaning of special category company

13.02 The following types of company are regarded as "special category companies":

Banking company: a company which is a recognised bank for the purposes of the Banking Act 1979 or is a licensed institution within that Act.

Insurance company: an insurance company to which Part II of the Insurance Companies Act 1982 applies.

Shipping company: a company which satisfies the Secretary of State that it ought in the national interest to be treated as an exempt shipping company. It is understood that there are very few such companies. After 1988 (the latest permitted by the Fourth Directive), such shipping companies will no longer be regarded as "special category".
[s257(1)]

Application of accounting requirements

13.03 Except as indicated below, sections 221 to 256 of the Act (see Chapters 2, 3 and 9) apply to a special category company and its accounts in the same way as for any other company [s257(2)].

13.04 The individual accounts of a special category company, and the group accounts of a holding company which is special category, or which has a subsidiary which is a special category company, may be prepared under the provisions set out below instead of those which apply in other cases. Where advantage is taken of this facility, the accounts must contain a statement that they are prepared under Chapter II of Part VII of the Companies Act 1985 [s257(3)]. The position where a company's individual accounts are prepared in accordance with Schedule 4 but are accompanied by group accounts prepared under Schedule 9 is sometimes referred to as a hybrid (see also para 9.04).

Special category individual accounts

13.05 Where a company which is special category chooses to prepare individual accounts which are special category, section 228 and Schedule 4 do not apply, but:

(1) the balance sheet must give a true and fair view of the state of affairs of the company as at the end of the financial year, and

(2) the profit and loss account must give a true and fair view of the company's profit and loss for the financial year.

[s258(1)]

The balance sheet and profit and loss account must instead comply with the requirements of Schedule 9, so far as applicable, but, except where expressly stated to the contrary, this is without prejudice to the general requirement for the accounts to give a true and fair view [s258(2),(3)].

13.06 The Secretary of State may, on the application or with the consent of the company's directors, modify in relation to the company any of the requirements (of Part VII Chapter II of the Act) as to the matters to be stated in a company's balance sheet or profit and loss account (except for the requirement to give a true and fair view), for the purpose of adapting them to the circumstances of the company [s258(4)]. There is no power to modify the requirements where a special category company chooses to prepare its accounts under the rules applicable to other companies.

13.07 A separate profit and loss account of the company does not have to be prepared where the company has subsidiaries and the profit and loss account is framed as a consolidated account dealing with all or any of the company's subsidiaries as well as the company and:

(1) complies with the requirements of the Act relating to consolidated profit and loss accounts (as those requirements apply in the case of special category companies), and

(2) shows how much of the consolidated profit and loss for the financial year is dealt with in the company's accounts.

[s258(5)]

Special category group accounts

13.08 Where a holding company which is special category, or any other holding company which has a subsidiary which is special category, chooses to prepare group accounts which are special category, they must give a true and fair view of the state of affairs and profit or loss of the company and the subsidiaries dealt with by those accounts as a whole, so far as concerns members of the holding company [s259(1)].

13.09 The group accounts, if prepared as consolidated accounts, must comply with Schedule 9 (so far as applicable), and if they are not prepared as consolidated accounts they must give the same or equivalent information. This is subordinate to the requirement for the group accounts to give a true and fair view [s259(3)]. The holding company may apply to the Secretary of State for the requirements of Schedule 9 to be modified in relation to the company for the purpose of adapting them to the company's circumstances [s259(4)].

Subsidiary with a different financial year

13.10 The Act specifies which accounts of a subsidiary should be used as the basis for incorporating the results and assets and liabilities of the subsidiary, where the financial year of that subsidiary does not coincide with the financial year of the holding company. Unless the Secretary of State permits otherwise, the accounts to be used are:

(1) where the subsidiary's financial year ends with that of the holding company, the accounts for that financial year, and

(2) if the financial years do not end on the same day, the accounts for the subsidiary's financial year ending last before that of the holding company.

[s259(2)]

These provisions are the same as for companies which are not special category.

Notes to special category accounts

13.11 The following requirements of Schedule 5 do not apply to special category accounts:

(1) disclosure of shareholdings in bodies corporate, not being subsidiaries (Sch 5 para 8), and

(2) detailed financial information about subsidiaries (Sch 5 Part III).

[s260(1)]

The above disclosures derive from the EEC Fourth Directive which the 1981 Act did not apply to special category companies.

Directors' report

13.12 Where a company's *individual* accounts are special category, the following applies with respect to the directors' report accompanying the accounts [s261(1)].

13.13 Information which is otherwise required to be given in the accounts, and allowed to be given in a statement annexed, may be given in the directors' report instead of in the accounts. If any information is so given, the report is treated as forming part of the accounts for the purposes of audit, except that the auditors must report on it only so far as it gives that information [s261(3)].

13.14 Where advantage is taken to show an item in the directors' report instead of in the accounts, the directors' report must also show the corresponding amount of that item for (or, as the case may require, as at the end of) the immediately preceding financial year, except where the amount would not have had to be shown had the item been shown in the accounts [s261(4)].

Matters to be disclosed

13.15 The matters which have to be disclosed in the directors' report where a company's individual accounts are special category are those set out in the following paragraphs.

13.16 Instead of containing a fair review of the development of the company's business during the year and of its position at the end of it, the directors' report must deal with the company's "state of affairs". The report must also state the amount (if any) which the directors recommend should be paid as dividend, and the amount (if any) which they propose to carry to reserves [s261(2)]. The requirements set out in paragraph 9.03(3) to (6),(8),(9),(11) to (13) of this book apply, except that a company does not have the option to show the particulars of directors' interests in shares and debentures in the notes to the accounts instead of in the directors' report. The applicable disclosures (which have to be given in relation to a company and, where required, its subsidiaries, if any) described in Chapter 9 are briefly:

(1) Names of directors.

(2) Principal activities.

(3) Significant changes in fixed assets.

(4) Difference, if material, between market value and book value of land and buildings.

(5) Directors' interests in group shares and debentures.

(6) Political and charitable contributions.

(7) Employment of disabled persons.

(8) Employee involvement.

(9) Employees' health, safety and welfare at work (not yet required).

Items (3) and (4) above do not apply if the company has the benefit of any provision of Part III of Schedule 9 as an insurance company or as an exempt bank or exempt shipping company.
[s261(5)]

Additional disclosures

13.17 Schedule 10 requires the directors' report to include additional disclosures but paragraphs 2 to 4 and 6 of that Schedule apply *only* where the company prepares group accounts which are special category [s261(6)]. The effect of this provision appears to be that the information required by Sch 10 para 2 (which relates to turnover and profitability of the company itself – see para 13.18(2) below) has to be given only in the rare case where the company submits special category group accounts which are not prepared as consolidated accounts. This represents a change from the law in force before the 1985 Act, because this information also had to be given by a company which was not a member of a group and whose turnover exceeded £1m.

13.18 The requirements are set out below:

Recent issues
(1) The following particulars must be given with respect to any issue of shares or debentures during the financial year:
   (a) reasons for making the issue,
   (b) classes of shares and debentures issued, and
   (c) as respects each class, the number (in the case of shares) or amount (for debentures) issued, and the consideration received by the company.
[Sch 10 para 1]

Turnover and profitability

(2) Where, in the opinion of the directors, the company has carried on business of two or more classes (other than banking, discounting or any other class which may be prescribed) which differ substantially from each other, there must be stated:

(a) the proportion of turnover attributable to each class, and

(b) for each class, the amount of the profit or loss before taxation attributable thereto.

[Sch 10 para 2]

Where a company has subsidiaries at the end of the year and prepares group accounts as consolidated accounts, the above information is required on a group basis only (that is in aggregate in respect of the company and its subsidiaries dealt with by the consolidated accounts) [Sch 10 para 3].

Classes of business which, in the opinion of the directors, do not differ substantially from each other, are to be treated as one class [Sch 10 para 4].

Labour force and remuneration

(3) Where the company's average number of employees is 100 or more, the average number of employees and their aggregate remuneration paid or payable in respect of the year must be stated [Sch 10 paras 5,7,8]. Where at the end of the financial year the company has subsidiaries, the information must, instead, relate to the persons employed by the group, where the average number is 100 or more [Sch 10 paras 6,8].

Exceptions

(a) Disclosure is not required where the (reporting) company is a wholly-owned subsidiary of a company incorporated in Great Britain.

(b) Persons who worked wholly or mainly outside the UK are not to be taken into account either in giving the prescribed particulars or in calculating the average number of employees.

[Sch 10 para 8]

Other material matters

(4) Particulars must be given of any other matters which are material for an appreciation of the state of the company's affairs by its members, provided the directors are of the opinion that disclosure will not be harmful to the business of the company or any of its subsidiaries [Sch 10 para 9].

Auditors' report

13.19 The provisions with regard to the auditors' report are set out in para 15.46.

CHAPTER 14

Oversea companies

14.01 This chapter describes the provisions of the Act in relation to the establishment by an "oversea company" of a place of business in Great Britain. They include registration with the registrar of companies, choosing an accounting reference date and filing of accounts (including, where appropriate, group accounts).

Meaning of oversea company

14.02 An "oversea company" is a company incorporated outside Great Britain which establishes, or which continues to have, a place of business in Great Britain. A "place of business" includes a share transfer or share registration office [s744]. A foreign company which carries on insurance business in Great Britain is regarded as an oversea company irrespective of whether it actually establishes a place of business here [Section 87 of the Insurance Companies Act 1982 as amended].

14.03 The establishment of a place of business is considered to be a question of fact and is typically determined by reference to such factors as the opening of premises and the employment of personnel. Thus, where an oversea company trades through a branch, it would have a place of business. The appointment of a representative in Great Britain should not in itself constitute the establishment of a place of business but if, for example, the representative takes premises in the name of the company, a place of business will have been established. An oversea company which carries on business through its British subsidiary is not, by reason only of that fact, regarded as having established a place of business.

Initial registration

14.04 Within one month of establishing a place of business in Great Britain (for example, a branch), an oversea company must register with the registrar of companies. This involves delivering to the registrar the following documents (all of which are available for inspection by the public):

(1) a certified copy of the charter, statutes or memorandum and articles of the company or other instrument constituting or defining the company's constitution and, if it is not in English, a certified translation into English,

(2) a return in the prescribed form (form number 691) containing:
    (a) a list of the names and addresses of the directors and secretary, and the nationality and business occupation of the directors,
    (b) a list of the names and addresses of one or more persons resident in Great Britain who are authorised to accept legal notices on behalf of the company,
    (c) a list of the documents filed under (1) above, and
    (d) a statutory declaration (by a director or secretary of the company or any person named in (b) above) stating the date on which the company's place of business in Great Britain was established.

[s691(1),(2), 709]

14.05 An oversea company would not be regarded as establishing a place of business in Great Britain merely by virtue of its having a subsidiary company which is incorporated in Great Britain.

14.06 The registration procedure would normally be carried out on behalf of the oversea company by lawyers or other professional advisers.

Registration of altered particulars

14.07 If there is any alteration to the matters set out in para 14.04 (1),(2)(a) or (b), the company is required (generally within twenty one days of the alteration) to deliver to the registrar of companies a return (form number 692) containing prescribed particulars of the alteration. Similar notification is required where the oversea company changes its corporate name [s692].

Display of corporate name

14.08 The corporate name and country of incorporation of an oversea company must be displayed conspicuously at every place where it carries on business in Great Britain. If the liability of the company's members is limited, this must also be stated. The foregoing particulars must also be stated in all bill-heads, letter paper, notices and other official publications of the company as well as in prospectuses inviting subscriptions for its shares or debentures in Great Britain [s693].

14.09 The registrar of companies has the power to regulate the name under which an oversea company may carry on business in Great Britain [s694].

Filing of accounts

14.10 Oversea companies are required to prepare, in respect of each accounting reference period, accounts which are (subject to specified exceptions – see para 14.12) in the same form, contain the same particulars and have annexed to them such documents, as would have been required if they were incorporated in Great Britain [s700(1)]. A copy thereof (together with a certified translation into English of any of the documents which are not in English) must be delivered to the registrar of companies (generally, within thirteen months after the accounting reference date), except where the company is an independent company with unlimited liability (see para 3.17 for a description of those circumstances) [s700(2),(3), 702]. All documents filed are available for inspection by members of the public [s709]. In practice, the registrar of companies will often be prepared to place on file accounts which are drawn up in accordance with comparable overseas standards.

14.11 The accounts to be filed are those for the company as a whole. Branch accounts are not sufficient for filing purposes, although they are usually required for tax purposes. Group accounts are required where at the end of the financial year an oversea company has subsidiaries, but this requirement is subject to the same exceptions as are available to British companies (see paras 2.19 and 2.20) [s700(1)].

However, it appears that the exemption for a company which is a wholly-owned subsidiary of another body corporate applies to an oversea company in the same way as it does to a British company; that is, if its parent is incorporated in Great Britain (see para 2.19), which is unlikely to be the case for the majority of oversea companies.

14.12 The Secretary of State has the power to modify the requirements for oversea companies or to exempt such companies from the requirements [s700(4),(5)]. Currently, the principal exceptions for oversea companies are that they are not required to follow the prescribed formats for the profit and loss account and balance sheet or the other disclosures which were introduced by the 1981 Act (and are now to be found in sections 228 and 230 and Schedule 4) but may continue to follow the same requirements as for special category companies (see Chapter 13). Furthermore, neither a directors' report nor an auditors' report has to be filed [S.I. 1982 No. 676].

14.13 The Act does not require a British branch of an oversea company to maintain accounting records or for them to be audited. However, many branches are audited in order to satisfy foreign regulatory or head office requirements.

Accounting reference date

Notification of accounting reference date

14.14 An oversea company must establish an accounting reference date, which will be used in determining the date in each year to which the accounts for filing with the registrar of companies will be made up and the time allowed for filing those accounts [s701(2)].

14.15 Unless it wishes automatically to be allocated 31st March as its accounting reference date, an oversea company must, within six months of establishing a place of business in Great Britain, give notice in the prescribed form (form number 701(2)) to the registrar of companies of its chosen accounting reference date [s701(2),(3)].

14.16 An oversea company's first accounting reference period is the period exceeding six months but not eighteen months which begins on a date chosen by the company (which must not be later than the date on which it established a place of business in Great Britain) and ends with its accounting reference date [s701(4)]. Later accounting reference periods are for twelve months beginning on the day following the end of an accounting reference period and ending with the company's accounting reference date [s701(5)].

Alteration of accounting reference period

14.17 An oversea company may give notice in the prescribed form to the registrar of companies altering its accounting reference date. The procedure to be followed is the same as for companies incorporated in Great Britain (see paragraphs 2.04 to 2.11) except that there is no restriction on the number of times an oversea company may have an extended accounting reference period (that is, one which exceeds twelve months but which does not exceed eighteen months) [s701(6)]. The forms for use are form 701(6)a for the alteration of a current accounting period and form 701(6)b for the retrospective alteration of the previous period.

Penalties

14.18 If an oversea company fails to comply with the requirements of the Act, it may incur penalties [s697, 703].

CHAPTER 15

Auditors

Annual appointment

15.01 Subject to the special provisions for dormant companies (see Chapter 12), at every general meeting at which accounts are laid in accordance with section 241, a company must appoint an auditor (or auditors) to hold office from the conclusion of that meeting until the conclusion of the next general meeting at which accounts are laid [s384(1)]. If an auditor is not appointed as required, the office of auditor becomes vacant and the company is required within one week to give notice of this fact to the Secretary of State who may appoint a person to fill the vacancy. If notice is not given, the company and every officer of it who is in default are liable to a fine and, for continued contravention, to a daily default fine [s384(5)].

15.02 At any time before the first general meeting at which accounts are laid, the directors may appoint a company's first auditors who will hold office until the conclusion of that meeting [s384(2)]. If the directors fail to exercise these powers, the company in general meeting may do so [s384(3)].

15.03 The directors or the company in general meeting may fill any casual vacancy in the office of auditor but, while any such vacancy continues, the surviving or continuing auditor or auditors (if any) may act [s384(4)]. Thus, if joint auditors were originally appointed, a casual vacancy in the office of one of those joint auditors should not prevent the other from continuing to act.

Remuneration

15.04 The auditor's remuneration (including expenses) must be fixed by the company in general meeting or in such manner as the company in general meeting may determine [s385(1),(3)]. The usual approach in practice is for the general meeting to give authority to the directors to fix the remuneration.

15.05 Where, however, the auditor is appointed by the directors (for example, as first auditor or to fill a casual vacancy) or by the Secretary of State, they may fix the remuneration [s385(2)].

Right to attend company meetings

15.06 A company's auditors are entitled to attend any general meeting of the company and to receive all notices of, and other communications relating to, any general meeting which a member of the company is entitled to receive, and to be heard at any general meeting which they attend on any part of the business of the meeting which concerns them as auditors [s387(1)].

15.07 An auditor who has been removed from office (see para 15.08) is entitled to attend:

(1) the general meeting at which his term of office would otherwise have expired, and

(2) any general meeting at which it is proposed to fill the vacancy caused by his removal,

and to receive all notices of, and other communications relating to, any such meeting which any member of the company is entitled to receive, and to be heard at any such meeting which he attends on any part of the business of the meeting which concerns him as former auditor of the company [s387(2)].

Removal of auditors

15.08 An auditor may be removed from office by an ordinary resolution of the company in general meeting notwithstanding anything in any agreement between the company and the auditor [s386(1)]. Where such a resolution is passed, the company must within fourteen days give notice thereof in the prescribed form (form number 386) to the registrar of companies [s386(2)]. The auditor may, however, still be entitled to compensation or damages in respect of the termination of his appointment as auditor or of any other appointment terminating with that of auditor [s386(3)]. Special notice (see below) must be given of any resolution to remove an auditor [s388(1)].

Special notice

15.09 Where a resolution requires special notice, notice of the intention to move the resolution must be given to the company at least twenty eight days before the meeting at which it is moved; the company in turn must give twenty one days notice to the members [s379(1),(2)]. Once the company receives notice of such a resolution it must send a copy of it to the auditor [s388(2)]. However, if after notice of the intention to move such a resolution has been given to the company, a meeting is called for a date twenty eight days or less after the notice has been given, the notice will be deemed to have been properly given, although not given within the time required [s379(3)]. This is designed to protect the position of the person giving the notice, so that it is not invalidated by the directors calling a meeting within a short period.

Safeguarding the position of the auditor

15.10 Special notice is required for a resolution at a general meeting of a company:

(1) appointing as auditor a person other than a retiring auditor, or

(2) filling a casual vacancy in the office of auditor, or

(3) reappointing as auditor a retiring auditor who was appointed by the directors to fill a casual vacancy, or

(4) removing an auditor before the expiration of his term of office.

[s388(1)]

15.11 On receipt of notice of such an intended resoltion, the company must forthwith send a copy thereof:
(a) to the person whom it is proposed to appoint or remove from office,
(b) to the retiring auditor (under (1) above), and
(c) where, under (2) or (3) above, the casual vacancy was caused by the resignation of an auditor, to the auditor who resigned.
[s388(2)]

15.12 Where notice is given of an intended resolution under 15.10(1) or (4) above, the retiring auditor or the auditor proposed to be removed may make written representations (not exceeding a reasonable length) with respect to the intended resolution; if the auditor requests their notification to members of the company, the company must (unless it received the representations too late) state, in the notice of resolution, that such representations have been made and send a copy of the representations to every member of the company to whom notice of the meeting is or has been sent [s388(3)]. If a copy of the representations is not sent to the members (either because they were received too late by the company or because of the company's default) the auditor may require the representations to be read out at the meeting [s388(4)]. If, on application to a court, the court considers that the right to make representations is being abused to secure needless publicity for defamatory matter, the representations need not be sent or read out. The court may order that the company's costs on the application be paid in whole or in part by the auditor [s388(5)].

Qualification for appointment

15.13 The Act sets out the qualifications which have to be obtained in order to be appointed as an auditor and also specifies the categories of person whom a company may not appoint as its auditor.

In order to be appointed as an auditor of a company, a person must:

(1) be a member of a body of accountants established in the UK which is recognised for this purpose by the Secretary of State (see 15.16 below), or

(2) hold a valid authorisation from the Secretary of State to be so appointed on the grounds of having similar qualifications obtained outside the UK, or

(3) retain an authorisation granted under section 161(1)(b) of the 1948 Act on the grounds of adequate knowledge and experience or pre-1947 practice.

[s389(1)]

15.14 The above does not apply to an auditor of an unlisted company who retains an authorisation under section 13(1) of the 1967 Act [s389(2)].

15.15 The Secretary of State may refuse an authorisation under 15.13(2) above, if it appears to him that the country in which the applicant's qualifications were obtained does not confer corresponding privileges on persons qualified in the UK [s389(5)].

Recognised bodies of accountants

15.16 The bodies of accountants whose members qualify under 15.13(1) above are:

(1) the Institute of Chartered Accountants in England and Wales,

(2) the Institute of Chartered Accountants of Scotland,

(3) the Chartered Association of Certified Accountants, and

(4) the Institute of Chartered Accountants in Ireland.

[s389(3)]

15.17   Auditors

The Secretary of State may, by statutory instrument, add or delete any body from the above list [s389(4)].

Persons not qualified to act

15.17 The following persons may not be appointed as auditor of a company:

(1) an officer or servant of the company,

(2) a person who is a partner of or in the employment of an officer or servant of the company, and

(3) a body corporate.

[s389(6)]

An "officer" of a company includes a director, manager or company secretary [s744]. Because an auditor is for some purposes regarded as an officer of the company, the Act provides that for the purpose of the foregoing an auditor of a company is not to be regarded as either an officer or a servant of it [s389(6)]. It follows that an auditor cannot also be secretary of the same company.

15.18 A person is also not qualified for appointment as auditor of a company if he is, under section 389(6), disqualified for appointment as auditor of any other body corporate which is that company's subsidiary or holding company or a subsidiary of that company's holding company, or would be so disqualified if the body corporate were a "company" [s389(7)].

Scottish firm

15.19 Notwithstanding any of the above provisions, a Scottish firm is qualified for appointment as auditor of a company only if all the partners are qualified for appointment as auditor of that company [s389(8)]. Such firms would, of course, be eligible to act as auditor for any British company and not just those registered in Scotland.

Appointment of a partnership under English law

15.20 Under English law, the appointment of a partnership to act as auditor, is taken to be an appointment of those of its partners who are individually qualified for appointment at the time the partnership is appointed.

Acting when disqualified

15.21 A person may not act as auditor of a company at a time when he

110

knows that he is disqualified for appointment to that office. If, to his knowledge, an auditor becomes disqualified during his term of office, he must immediately vacate his office and give notice in writing to the company that he has resigned because of that disqualification [s389(9)]. Contravention of these provisions carries a penalty [s389(10)].

Resignation

15.22 An auditor may resign his office by depositing a notice in writing to that effect at the company's registered office; this brings his term of office to an end on the date on which the notice is deposited or on such later date as may be specified in the notice [s390(1)]. As noted earlier, an auditor's term of office expires automatically at the conclusion of the general meeting at which the accounts, on which he was appointed to report, are laid. Thus, if an auditor has completed an audit but does not wish to seek reappointment for a further term, "resignation" is *not* required.

15.23 An auditor's notice of resignation is not effective unless it contains either:

(1) a statement to the effect that there are no circumstances connected with his resignation which he considers should be brought to the notice of the members or creditors of the company, or

(2) a statement of any such circumstances.

[s390(2)]

15.24 The company is required, within fourteen days, to send a copy of the notice of resignation to the registrar of companies and, if the notice contained a statement of circumstances connected with his resignation, also to every person who is entitled to receive copies of the accounts [s390(3)].

15.25 If, however, the company or any person claiming to be aggrieved applies to a court within fourteen days of the receipt of the notice by the company, and the court decides that the statement is being used to secure needless publicity for defamatory matter, the court may direct that the statement need not be sent out. The court may also order that the company's costs on the application are to be paid in whole or in part by the auditor [s390(4),(5)]. Within fourteen days of the court's decision, the company must send a statement setting out the effect of the order (where the court makes an order) or (where there is no order) a copy of the auditor's notice containing the statement, to the registrar of companies and those persons entitled to be sent copies of the accounts [s390(6)].

15.26 The Act provides for penalties for contravention of the requirements relating to the circulation by the company of copies of the auditor's
statement and of the effect of the court order [s390(7)].

Auditor may requisition meeting

15.27 Where the auditor's notice of resignation contains a statement
giving the circumstances of his resignation (see para 15.23), the auditor
may, in writing, call on the directors to convene forthwith an extraordinary general meeting of the company to consider the matter
[s391(1)]. If, within twenty one days of being called upon to do so, the
directors do not convene a meeting to be held twenty eight days or less
after the date on which the notice convening the meeting is given, every
director who failed to take all reasonable steps to ensure that a meeting
was convened as required, is liable to a fine [s391(4)].

Circulation of additional statement

15.28 The auditor is also entitled to request the company to circulate to its
members, before the general meeting at which his term of office would
otherwise have expired or before any general meeting at which it is
proposed to fill the vacancy caused by his resignation or convened on his
requisition, a written statement (not exceeding a reasonable length) of
the circumstances connected with his resignation [s391(2)]. Unless it is
received too late, the company is required to state in the notice of the
meeting that a statement has been made and to send a copy of the
statement to every member to whom notice of the meeting is or has been
sent [s391(3)].

15.29 If a copy of the statement is not sent out because it was received too
late or because of the company's default, the auditor may (without
prejudice to his right to be heard orally) require the statement to be read
out at the meeting [s391(5)].

15.30 Copies of a statement need not be sent out and the statement need
not be read out at the meeting if, on the application either of the company
or of any other person who claims to be aggrieved, the court is satisfied
that these rights are being abused to secure needless publicity for
defamatory matter. The court may order the company's costs on such an
application to be paid in whole or in part by the auditor [s391(6)].

Attendance at meetings

15.31 An auditor who has resigned is entitled to attend any such meeting
as is mentioned in para 15.28 above and to receive all notices of, and other
communications relating thereto, which any member of the company is

entitled to receive and to be heard at any such meeting on any part of the business of the meeting which concerns him as former auditor of the company [s391(7)].

Auditors' powers

In relation to the company

15.32 An auditor has a right of access at all times to the company's books, accounts and vouchers, and is entitled to require from the officers of the company such information and explanations as he considers necessary for the performance of his duties [s237(3)].

In relation to subsidiaries

15.33 Where a holding company has a subsidiary which is incorporated in Great Britain, the subsidiary and its auditors have a duty to provide any information and explanation which the holding company's auditors may reasonably require for the purposes of their duties as auditors of the holding company [s392(1)(a)]. Where the subsidiary is incorporated elsewhere, the holding company must take all such steps as are reasonably open to it to obtain from the subsidiary such information and explanation [s392(1)(b)].

15.34 If a subsidiary or holding company fails to comply with these requirements, the subsidiary or holding company and every officer of it who is in default is liable to a fine. If an auditor of a subsidiary fails without reasonable excuse to provide the information and explanations required, he is liable to a fine [s392(2)].

False statements to auditors

15.35 An officer of a company risks imprisonment or a fine or both if he knowingly or recklessly makes to the company's auditors a statement (whether orally or in writing) which conveys or purports to convey any information or explanation which the auditors require, or are entitled to require, as auditors of the company, and which is misleading, false or deceptive in a material particular [s393].

Auditors' report on the accounts

15.36 The following paragraphs set out the requirements in relation to the report by the auditors on a company's accounts. The special auditors' report on "modified" accounts is described in paragraphs 12.21 and 12.22. The position of "special category companies" which take advantage of the disclosure exemptions in Part III of Schedule 9 is considered in paragraph 15.46.

Requirement to report

15.37 The Act places a statutory duty on a company's auditors to make a report to the members on "the accounts examined by them, and on every balance sheet and profit and loss account, and on all group accounts, copies of which are to be laid before the company in general meeting during their tenure of office" [s236(1)].

15.38 As noted earlier, a copy of the auditors' report must be attached to the accounts [s239] and must be read out (but not necessarily by the auditors) at the general meeting at which the accounts are laid and must be open to inspection by members at that meeting [s241(2)].

Contents of report

15.39 The report of the auditors must state:

(1) whether, in their opinion, the company's balance sheet and profit and loss account and (if it is a holding company submitting group accounts) the group accounts have been properly prepared in accordance with the Companies Act 1985, and

(2) whether, in their opinion, a true and fair view is given:
    (a) in the balance sheet, of the state of the company's affairs at the end of the financial year,
    (b) in the profit and loss account (if not framed as a consolidated account), of the company's profit or loss for the financial year, and
    (c) in the case of group accounts, of the state of affairs and profit or loss of the company and its subsidiaries dealt with by those accounts, so far as concerns members of the company.

[s236(2)]

Other matters which may have to be reported

15.40 The Act specifies other matters which the auditors must consider but which must be referred to in their report only if they form a negative opinion thereon.

Consistency of directors' report with accounts
15.41 Except where a company's individual accounts are special category, the auditors are required to consider whether the information given in the

114

directors' report is consistent with the accounts for the financial year to which the directors' report relates. If they are of the opinion that it is *not* consistent, they must state this in their report [s237(6), 261(7)].

Accounting records

15.42 The auditors must carry out such investigations as are necessary to enable them to form an opinion as to:

(1) whether proper accounting records (see Chapter 16) have been kept by the company and proper returns adequate for their audit have been received from branches not visited by them, and

(2) whether the company's balance sheet and its profit and loss account (if not prepared as a consolidated account) are in agreement with the accounting records and returns.

[s237(1)]

15.43 If the auditors form a negative opinion in relation to any of these matters, they must state that fact in their report [s237(2)].

Information and explanations not received

15.44 If the auditors fail to obtain all the information and explanations which, to the best of their knowledge and belief, are necessary for the purposes of their audit, they must state that fact in their report [s237(4)].

Remuneration of and transactions with directors and employees

15.45 If the requirements of the Act relating to the disclosure of directors' and higher paid employees' remuneration, and the disclosure of particulars of transactions with directors and officers are not complied with in the accounts, the auditors are required to include in their report, so far as they are reasonably able to do so, a statement giving the required particulars [s237(5)].

Special category companies

15.46 The auditors' report on the accounts of special category companies would be in the same format as for other companies, except where a special category company is entitled to, *and has availed itself of,* the benefit of any of the provisions of Part III of Schedule 9 (disclosure exceptions) [s262(1)].

15.47 In such a case, the requirements set out in para 15.39(2) above do not apply. The report of the auditors must state whether, in their opinion, the company's balance sheet and profit and loss account and (if it is a holding company submitting group accounts) the group accounts have been properly prepared in accordance with the Companies Act 1985 [s262(2)].

15.48 The provisions set out in paragraphs 15.42 to 15.45 apply also to all audits of special category companies.

15.49 Two observations in relation to the above may be made. Firstly, although the directors of companies which take advantage of the disclosure exemptions are still required to prepare accounts which give a true and fair view [s258, 259], the auditors are not required to express an opinion on their truth and fairness. Secondly, the above provisions apply only where the company itself is entitled to and makes use of the disclosure exemptions and not simply where the group accounts include a subsidiary which has done so.

The requirements for the accounts of special category companies are described in Chapter 13.

CHAPTER 16

Accounting records

16.01 The Act requires every company to "cause" accounting records to be kept; it also specifies the minimum contents of such records and the period for which they must be retained. The use of the word "cause" would appear to be intended, inter alia, to permit a company to engage someone other than an employee of the company to make the actual entries in the accounting records.

Contents of accounting records

16.02 The accounting records must be sufficient to show and explain the company's transactions and must be such as to:

(1) disclose with reasonable accuracy, at any time, the financial position of the company at that time, and

(2) enable the directors to ensure that any balance sheet and profit and loss account, which they prepare under Part VII of the Act, comply with the requirements of the Act as to their form, content and otherwise.

[s221(2)]

16.03 The accounting records must, in particular, contain:

(1) entries from day to day of all sums of money received and expended by the company, and the matters in respect of which the receipt and expenditure takes place, and

(2) a record of the assets and liabilities of the company.

[s221(3)]

16.04 In addition, where the company deals in goods, the accounting records must contain:

(1) statements of stock held by the company at the end of each financial year of the company,

(2) all statements of stocktakings from which any such statement of stock has been or is to be prepared, and

(3) except in the case of goods sold by way of ordinary retail trade, statements of all goods sold and purchased, showing the goods and the buyers and sellers in sufficient detail to enable all these to be identified.

[s221(4)]

16.05 The Act sets out the basic requirements for the accounting records which are to be maintained by a company but does not prescribe the form that those records should take. This will depend on many factors, not least of which will be the size of the company and the degree of sophistication required for internal management purposes. It is permissible for data to be recorded otherwise than in legible form provided it is capable of being reproduced in legible form [s722,723].

16.06 In 1977 the Auditing Practices Committee of the Consultative Committee of Accountancy Bodies sought counsel's opinion on various points concerning accounting records. A summary of the points raised and the opinions received was published in issue 6 (winter 1977/78) of "True and Fair". In relation to the question as to what are accounting records, the summarised opinion was:

> "Accounting records comprise the orderly collection and identification of the information in question, rather than a mere accumulation of documents. The accounting records need not be in book form, they may take the form of, for example, a loose-leaf binder or computer tape. It will even be sufficient if the books of prime entry are in the form of a secure clip of invoices with an add-list attached. The essence of the matter is that the information recorded is organised and labelled so as to be capable of retrieval. A carrier-bag full of invoices will not suffice."

Location and inspection of accounting records

16.07 A company's accounting records must be kept at the company's registered office or such other place as the directors consider fit. They must at all times be open to inspection by the company's officers [s222(1)]. A member of a company does not enjoy such a statutory right of inspection; article 109 of Table A (as set out in S.I. 1985 No. 805) states that "No member shall (as such) have any right of inspecting any accounting records or other book or document of the company except as conferred by statute or authorised by the directors or by ordinary resolution of the company".

16.08 If accounting records are kept at a place outside Great Britain, accounts and returns with respect to the business dealt with in those accounting records must be sent to, and kept at, a place in Great Britain, and must at all times be open to inspection by the company's officers [s222(2)].

16.09 These accounts and returns must be such as to:

(1) disclose with reasonable accuracy the financial position of the business in question at intervals of not more than six months, and

(2) enable the directors to ensure that the company's balance sheet and profit and loss account comply with the requirements of the Act as to the form and content of company accounts and otherwise.

[s222(3)]

Retention of accounting records

16.10 A company's accounting records must be retained for three years by a private company and for six years by a public company. The period is calculated from the date on which the records were made. This is subject to any direction as to the disposal of records which may be given under the winding-up rules [s222(4), 663]. The foregoing does not apply to the various registers which the Act requires a company to maintain (for example, the register of directors' interests in shares and debentures of group companies) and which must generally be retained indefinitely.

Penalties

16.11 There are penalties for non-compliance with the above provisions [s223].

CHAPTER 17

Publication of accounts

17.01 This chapter sets out the procedure which has to be followed when a company publishes its accounts or an abridged version thereof.

Definition of "publish"

17.02 A company is regarded as publishing any balance sheet or other account if it publishes, issues or circulates it or otherwise makes it available for public inspection in a manner calculated to invite members of the public generally, or any class of members of the public, to read it [s742(5)]. "Public" has a wide meaning in law and would prima facie include special groups such as employees or customers.

Publication of full company accounts

17.03 "Full individual accounts" means the full version of a company's individual accounts (thus excluding any group accounts) *or*, if it is entitled to deliver modified individual accounts to the registrar of companies, either the modified version or the full version, together with (in both cases) its directors' report except where it is exempt (for example, as a small company) from the requirement to deliver a copy of that report to the registrar of companies [s254(1)].

17.04 "Full group accounts" means the full version of a company's group accounts or, if it is entitled to deliver modified group accounts to the registrar of companies, either the full version or the modified version [s254(1)].

17.05 If a company publishes (for example, in brochures for publicity purposes) full individual accounts, it must also publish therewith:

(1) the auditors' report (under section 236) or, where those accounts are modified accounts, the special report of the auditors [s254(1),(2),(5), Sch 8 para 10], and

(2) where the company is required to prepare group accounts, its group accounts (which may be modified accounts but only if the individual accounts are modified) [s254(1),(3)].

17.06 If a company publishes the full or modified version of its group accounts otherwise than together with its individual accounts, it must also publish with them the auditors' report (under section 236) or, where those group accounts are modified, the special report of the auditors [s254(1), (4),(5) Sch 8 para 10].

17.07 A company which contravenes any of the above provisions, and any officer who is in default, is liable to a fine [s254(6)].

Publication of abridged accounts

17.08 The rules set out below apply where a company publishes "abridged accounts"; that is, where a company publishes, otherwise than as part of full individual or group accounts to which section 254 applies, any balance sheet or profit and loss account relating to a financial year of the company or purporting to deal with any such financial year [s255(1)].

17.09 In relation to accounts published by a holding company, the above reference to a balance sheet or profit and loss account includes an account in any form purporting to be a balance sheet or profit and loss account for the group consisting of the holding company and its subsidiaries [s255(2)].

17.10 Where a company publishes abridged accounts, they must be accompanied by a statement indicating in relation to each financial year dealt with by the abridged accounts:

(1) that the accounts are not full accounts,

(2) whether full individual or full group accounts (according as the abridged accounts deal solely with the company's own affairs or with the affairs of the company and any subsidiaries) have been delivered to the registrar of companies (or, in the case of an unlimited company which is exempt from the requirement to deliver accounts, that the company is so exempt),

(3) whether the auditors have reported (under section 236) on the company's accounts for any financial year with which the abridged accounts purport to deal, and

(4) whether that report was unqualified (that is, a report without qualification to the effect that the auditors were of the opinion that the accounts gave a true and fair view and were properly prepared in accordance with the provisions of the Companies Act 1985).

[s255(3)]

17.11   Publication of accounts

17.11 It is evident that where the abridged accounts deal with more than one financial year (for example, where, for comparative purposes, the preceding year's results are also given) the statements under 17.10(2),(3) and (4) above must refer to each of those financial years.

17.12 Where a company publishes abridged accounts, it is not permitted to publish the auditor's report [s255(4)]. This is to avoid giving the impression that the abridged accounts constitute the company's full accounts which give a true and fair view.

17.13 A company which contravenes any of the above provisions, and any officer who is in default, is liable to a fine [s255(5)].

17.14 Section 255 applies to all UK companies, including "special category companies" (that is, banks, insurance and exempt shipping companies) which prepare accounts on the "old" basis under Schedule 9, but it does not apply to oversea companies publishing abridged accounts in the UK.

17.15 It is evident that to fall within the ambit of section 255, an abridged profit and loss account would be one which covers a full statutory accounting period of a company and an abridged balance sheet would be one which is made up as at the same date as the statutory balance sheet. What is not clear is how much information is necessary to constitute abridged "accounts". For example, a reference to a profits figure on its own would hardly constitute a profit and loss account, but as soon as two or more figures (such as turnover and profit) are put into relation with each other, the result may come within the ambit of section 255.

17.16 "Abridged accounts" would appear to include preliminary or interim announcements to The Stock Exchange which contain a *full year's* figures (whether for the current year or as comparatives), accounts appearing in prospectuses, class 1 circulars and offer documents, annual reports to employees containing summary accounts, five or ten year summaries published in annual reports or other circulated material.

CHAPTER 18

Annual return and annual general meeting

Annual return

Requirement to prepare

18.01 Every company is required, at least once in every calendar year, to make an annual return [s363(1), 364(1)]. A company need not make a return either in the year of its incorporation or, if it is not required by the Act (section 366) to hold an annual general meeting during the following year, in that year [s363(3), 364(2)].

18.02 The particulars to be given in an annual return depend upon whether or not the company has a share capital. The return must be in the prescribed form (form number 363; previously, there were two separate forms, form number 6a for a company having a share capital and form number 7 for a company not having a share capital) [s363(2), 364(1)].

Period for completion and submission

18.03 A company's annual return must be completed within 42 days of the annual general meeting and a copy of the return, signed both by a director and by the company secretary, must be forwarded without delay to the registrar of companies [s365(1),(2)]. The fee to be paid when submitting the return is currently £20.

Contents

18.04 As noted, companies have to use the prescribed form (available from legal stationers or free of charge from the registrar of companies) for their annual return. This chapter therefore sets out only briefly the information to be given in the annual return. The contents of the annual return are regulated by sections 363 and 364 and Schedule 15 of the Act. The amount of information to be given by a company depends on whether the company has or does not have a share capital.

Company having a share capital

18.05 The information to be disclosed in the annual return of a company having a share capital is, broadly:

(1) The address of the registered office of the company.

(2) The address of the place where the register of members is kept, if other than at the registered office.

(3) The address of the place where the register of holders of debentures (or any duplicate of the whole or part thereof) is kept, if other than at the registered office.

(4) A summary of the company's share capital, giving prescribed particulars.

(5) The total amount of the company's indebtedness in respect of all mortgages and charges.

(6) Names and addresses of and number of shares held by persons who were members of the company on the fourteenth day after the company's annual general meeting for the year.

(7) The particulars, required to be contained in the company's register of directors and secretaries, with respect to the persons who at the date of the return were a director or secretary of the company.

Company not having a share capital

18.06 The requirements set out in 18.05(1),(2),(3),(5) and (7) above apply to the annual return of a company not having a share capital [s364(1)].

Shadow director

18.07 For the purposes of an annual return, a shadow director (see para 27.04) is deemed to be a director and an officer [s363(8), 364(5)].

Penalties

18.08 There are penalties for not complying with the requirements for an annual return [s363(7), 364(4), 365(3)].

Annual general meeting

Requirement to hold a meeting

18.09 Every company must hold an annual general meeting (AGM) in each calendar year and not more than fifteen months may elapse between the date of one AGM and that of the next [s366(1),(3)]. The notice of the meeting must specifically state that it is to be the AGM [s366(1)].

18.10 So long as a newly incorporated company holds its first AGM within eighteen months of its incorporation, it need not hold it in the year of its incorporation or in the following year [s366(2)]. Thus, for example, if a company is incorporated on 1st August 1985, it need not hold its first AGM in either 1985 or 1986 but must do so by the end of January 1987.

18.11 Twenty one days notice is required to be given when calling an AGM, unless the company's articles provide for a longer period of notice [s369(1),(2)]. If an AGM is called by shorter notice, it will be deemed to have been properly called if this is agreed by all the members who are *entitled* to attend and vote at the AGM [s369(3)]. Thus, approval is required irrespective of whether or not they actually attend the meeting. The provisions of the Act relating to entitlement to receive notice and the method by which it is to be given, proxies, minutes of and the conduct of meetings are outside the scope of this book.

Power of Secretary of State to call a meeting

18.12 If a company fails to hold an AGM as required, any member of the company may apply to the Secretary of State who may, on such terms as he considers expedient, call or direct the calling of a general meeting of the company [s367(1)]. The Secretary of State may direct that only one member of the company present in person or by proxy shall be deemed to constitute a meeting [s367(2)]. A meeting called by the Secretary of State will normally be deemed to be an AGM of the company; however, where the meeting is not held in the year in which the default occurred, the meeting will not be treated as the AGM for the year in which it is actually held unless, at that meeting, the company resolves that it be so treated [s367(4)]. A copy of any such resolution must be forwarded within fifteen days to the registrar of companies [s367(5)].

Penalties

18.13 Provision is made for the imposition of a fine where the above requirements are not complied with [s366(4), 367(3),(5)].

CHAPTER 19

Share premium and merger relief

19.01 The 1981 Act introduced specified exceptions to the rule set out in the 1948 Act that where a company issues shares at a premium, whether for cash or otherwise, the premium must be credited to the share premium account, which is subject to restrictions as to its use. The primary exception relates to share-for-share takeovers. The exceptions were included in the 1981 Act following the decision in *Shearer v Bercain Limited [1980] 3 All E.R.295.*

19.02 The judgement held that section 56 of the 1948 Act (now section 130 of the 1985 Act) requires that a "true value" must be attributed to non-cash assets (for example, shares in another company) acquired in consideration for the issue of shares and that any excess of this "true value" over the nominal value of the shares issued must be transferred to the share premium account, which is not distributable. The case did not define "true value", though normally it would be construed as meaning the value on an open market arm's length basis of the assets acquired. The judgement also held that the 1948 Act prohibited a holding company from regarding a dividend it receives out of the pre-acquisition profits of a subsidiary as being distributable by the parent.

19.03 One of the more important practical effects of the decision was its impact on share-for-share exchanges (that is, where one company issues its shares in exchange for shares in another company). In requiring such transactions to be accounted for in the parent company's individual accounts on the basis of a true value of the consideration received, the case had the effect of making it impossible for the parent's consolidated accounts to be prepared on the basis of "merger" accounting, consequently requiring the adoption of "acquisition" accounting under which the pre-acquisition profits of an acquired company would not form part of the post-combination accumulated profits of the group.

19.04 Furthermore, the recognition of the share premium on the issue of the shares (with the consequent increase in the amount at which the shares in the subsidiary would be stated in the parent's individual accounts) has the effect of preventing the onward distribution by the parent of any dividends it receives from the acquired company which are paid out of its accumulated profits at the date of the acquisition of the shares (that is, "pre-acquisition" profits), because such amounts would have to be applied in reducing the cost of the shares in the subsidiary.

19.05 The 1981 Act introduced relief from the requirement to recognise share premium in defined circumstances. The circumstances in which the "merger relief", as it is referred to in the Act, are available were later extended by statutory instrument. The 1981 Act also removed the provision which was regarded as generally prohibiting a holding company from distributing a dividend received out of the pre-acquisition profits of a subsidiary. The availability of merger relief does not depend on whether "merger accounting" (which is governed by SSAP 23) is adopted in the group accounts.

19.06 Before considering merger relief, it is appropriate to look at the requirement to recognise, and the permitted uses of, the share premium account.

"The share premium account"

19.07 If a company issues its shares at a premium, whether for cash or otherwise, an amount equal to the premium must be transferred to "the share premium account" [s130(1)]. The share premium account may be used for the following purposes only:

(1) in paying up unissued shares to be allotted as fully paid bonus shares to members of the company,

(2) in writing off:
  (a) the company's preliminary expenses, or
  (b) the expenses of, or the commission paid or discount allowed on, any issue of shares or debentures of the company, and

(3) in providing for the premium payable on redemption of debentures of the company.

[s130(2)]

19.08 Except for the above permitted applications, the provisions of the Act relating to the reduction of a company's share capital (which are outside the scope of this book) apply as if the share premium account were part of its paid up capital [s130(3)].

Merger relief – ninety per cent acquisitions

19.09 Except for cases to which section 132 applies (group reorganisations – see paras 19.18 to 19.24), the following provisions apply where the issuing company (referred to below as the "acquiring company") has secured at least a ninety per cent equity holding in another company (or body corporate) in pursuance of an arrangement providing for the issue of equity shares in the acquiring company in return for the issue or transfer to it of equity shares in that other company (or body corporate) or the cancellation of any such shares not held by the company [s131(1), 133(4)].

19.10 Where the equity shares in the acquiring company are issued at a premium, section 130 of the Act does not apply to the premium and, consequently, the premium is not required (or permitted) to be transferred to "the share premium account" [s131(2)].

19.11 The arrangement referred to in para 19.09 above may provide *also* for the allotment of shares (that is, equity or non-equity shares) in the acquiring company in consideration for the issue or transfer to the acquiring company of *non-equity* shares in the other company (or body corporate) or the cancellation of any such shares not held by the acquiring company. In such cases, the relief from section 130 of the Act extends to those shares allotted by the acquiring company [s131(3), 133(4)].

19.12 The acquiring company is regarded as having secured in pursuance of an arrangement at least a ninety per cent equity holding in another company (or body corporate) if, as a result of *that* arrangement, it holds, in aggregate, ninety per cent or more of the nominal value of its equity share capital (whether or not all or any of those shares were acquired in pursuance of the arrangement in question) [s131(4), 133(4)].

19.13 Where the equity share capital of the company (or body corporate) being acquired is divided into different classes of shares, the ninety per cent holding must be obtained in respect of each class of equity before merger relief is available [s131(5), 133(4)].

19.14 For the purpose of the above provisions, any shares in the company (or body corporate) being acquired which are held by, or by the nominee of, the acquiring company's holding company, subsidiary or fellow subsidiary, are regarded as being held by the acquiring company [s131(6), 133(4)].

Mixed consideration

19.15 Merger relief under section 131 is available also where, under the arrangement, the acquiring company provides other consideration (for example, a cash payment or the issue of loan stock) in addition to an issue of its own shares.

Demergers

19.16 Section 131 covers both mergers and acquisitions following demergers; that is, where a holding company disposes of its shares in a subsidiary by a dividend in specie to its own members who then exchange the shares they receive for shares in another company. For example, where company A owns companies B and C, and company D acquires the shares in C with the consideration being the issue of shares in D to the members of A.

Piecemeal acquisitions

19.17 The Act is worded in such a way that the merger relief is available only in respect of acquisitions in pursuance of the particular arrangement which brings the holding up to the required ninety per cent threshold. For example, if in pursuance of two separate arrangements a company acquires in another company firstly an eighty per cent holding and then a further ten per cent holding, the relief from the requirement to transfer the premium to the share premium account is available only in respect of the second (ten per cent) acquisition (although the ten per cent need not be acquired all at one time provided all of it was acquired in pursuance of the same arrangement). In share-for-share exchanges where less than ninety per cent of the equity is acquired, a true value must be attributed to the shares acquired. If this exceeds the nominal value of the shares issued by the acquiring company, the difference must be recorded in the share premium account. The use of fair values will usually also give rise to an amount for (positive or negative) goodwill in the consolidated accounts, to the extent of any difference between the fair values attributable to the separable net assets of the acquired company and the value attributable to its equity in aggregate. The accounting treatment of goodwill arising on consolidation is dealt with in paras 5.25 to 5.29.

Merger relief – group reorganisations

19.18 Companies do not have a choice as to whether to regard a transaction as coming within the scope of sections 131 or 132. If the transaction is a group reorganisation in circumstances to which the following paragraphs apply, section 132 applies to the exclusion of section 131 [s131(1), 132(8)].

19.19 Section 132 applies where the issuing company is a wholly-owned subsidiary of another company or body corporate ("the holding company") and allots shares to:

(1) the holding company, or

(2) another wholly-owned subsidiary of the holding company,

in consideration for the transfer to the issuing company of assets, other than cash, which belong to any company or body corporate ("the transferor company") which is a member of the group of companies which comprises the holding company and its wholly-owned subsidiaries [s132(1), 133(4)]. Assets other than cash would, of course, include shares in another company.

19.20 Where the shares are issued at a premium, the issuing company is not required to transfer any amount in excess of "the minimum premium value" to the share premium account [s132(2)].

19.21 The minimum premium value is the amount (if any) by which the "base value" of the consideration for the shares allotted exceeds their aggregate nominal value [s132(3)].

19.22 The "base value" of the consideration for the shares allotted is the amount by which:

(1) the cost to the transferor company of the assets transferred or the amount at which they are stated in the transferor's accounting records immediately prior to the transfer (whichever is the less), exceeds

(2) the amount at which the liabilities assumed are stated in the transferor company's accounting records immediately prior to the transfer.

[s132(4), (5)]

19.23 The above provisions apply only where the issue of shares took place on or after 21st December 1984 [s132(6)]. Similar provisions, under section 38 of the 1981 Act, which relate only to share-for-*share* transactions which took place between 4th February 1981 and 20th December 1984, are set out in Schedule 25 of the Act [s132(7)].

19.24 The provisions of (what is now) section 132 were introduced in December 1984 after a favourable response to a Consultative Document (issued in August 1983) which proposed to extend the merger (share premium) relief available in group reconstructions to the transfer of any non-cash asset (and not just the shares in another subsidiary in the same group) between wholly-owned companies in the same group.

Distributability of pre-acquisition profits

19.25 The question as to whether a dividend paid by a subsidiary to its parent company is available for onward distribution by that parent depends, inter-alia, on whether receipt of the dividend can be regarded as giving rise to a realised profit for the parent and not simply on whether it derives from pre- or post acquisition profits. The rules governing the distribution of profits are described in Chapter 20. The possible interaction between distributable profits and the use of merger accounting in group accounts is considered in para 19.32 below.

19.26 Before the 1981 Act, dividends received by holding companies out of the pre-acquisition profits of their subsidiaries were, generally, not regarded as being available for distribution by the holding company. The exception to this rule was where share premium was not recorded in the acquiring company's balance sheet because the consolidated accounts were prepared on the basis of merger accounting. Furthermore, a provision in Schedule 8A of the 1948 Act (now Schedule 9 of the 1985 Act and which applies only to special category companies) was interpreted by the judge in the Bercain case (see para 19.01) as prohibiting a holding company from regarding as distributable any dividends it receives out of the pre-acquisition profits of its subsidiaries, except as allowed in that provision. The exceptions were certain types of group reconstruction broadly similar to the (now repealed) section 38 or the 1981 Act (see para 19.23). The position was remedied in the 1981 Act by removing, with retrospective effect, the offending paragraph from Schedule 8A.

Cost of shares acquired

19.27 As a necessary corollary to the relaxations on share premium where, by virtue of sections 131 or 132, a company is not required to include an amount in its share premium account, that amount may also be disregarded in determining the amount at which the shares or other consideration acquired are to be stated in the company's individual balance sheet [s133(1)]. Thus, in such a share for share acquisition, the cost of the shares acquired may be stated as being equal to the nominal value of the shares issued for their acquisition plus, if the arrangement is a group reorganisation (see para 19.18), any share premium which the acquiring company is obliged to recognise in its accounts. This facilitates the accounting treatment of dividends received out of pre-acquisition profits which would otherwise have to be applied in reducing the carrying amount of the investment in the shares. The distribution of profits (which would include dividends received out of the pre-acquisition profits of a subsidiary) is governed by the rules set out in Part VIII of the 1985 Act (see Chapter 20); in particular, only realised profits are regarded as distributable. It appears that where the receipt of such dividends leaves intact the carrying value of the investment in the subsidiary, the dividends received may be regarded as realised profits in the hands of the holding company. This matter is considered further in para 19.31 and 19.32 below.

Merger accounting

19.28 For accounting periods beginning on or after 1st April 1985, "merger accounting" is governed by SSAP 23, which sets out the conditions which must be met if groups wish to adopt merger accounting. "Merger accounting" is a technique used in preparing consolidated accounts and should not be confused with the statutory "merger relief" (share premium relief), described earlier in this chapter, which is concerned principally with the recording of the acquisition of a subsidiary in a parent company's individual accounts. The statutory "merger relief" is not dependent on the use of merger accounting in the group accounts.

19.29 In order to be able to adopt merger accounting in the consolidated accounts, it must be permissible, in the individual accounts of the acquiring company, to record the shares as having been issued at their nominal value, with no recognition (in the share premium account) of any excess of the value of the consideration received (that is, shares in another company) over the nominal value of the shares issued. Thus, the cost of the shares acquired would be recorded at the nominal value of the shares issued which, in a group reorganisation, would often be the same as that of the shares being acquired. To the extent of the merger relief available, any dividends received out of the accumulated profits at the date of acquisition of the shares (pre-acquisition profits) would be regarded as being distributable by the parent company and its group accounts would be prepared on the basis of the distributability of those pre-acquisition profits.

19.30 In some cases where the statutory merger relief is available, the business combination may not qualify under SSAP 23 to be accounted for in the group accounts on the basis of "merger accounting" but, instead, "acquisition accounting" would have to be followed. In such a case the group accounts would reflect a "merger reserve" equal to the amount of the share premium which, by virtue of the statutory merger relief, is not recorded in the share premium account in the parent's individual balance sheet. The reason for this is that the conditions for statutory merger relief (para 19.09) are not identical to those for merger accounting under SSAP 23. In particular, the latter does not permit merger accounting where more than 10% of the fair value of the total consideration given by the acquiror for the equity share capital (including that given for shares already held) is not in the form of equity share capital (for example, the acquiror may make a significant cash payment).

Distributable profits

19.31 Paragraph 1 of the Introduction to SSAP 23 states that the standard deals only with accounting in group accounts and not with the individual accounts of the parent company but notes that "guidance" on this matter is contained in the Appendix. Paragraph 1 of the Appendix then states that it would be "normal practice", where a business combination falls outside the criteria for the use of merger accounting in the consolidated accounts, for the holding company's individual balance sheet to reflect a "merger reserve" which would be equivalent to the amount of the merger relief obtained.

19.32 The Appendix then goes on (in paragraph 4) to cast doubts on whether this merger reserve (which the law does not require to be created) becomes realised on receipt by the parent of a dividend out of the pre-acquisition profits of the subsidiary which this reserve represents. The statement thus raises doubts where there should be none. It seems implausible that the book-keeping treatment can negate the plain intention of the merger relief provisions of the Act; that is, to permit a parent company to regard as a realised profit a dividend it receives out of the pre-acquisition profits of a subsidiary to the extent that it is represented by statutory "merger relief" obtained by the parent. Where the merger relief is shown in the parent company's individual balance sheet as a "merger reserve" under the circumstances envisaged in the Appendix, it is concluded that this reserve becomes realised on the receipt of a dividend out of the subsidiary's (pre-acquisition) profits which it represents.

CHAPTER 20

Distribution of profits and assets

20.01 The 1980 Act introduced into statute law specific regulations relating to the distribution of profit. The 1981 Act included a few modifications to these regulations. Previously, the only definitions of distributable profit in UK company law (other than in a company's memorandum or articles) were to be found in case law. In particular, English law (but not Scottish law) had allowed the distribution of unrealised profits under certain circumstances. Distributions are now restricted to those permitted by the 1985 Act subject to any further restrictions which may be included in a company's articles of association and any case law of continuing effect.

20.02 The statutory rules for distributions may be summarised as follows:

- The basic calculation of "profits available for distribution" is by reference to the excess of realised profits over realised losses as included in the accounts. There is an additional restriction for public companies. A public company may not let a distribution reduce its net assets to below the amount of its called-up share capital and undistributable reserves.

- A public company which is an "investment company" as defined (principally listed investment trusts) may distribute the excess of its realised revenue profits over its realised and unrealised revenue losses, but may not let a distribution reduce the value of its assets to below 1½ times its liabilities.

These statutory rules are described in greater detail below.

Definition of distribution

20.03 "Distribution" means every description of distribution of a company's assets to its members, whether in cash or otherwise, *except* distribution by way of:

(1) an issue of shares as fully or partly paid bonus shares,

(2) the redemption or purchase of any of the company's own shares out of capital (including the proceeds of any fresh issue of shares) or out of unrealised profits in accordance with the provisions of the Act,

(3) the reduction of share capital by extinguishing or reducing the liability of any of the members on any of the company's shares in respect of share capital not paid up, or by repaying paid up share capital, and

(4) a distribution of assets to members of the company on its winding up.

[s263(2)]

Profits available for distribution

20.04 A company may not make a distribution except out of profits available for the purpose [s263(1)]. Profits available for distribution are defined as the aggregate of:

(1) accumulated "realised profits" not previously distributed or capitalised, less

(2) accumulated "realised losses" so far as not previously written off in a reduction or reorganisation of capital duly made.

This is subject to the special rules for investment companies [s263(3)].

20.05 A company's memorandum or articles may be more restrictive regarding the sums out of which, or the cases in which, a distribution may be made [s281].

20.06 Where, after making all reasonable enquiries, the directors of a company are unable to determine whether a particular profit or loss made before 22nd December 1980 is realised or unrealised, they may treat the profit as realised and the loss as unrealised [s263(5)].

Bonus issues

20.07 A company is not permitted to apply an unrealised profit in paying up debentures or any amounts unpaid on its issued shares [s263(4)]. In other words, unrealised profits cannot be used to reduce any outstanding amounts due from share – or debenture holders. Article 110 of Table A* (previously article 128 of Table A in the 1948 Act) allows realised profits to be applied in paying up amounts unpaid on shares or in issuing to members fully paid shares or debentures. No mention is made in article 110 of the issue of partly paid shares or debentures by way of a bonus.

* As set out in S.I. 1985 No. 805

20.08 Where immediately before 22nd December 1980 a company was authorised by its articles to apply its *unrealised* profits in paying up in full or in part unissued shares to be allotted to members of the company as fully or partly paid bonus shares, that provision continues (subject to any alteration of the articles) as authority for those profits to be so applied after that date [s278]. This authority does not extend to debentures. Article 110 of Table A (previously article 128A of Table A in the 1948 Act) continues this authority but only in respect of fully paid bonus shares. A company's unrealised profits would include any unrealised credit balance on its "revaluation reserve".

Restriction on distributions by public companies

20.09 A public company may make a distribution only if at the time the amount of its net assets is not less than the aggregate of its called-up share capital and undistributable reserves and then only if, and to the extent that, the distribution does not reduce the amount of the company's net assets to below that aggregate. This rule is made subject to the special rules for investment companies [s264(1)]. "Net assets" means the aggregate of the company's assets less the aggregate of its liabilities. "Liabilities" include provisions for liabilities and charges [s264(2)].

20.10 A public company may not include any uncalled share capital as an asset for this purpose [s264(4)]. However, share capital which is called but unpaid would be regarded as an asset, if the amount in question is considered to be recoverable.

20.11 A company's undistributable reserves are:

(1) the share premium account,

(2) the capital redemption reserve,

(3) the net credit balance representing unrealised profits not capitalised less unrealised losses not previously written off in a reduction or reorganisation of capital duly made, and

(4) any other reserve the distribution of which is prohibited by any other enactment or by the company's memorandum or articles.

[s264(3)]

20.12 For the purpose of (3) above, the term "capitalisation" does not include a transfer, on or after 22nd December 1980, of profits to the capital redemption reserve [s264(3)]. The reason for this appears to be because transfers to capital redemption reserve, which are required where a company purchases or redeems its own shares out of profits, have to be made out of profits available for distribution and that, as from that date, unrealised profits are not available for distribution.

20.13 An effect of item 20.11(3) above is that any excess of recorded unrealised losses over recorded unrealised profits on revaluations of fixed assets (that is, an overall debit balance on revaluation reserve) must be deducted by a public company from its realised profits less realised losses to arrive at the amount available for distribution.

20.14 A further practical effect is that where a public company has revalued an asset (which it still holds and is still shown in the balance sheet at the revalued amount) and has distributed a dividend out of the resulting unrealised surplus (which before 22nd December 1980 was permitted under English law in certain circumstances), those distributions must be covered by realised profits before any further distribution can be paid, because the Act still regards the revaluation surplus as an accumulated unrealised profit. When the asset is sold, the deemed surplus will, of course, no longer be regarded as unrealised, although it will not actually result in an increase in the company's realised profits (unless and to the extent that the asset is sold for an amount above its book value).

20.15 Example 1 illustrates the effect of the distribution rules on public and private companies.

Example 1:

Calculation of distributable profit

Assume:

	X		Y	
Share capital		£50		£50
Unrealised surplus/(deficit) on revaluation of all fixed assets		40		(40)
Realised profits	70		70	
Realised losses	(20)	50	(20)	50
Total share capital and reserves/net assets		£140		£60

Distributable profit if the company is a private company:

	X Ltd	Y Ltd
Realised profits	£70	£70
less		
Realised losses	(20)	(20)
Distributable profit	£50	£50

The revaluation deficit in Y Ltd is ignored only because it arose on a revaluation of *all* its fixed assets [s275(1)]. If it arose as a result of a partial revaluation only, it would be regarded as a realised loss and therefore deductible in arriving at distributable profit, which would then be £10.

Example 1 continued
Distributable profit if the company is a
public company: X PLC   Y PLC
Distributable profit restricted to:
Net assets,   £140   £60
   less aggregate of:
Share capital, and   £(50)   £(50)
undistributable reserves   (40)   (90)   –   (50)
Distributable profit   £50   £10

The unrealised revaluation deficit in Y PLC does not form part of its
undistributable reserves (see para 20.13).

Meaning of realised profits and losses

20.16 The definition of "realised profits" is to be found in Schedule 4 para
91 of the Act and, by virtue of section 742(6), applies also for the purpose
of calculating a company's distributable profits. This calculation will be
based on the individual accounts of the company (see para 20.26). A
company's realised profits are those profits which are treated as realised
profits in the accounts, in accordance with principles generally accepted
with respect to the determination of realised profits for accounting
purposes at the time when those accounts are prepared [s742(6), Sch 4
para 91]. It thus appears that it would not be necessary to adjust the
amount of the profits treated as realised in the accounts used as the basis
for a proposed distribution where generally accepted accounting
principles change between the time the accounts are prepared and the
date of a distribution based on those accounts.

20.17 "Realised losses" are *not* similarly defined, but the Act does state
that any "provision" (as defined in Sch 4 paras 88,89)*, other than one in
respect of a diminution in value of a fixed asset appearing on a revaluation
of all the fixed assets† of the company, or of all its fixed assets other than
goodwill, is to be treated as a realised loss [s275(1)]. The exception, which
does *not* extend to the annual depreciation charge, is available to both
public and private companies but, for public companies, is effectively
limited to the extent of the company's unrealised revaluation surpluses (if
any), because such companies have to satisfy the "net assets" test,
described in para 20.09. The exception appears to relate back to a
distinction made in case law between losses of fixed capital and losses of
circulating capital, where the former did not have to be made good.

---

*   For special category accounts read "(within the meaning of Schedule
    9)" [s279, Sch 11 para 7].
†   For special category accounts "fixed assets" are defined to include any
    other asset which is not a current asset (so-called "in between" assets)
    [s279, Sch 11 para 7].

20.18 For the operation of this exception, it is *not*, however, necessary for a revaluation of all the fixed assets to be incorporated in the accounts. The other assets which have not actually been revalued in the accounts will be regarded as having been revalued at that time if their value is "considered" by the directors, who must be satisfied that their aggregate value at that time is not less than the aggregate amount at which they are stated in the accounts [s275(4),(5)]. That is, there must not be an unrecorded net deficit on the assets not actually revalued in the accounts. Thus, for example, in order for a provision for diminution in the value of some fixed assets to be regarded as an unrealised loss, it is necessary only for the directors to "consider" the value of the remaining fixed assets (excluding goodwill if they so wish) as at the time the provision is made.

20.19 In order to take advantage of these provisions, this "consideration" of value must be described in a note to the accounts which should state that:

(1) the directors have at a particular time considered the value of fixed assets without actually revaluing them,

(2) the directors are satisfied that the aggregate value of those assets at the time is or was not less than the aggregate amount at which they are or were for the time being stated in the company's accounts, and

(3) that the relevant items (see para 20.26) are stated in the accounts on the basis that a revaluation of the company's fixed assets (which would include the assets in question) took place at that time.

[s275(6)]

Depreciation of revalued assets

20.20 Where a company has revalued a fixed asset which, on revaluation, gave rise to an unrealised profit, it would charge depreciation on the revalued amount to the profit and loss account (such provisions being regarded as a realised loss – see para 20.17). In such cases, an amount equal to the amount by which the charge for depreciation exceeds the charge that would have been made had the asset not been revalued, is treated as a realised profit (that is, the "extra" depreciation written off may be added back to realised profits for the purpose of calculating distributable profits) [s275(2)]. Many companies reflect this in their accounts by making an annual transfer between reserves.

Cost of asset not available

20.21 Where there is no record of the original cost of an asset, or a record cannot be obtained without unreasonable expense or delay, then for the purpose of determining whether the company has made a profit or loss in respect of that asset, its cost is taken to be the value ascribed to it in the earliest available record of its value made on or after its acquisition by the company [s275(3)].

Development costs

20.22 Where development costs are shown as an asset in a company's accounts, the amount shown must be treated as a realised loss (or, in the case of an investment company, as a realised revenue loss) [s269(1)]. This does not apply:

(1) to any part of the amount shown which represents an unrealised profit arising on a revaluation of those costs, or

(2) (a) if there are "special circumstances" which justify the directors in deciding that the amount should not be so treated, and
   (b) the note to the accounts which gives the reasons for showing development costs as an asset (see para 5.20) states also that the amount is not to be treated as a realised loss (or realised revenue loss) and explains the circumstances relied upon to justify the decision of the directors to that effect.

[s269(2)]

The above does not apply where the company's (individual) accounts are special category (see Chapter 13) [s279, Sch 11 para 3].

20.23 The "special circumstances" are not defined but, if development costs are carried forward in accordance with the criteria set out in SSAP 13, the directors should be able to justify their not being treated as a realised loss for distribution purposes.

Distributions in kind

20.24 A feature of most demergers is the distribution of non-cash assets (particularly shares in another company in the same group). In order that the prohibition on the distribution of unrealised profits does not unduly inhibit demergers, the Act provides that where a company makes a distribution of or including a non-cash asset which contains an element of unrealised profit (for example, a surplus on revaluation), that profit is to be treated as a realised profit for the purposes of determining the lawfulness of the distribution and, where the accounts have to comply with Schedule 4, for the inclusion of the profit as realised in the profit and loss account [s276]. Thus, it is likely for accounting purposes that in such cases the unrealised profit will be transferred from the revaluation reserve to the profit and loss account.

Accounts supporting a distribution

20.25 The Act sets out the procedure which must be followed in determining whether a company may make a proposed distribution without contravening the rules.

20.26 The amount of a distribution which may be made is determined by reference to the following items as stated in the company's individual (not group) accounts:

(1) profits, losses, assets and liabilities,

(2) provisions* of any of the kinds mentioned in paragraphs 88 and 89 of Schedule 4 (depreciation, diminution in value of assets, retentions to meet liabilities, etc.), and

(3) share capital and reserves (including undistributable reserves).

[s270(2)]

20.27 The determination of whether a company may make a proposed distribution is normally to be made on the basis of the company's audited individual accounts in respect of the last preceding accounting reference period for which accounts have been laid before the company in general meeting (or, where the company's individual accounts are special category, which have been laid or delivered to the registrar of companies) [s270(3), 279, Sch 11 para 4]. These accounts are referred to below as the "last annual accounts".

20.28 Where a distribution would be found to contravene the distribution rules if reference were made only to the company's last annual accounts (for example, where a proposed interim dividend exceeds the distributable profits, less any subsequent distribution of those profits, calculated by reference to those accounts) the company must prepare "interim accounts", "such as to enable a reasonable judgement to be made" [s270(4)]. If the last annual accounts show sufficient distributable profits to support a proposed distribution but the directors are aware that this position has been eroded by subsequent losses, it appears that s270(4) does not apply (because by reference only to those accounts the distribution would be lawful). However, it would obviously be imprudent for directors to declare a dividend in excess of the estimated distributable profits at the time of the declaration. In particular, if such an action were to be regarded as carrying on business with intent to defraud creditors, consenting directors may be liable to imprisonment or a fine or both, and in a winding-up may be liable for the debts of the company [s458, 630].

---

* Provisions within the meaning of Schedule 9 in the case of special category accounts [s279, Sch 11 para 4].

20.29 There is a similar requirement for the preparation of "initial accounts" where a distribution is proposed to be declared during the company's first accounting reference period or before any accounts are laid (or filed in the case of special category accounts) in respect of that period [s270(4), 279, Sch 11 para 4].

20.30 Distributions which have already been made on the basis of these accounts must be allowed for in determining whether subsequent distributions based on those accounts are lawful [s274(1)]. This applies also to various types of financial assistance [s274(2)].

20.31 The distribution rules are treated as contravened if the requirements in relation to the relevant accounts are not fulfilled [s270(5)].

Requirements for accounts supporting a distribution

Last annual accounts
20.32 The accounts must have been properly prepared in accordance with the Act, or have been so prepared except for matters which are not material for determining, by reference to the relevant items in the accounts (see para 20.26), whether the distribution would contravene the relevant provisions of the Act. In addition, the balance sheet must give a true and fair view of the state of the company's affairs as at the balance sheet date and the profit and loss account must give a true and fair view of the company's profit or loss for the period covered by the accounts [s271(2)]. The requirement for the accounts to give a true and fair view does not apply where the company is entitled to avail itself, and has availed itself, of any of the provisions of Part III of Schedule 9 [s279, Sch 11 para 5].

20.33 The auditors must have reported on the accounts. Their report must either be unqualified (that is, a report without qualification to the effect that in the auditors' opinion the accounts have been properly prepared in accordance with the Act) or, if it is qualified, the auditors must have stated in writing, either at the time of the report or subsequently, whether, in their opinion, the subject matter of their qualification is material for determining by reference to the relevant items (see para 20.26), whether the distribution would contravene the provisions of the Act [s271(3),(4)]. A copy of this statement must have been laid before the company in general meeting [s271(4)]. In the case of a special category company, a copy of the auditors' statement must have been laid before the company in general meeting or have been delivered to the registrar of companies, according as those have been laid or filed [s279, Sch 11 para 5].

20.34 The auditors' statement may relate either to a specific proposed distribution or generally to distributions (although in this case it is likely that a "clearance" threshold would be stated) [s271(5)].

Interim accounts
20.35 There are provisions relating to interim accounts prepared by public companies (but *not* by private companies) to support a proposed distribution.

20.36 Similar conditions to those set out in para 20.32 apply, and therefore the accounts must give a true and fair view and comprise a balance sheet, profit and loss account, and related notes specified in Schedule 4 to the Act. Disclosures required under other provisions of the Act (for example, directors' remuneration under Schedule 6) are *not* required. Where the accounts are special category, they must comply with Schedule 9 instead of Schedule 4. The balance sheet must be signed by the directors in accordance with section 238 (see para 3.02) and a copy of the accounts must have been delivered to the registrar of companies prior to the distribution [s272, 279, Sch 11 para 6]. The accounts do not have to be audited and thus paras 20.33 and 20.34 do not apply.

Initial accounts
20.37 Section 273 applies in relation to initial accounts prepared by a public company to support a proposed distribution; there are no regulations relating to the initial accounts of private companies.

20.38 The regulations are broadly the same as those relating to the last annual accounts. The balance sheet must also have been signed by the directors in accordance with section 238 [s273, 279, Sch 11 para 6]. A copy of the accounts, the auditors' report and (if the auditors' report was qualified) of the auditors' statement must have been delivered to the registrar of companies [s273(6),(7)].

Investment companies

20.39 Investment companies (as defined below) have the option of following the normal rules relating to distributions (that is, in sections 263 and 264) or of following the special rules for investment companies. For all practical purposes, the rules apply only to listed investment trust companies.

Definition

20.40 An investment company is a public company which has given notice (which has not been revoked) in the prescribed form (form number 266(1)) to the registrar of companies of its intention to carry on business as an investment company, and has thereafter complied with the following conditions:

(1) its business consists of investing its funds mainly in securities with the aim of spreading investment risk and giving its members the benefit of the results of the management of its funds,

(2) none of its holdings in companies (other than investment companies) represents more than 15% by value of its (the investing company's) total investments.

(3) distribution of capital profits is prohibited by its memorandum or articles of association, and

(4) it has not retained, in respect of any accounting reference period, more than 15% of its income from securities (unless required to do so by the Act).

[s266(1),(2)]

20.41 A company may at any time cease to be an investment company by giving notice thereof in the prescribed form (form number 266(3)) to the registrar of companies [s266(3)].

Permitted distributions

20.42 Subject to the conditions described below, an investment company has the option to make a distribution out of its accumulated realised revenue profits not previously distributed or capitalised less its accumulated revenue losses (whether realised or unrealised) so far as not previously written off in a reduction or reorganisation of capital duly made:

(1) if at that time the amount of its assets is at least equal to one and a half times its total liabilities (including provisions for liabilities and charges), and

(2) if, and to the extent that, the distribution does not reduce the amount of its assets to less than one and a half times its liabilities (including such provisions).

[s265(1),(2), 279, Sch 11 para 2]

20.43 Thus, realised capital losses need not be deducted in arriving at distributable profits and realised capital profits are not distributable except on winding up. This option may be exercised notwithstanding the provisions of section 264 which restrict distributions by public companies (see para 20.09).

20.44 Uncalled share capital is not to be regarded as an asset of the company for these purposes [s265(3)].

20.45 The difference between the rules for ordinary public companies and the option for investment companies is illustrated by Example 2.

Example 2:

Calculation of distributable profit – investment company compared with ordinary public company.

Assume:

		X		Y
Share capital	A	£100		£50
Unrealised capital profits	B	–	40	
Unrealised capital losses	C	(80)		–
Unrealised revenue losses	D	(10)		(10)
		(90)		30
Realised revenue profits	E	100	70	
Realised revenue losses	F	(40)	(20)	
Realised capital profits	G	40	20	
		100		70
Total share capital and reserves/net assets	H	110		150
Total liabilities	J	110		240
Total assets	K	£220		£390

If the company is an ordinary public company:

		X PLC		Y PLC	
Distributable profit restricted to:					
Net assets,	H		£110		£150
less aggregate of:					
Share capital, and	A	£(100)		£(50)	
undistributable reserves	B/C	–		(40)	
(net credit balances only)			(100)		(90)
Distributable profit			£10		£60

If the company is an investment company, and is therefore prohibited by its memorandum and articles from distributing its capital profits, those capital profits must be excluded, giving the following result assuming that advantage is *not* taken of the alternative provisions of section 265.

		X PLC (Investment company)	Y PLC (Investment company)
Distributable profit for an ordinary public company, less		£10	£60
realised capital profits	G	(40)	(20)
Distributable profit		–	£40

Example 2 (continued):

Under section 265, an investment company may calculate its distributable profit as follows:

		X PLC (Investment company)		Y PLC (Investment company)	
Distributable profit is the lesser of:					
(1) Realised revenue profits	E		£100		£70
less: Realised revenue losses,	F	£(40)		£(20)	
and Unrealised revenue losses	D	(10)		(10)	
			(50)		(30)
			£50		£40
and:					
(2) Excess of total assets	K		220		390
over 1½ times total liabilities	J		(165)		(360)
			£55		£30
Distributable profit			£50		£30

In this example, it is likely that X PLC would take advantage of the provisions of section 265 because it results in a higher amount of distributable profit, while Y PLC would not.

20.46 The conditions which must be fulfilled before an investment company may make a distribution under the above provisions are:

(1) it must be listed on a recognised stock exchange (currently only The Stock Exchange),

(2) during the period starting with the first day of the company's accounting reference period which immediately precedes that in which the distribution is to be made* and ending with the date of the distribution, the company has not:
  (a) distributed any of its capital profits, or
  (b) applied any unrealised profits or any capital profits (realised or unrealised) in paying up debentures or any amounts unpaid on any of its issued shares, and

(3) the company has given to the registrar of companies the requisite notice (see para 20.40) of its intention to carry on business as an investment company:
  (a) before the beginning of the immediately preceding accounting reference period, or

---

* Where the distribution is to be made in the company's first accounting reference period, the first day of that period.

(b) if the company was incorporated on or after 22nd December 1980, as soon as may have been reasonably practicable after the date of its incorporation.

[s265(4),(5),(6)]

Special category accounts

20.47 Where the company's individual accounts are special category, in determining capital and revenue profits and losses, an asset which is not a fixed asset or a current asset is to be treated as a fixed asset [s265(7), 279, Sch 11 para 2]. The only companies which are thought likely to qualify both as special category and as an investment company would be those of the nature of investment banks.

Extension to other companies

20.48 The Secretary of State may by statutory instrument extend these provisions to companies whose principal business is investing their funds in securities, land and other assets with the aim of spreading investment risk and giving their members the benefit of the results of the management of the assets [s267(1)]. The statutory instruments may make different provisions for different classes of companies and may contain such transitional and supplemental provisions as the Secretary of State considers necessary [s267(2)].

Letters and order forms

20.49 The business letters and order forms of an investment company must indicate its status [s351(1)(c)].

Insurance companies with long term business

20.50 Where an insurance company carries on long term business as defined in the Insurance Companies Act 1982, an amount properly transferred to the profit and loss account of an insurance company from a surplus in the long term business fund or funds of the company and any deficit in those funds are to be treated respectively as a realised profit and a realised loss [s268(1),(3)]. A "surplus" refers to an excess of the assets representing those funds over the liabilities attributable to long term business as shown by an actuarial investigation in accordance with sections 18 or 42 of the Insurance Companies Act 1982. A "deficit" is to be construed accordingly [s268(2),(3)].

Consequences of an unlawful distribution

20.51 Where a distribution or part of one made by a company to one of its members is made in contravention of the Act and, at the time of the distribution, the member knows or has reasonable grounds for believing that this is the case, he is liable to repay it (or part of it, as the case may require) to the company or, where the distribution was other than in cash, to pay the company a sum equal to the value of the distribution (or part of it) at the time of the distribution [s277(1)]. The foregoing is without prejudice to any other obligation imposed on a member to repay a distribution unlawfully made to him [s277(2)].

20.52 The above does not, however, apply in relation to financial assistance given by a company in contravention of section 151, or any payment made by a company in respect of the redemption or purchase by the company of shares in itself [s277(2)].

20.53 The liability of directors for unlawful distributions is not specifically dealt with by the Act. Paragraph 20.28 above considers briefly the position where a company carries on business with intent to defraud creditors. It is also possible that directors who are parties to an unlawful distribution may be liable to repay the amount to the company.

CHAPTER 21

Reregistration of private and public companies

21.01 The Act allows a private company to alter its status and become a public company, provided that prescribed conditions are met and the reregistration procedure is correctly followed. The principal conditions which must be met are that the company has issued share capital of at least £50,000 and does not have a realised deficit on its reserves. Thus, where a company is formed with the intention of "going public" before it has generated sufficient income to cover its expenses it should, if possible, be formed as a public company at the outset, thereby avoiding the possibility of not being permitted to reregister as public because of having a realised deficit on its reserves.

21.02 The Act also permits a public company to reregister as a private company and sets out the procedure to be followed.

Reregistration of a private company as a public company

21.03 A private company having a share capital may reregister as a public company if it passes a special resolution to be reregistered and makes an application to the registrar of companies, enclosing the required documentation [s43(1)].

21.04 A company may not reregister if it has previously *reregistered* as unlimited [s43(1)]. The position of an unlimited company wishing to reregister as a public (limited) company is described in para 21.25.

21.05 The special resolution to reregister must:

(1) alter the company's memorandum to state that the company is to be a public company,

(2) alter the company's memorandum to bring it into conformity with the form and substance of the memorandum for a public company (including a change of its name so that it ends with the words "public limited company" or the permitted abbreviation "p.l.c."), and

(3) alter the company's articles as appropriate in the circumstances. [s43(2)]

21.06 A copy of the special resolution must be filed with the registrar of companies within fifteen days of its being passed [s380(1),(4)].

21.07 The application must be in the prescribed form (form number 43(3)) and be signed by a director or secretary of the company. It must be accompanied by the following documents:

(1) a printed copy of the duly amended memorandum and articles,

(2) a copy of a balance sheet of the company made up to a date not more than seven months before the company's application for reregistration (the "relevant balance sheet") together with a copy of an unqualified report (see para 21.10) by the company's auditors in relation to that balance sheet,

(3) a copy of a statement by the auditors that, in their opinion, the relevant balance sheet shows that, at the balance sheet date, the amount of the company's net assets was not less than the aggregate of its called-up share capital and undistributable reserves (see para 20.09),

(4) where required (see para 21.22), a copy of the valuation report on the non-cash consideration received for shares allotted, and

(5) a statutory declaration, in the prescribed form (form number 43(3)(e)), by a director or secretary of the company:
   (a) that the special resolution has been passed and that the requirements as to share capital and, where appropriate, valuation of non-cash consideration have been satisfied, and
   (b) that between the balance sheet date and the application for reregistration, there has been no change in the financial position of the company that has resulted in the amount of the company's net assets becoming less than the aggregate of its called-up share capital and undistributable reserves.

[s43(3),(4),(5)]

21.08 Thus, the relevant balance sheet referred to above is a balance sheet of the company to be reregistered (a consolidated balance sheet is not required, nor will one fulfil the above requirements). This balance sheet may be the balance sheet prepared at the end of the most recent financial year (provided that was within seven months of the application) or a balance sheet prepared especially for the reregistration. The balance sheet should include the related "notes" required by Schedules 4 or 9 respectively.

21.09 It follows that if the company has accumulated realised losses (however small) it would not normally meet the test in 21.07(3) above and would therefore be denied reregistration.

Meaning of unqualified report

21.10 The reference to an "unqualified report" by the company's auditors in relation to the "relevant balance sheet" has the meaning set out in the paragraphs which follow.

21.11 If the balance sheet was prepared in respect of an accounting reference period of the company, it means a report by the company's auditors stating, without material qualification, that in their opinion the balance sheet:

(1) has been properly prepared in accordance with the Companies Act 1985, and

(2) gives a true and fair view of the state of the company's affairs as at the balance sheet date.

[s46(2)]

21.12 In any other case, it means a report by the auditors stating, without material qualification, that in their opinion the balance sheet:

(1) complies with the applicable "accounting provisions" (see para 21.14 below), and

(2) gives a true and fair view of the state of the company's affairs as at the balance sheet date.

[s46(3)]

21.13 In both of the above two cases, where the balance sheet is that of a special category company (see Chapter 13) which is entitled to, and has availed itself of, any of the disclosure exceptions in Part III of Schedule 9, the auditors' report is not required to state that the balance sheet gives a true and fair view [s46(4)].

21.14 The accounting provisions referred to above are sections 228 and 238(1) (contents, form and signing of accounts – see Chapters 2 and 3) and, where applicable, section 258 (contents and form of special category accounts – see Chapter 13) [s46(3)]. The balance sheet should include the related "notes" required by Schedules 4 or 9 respectively.

21.15 In the second case (para 21.12 above), because the balance sheet is not prepared in respect of an accounting reference period, the accounting provisions are deemed to have effect with such modifications as are necessary [s46(6)].

Meaning of "material qualification"

21.16 An audit qualification is not material if, but only if, the auditors state in their report that the matter giving rise to the qualification is not material for the purpose of determining (by reference to the balance sheet) whether, at the balance sheet date, the amount of the company's net assets was not less than the aggregate of its called up share capital and undistributable reserves [s46(5)].

Requirements as to share capital

21.17 For a private company to be reregistered as a public company, all of the following conditions with respect to its share capital must be satisfied at the time the special resolution is passed [s45(1)]. That is (subject to the exceptions set out below):

(1) The nominal value of the company's allotted share capital must be at least the "authorised minimum" (currently £50,000 but the Secretary of State has the power to alter it – s118).

(2) Each of the company's allotted shares must be paid up at least as to one-quarter of its nominal value and the whole of any premium on it.

(3) If any shares in the company or any premium on them have been fully or partly paid up by an undertaking given by any person that he or another should do work or perform services (whether for the company or any other person), the undertaking must have been performed or otherwise discharged.

(4) If shares have been allotted as fully or partly paid up as to their nominal value or any premium on them otherwise than in cash, and the consideration for the allotment consists of or includes an undertaking to the company (other than to do work or perform services), then either:
   (a) the undertaking must have been performed or otherwise discharged, or
   (b) there must be a contract between the company and some person pursuant to which the undertaking is to be performed within five years from the time the special resolution is passed.

[s45(2),(3),(4)]

Exceptions

21.18 The above provisions for the reregistration of a private company were originally included in the 1980 Act. In order to provide companies existing at the time with some relief from the conditions imposed, the exceptions set out in the following paragraph were granted.

21.19 In determining whether the conditions in para 21.17(2),(3) and (4) above are complied with, the following shares may be disregarded:

(a) any share which was allotted before 22nd June 1982 (but see below for restriction), and

(b) any share which was allotted under an employees' share scheme and which would prevent the company from being reregistered because those shares do not satisfy the conditions in para 21.17(2) above.

[s45(5)]

21.20 However, any share which is disregarded as above must also be disregarded in determining whether the company has the minimum share capital required by para 21.17(1) above [s45(7)].

21.21 Shares must not be disregarded by virtue of 21.19(a) above if the aggregate of their nominal value is more than one-tenth of the nominal value of the company's allotted share capital, and for this purpose the allotted share capital is treated as not including any shares disregarded under 21.19(b) above [s45(6)].

Report on shares issued for a consideration other than cash

21.22 As noted in Chapter 22, where a public company (but not a private company) allots its shares for a consideration other than cash, it must obtain an independent accountant's report on the value of that consideration [s103]. However, where a private company wishes to reregister as a public company and it has, between the date as at which the relevant balance sheet was prepared and the passing of the special resolution to reregister, allotted shares which were fully or partly paid up (as to their nominal value or any premium) otherwise than in cash, such an independent accountant's report is required before the company may be reregistered. Furthermore, the report must have been made to the company during the six months immediately preceding the allotment of the shares [s44(1),(2)].

Exceptions

21.23 Where an amount standing to the credit of the profit and loss account or any other reserve of the company has been applied in paying up, to any extent, any of the shares allotted or any premium on those shares, the amount applied is not regarded as consideration for the purpose of para 21.22 above and, therefore, a report on its value is not required [s44(3)].

21.24 A report is not required in the following cases, described briefly below, which are the same as the exceptions for a public company which issues shares for a non-cash consideration (see Chapter 22). A full description of the exception will be found in the paragraphs indicated.

(1) Where shares are allotted in pursuance of an offer to acquire all of the shares (or all those of a particular class) in another company or body corporate which are not already held by the acquiring company or, if it is a member of a group, by another member of that group (see paras 22.03 and 22.04).

(2) In a merger (as defined) with another company or body corporate; that is, where a company acquires all the assets and liabilities of another company or body corporate in exchange for the issue of shares in the acquiring company to shareholders of the other, with or without any cash payment.

[s44(4) to (7)]

Unlimited company reregistering as public

21.25 An unlimited company is a form of private company [s1(3)]. Limited companies can generally reregister as unlimited and unlimited companies can generally reregister as limited; however, only one such change of status is permitted [s49(2), 51(2)]. An unlimited company, which has a share capital, may reregister as a *public* limited company provided that it has not previously changed its status from limited to unlimited [s43(1)]. The requirements set out in this chapter apply with the following modification; that is, the special resolution must, in addition to the other requirements:

(1) state that the liability of the members is to be limited by shares, and what the company's share capital is to be, and

(2) make such alterations in the company's memorandum as are necessary to bring it in substance and in form into conformity with the requirements of the Act with respect to the memorandum of a company limited by shares.

[s48(2)]

When reregistration becomes effective

21.26 Reregistration as a public company is effective only when the registrar of companies issues the company with a (revised) certificate of incorporation stating that the company is a public company [s47(1),(4)]. Any alterations in the memorandum and articles set out in the special resolution take effect at the same time [s47(4)].

Reregistration of a public company as a private company

21.27 The Act permits a public company to reregister as a private company by following a prescribed procedure. The company must pass a special resolution to this effect, and the resolution must alter the company's memorandum so that it no longer states that the company is to be a public company. The resolution must also make any other alterations in the company's memorandum and articles as are requisite in the circumstances [s53(1),(2)]. An application in the prescribed form (form number 53), which must be signed by a director or by the secretary of the company, must be delivered to the registrar of companies. This must be accompanied by a printed copy of the memorandum and articles of the company as altered by the resolution [s53(1)]. A copy of the special resolution must be filed with the registrar of companies within fifteen days of its being passed [s380(1),(4)].

21.28 There is a safeguard whereby members who did not consent to or vote in favour of such a resolution may apply within twenty eight days to the court to have it set aside. Application must be made by:

(1) the holders of not less than in aggregate five per cent of the nominal value of the company's issued share capital or any class thereof (or if the company is not limited by shares, by not less than five per cent of its members), or

(2) by not less than fifty members of the company.

[s54(2),(3)]

21.29 Reregistration is effective on the issue by the registrar of a revised certificate of incorporation for the company [s55].

CHAPTER 22

Accountant's report on shares issued by a public company for a non-cash consideration

Requirement for a report

22.01 Subject to specified exceptions, a public company may not allot any shares as fully or partly paid up (as respects nominal value or premium) otherwise than in cash unless:

(1) that consideration has been independently valued,

(2) a report with respect to its value has been made to the company during the six months immediately preceding the allotment of the shares, and

(3) a copy of the report has been sent to the proposed allottee.

The appointment of the independent valuer and the report must be made in compliance with section 108 of the Act (see para 22.08) [s103(1)].

Exceptions

Bonus issues
22.02 The application of any amount standing to the credit of any of the company's reserves or profit and loss account, in paying up (wholly or partly) the nominal value or premium on shares to be allotted to its members does not count as consideration for the allotment and accordingly the requirements of the previous paragraph do not apply to the amount so applied [s103(2)].

Acquisition of shares
22.03 Subject to the conditions set out below, a report is also not required under an arrangement whereby a company allots shares on terms that the whole or part of the consideration for the shares allotted is to be provided by the transfer to the company (or the cancellation) of all or some of the

156

shares, or of all or some of the shares of a particular class, in another company or body corporate. The exception is available whether or not the arrangement also provides for the issue to the acquiring company of shares, or of shares of any particular class, in that other company or body corporate [s103(3),(7)].

22.04 To qualify for the exception, the arrangement must be open to all the holders of the shares in the other company or body corporate (or, where the arrangement applies only to shares of a particular class, to all the holders of shares of that class). In determining whether this is the case, the following shares are to be disregarded; that is, shares held by or by a nominee of the acquiring company (that is, the company proposing to allot shares), or by a nominee of a company (or body corporate) which is the acquiring company's holding company or subsidiary or a company (or body corporate) which is a subsidiary of its holding company [s103(4),(7)].

"Mergers"
22.05 A report is not required in a proposed "merger"; that is, where there is a proposed allotment of shares (or other securities) by a company to the shareholders of another company (or body corporate) in exchange for all the assets and liabilities of that other company (or body corporate), with or without a cash payment to those shareholders [s103(5),(7)]. The type of merger referred to here is not the SSAP 23 type of merger but is the subject of the EEC Third Directive on Company Law which is awaiting enacting legislation in the UK.

Effect of contravention

22.06 If a company allots shares in contravention of the provisions set out in para 22.01 above and cithcr:

(1) the allottee has not received the valuer's report, or

(2) there has been some other contravention of section 103 or 108 of the Act which the allottee knew or ought to have known amounted to a contravention,

the allottee is liable to pay the company an amount equal to the nominal value of the shares and the whole of any premium (or, if the case so requires, so much thereof as is treated as paid up by the consideration) with interest at the "appropriate rate" [s103(6)]. The appropriate rate means five per cent per annum or such other rate as may be prescribed by statutory instrument [s107].

22.07 Section 113 sets out the circumstances in which the court may grant exemption (either in whole or in part) from this liability.

Independent valuer's report

22.08 The report (required by sections 44 and 103 of the Act – see paras 21.22 and 22.01) on the value of non-cash consideration for an allotment of shares, must be made by an independent person (referred to hereafter as "the valuer") who is qualified at the time of the report to be appointed, or continue to be, an auditor of the company [s108(1)]. Usual practice is for a company's own auditors to issue the report.

22.09 In giving his report, the valuer need not himself value the consideration; where it appears to him to be reasonable, he may arrange for or accept a valuation of the consideration, or part of it, made by another person who must appear to the valuer to have the requisite knowledge and experience for the task. That other person must report to the valuer so as to enable him to make his own report and must not be:

(1) an officer or servant of the company or any other body corporate which is that company's subsidiary or holding company or a subsidiary of that company's holding company, or

(2) a partner or employee of such an officer or servant.

[s108(2)]

For this purpose, an officer or servant does not include an auditor [s108(3)].

Contents of valuer's report

22.10 The valuer's report is required to state:

(1) the nominal value of the shares to be wholly or partly paid for by the consideration,

(2) the amount of any premium payable on the shares,

(3) the description of the consideration and, in respect of that part of the consideration which he himself has valued, a description thereof, the method used to value it and the date of the valuation, and

(4) the extent to which the nominal value of the shares and any premium are to be treated as paid up:
    (a) by the consideration, and
    (b) in cash.

[s108(4)]

22.11 Where the consideration or part of it is valued by a person other than the valuer himself, the valuer's report must state that fact and also:

(1) the name of the other person and what knowledge and experience he has to carry out the valuation, and

(2) describe so much of the consideration as was valued by the other person and the method used to value it, and specify the date of the valuation.

[s108(5)]

22.12 Additionally, the valuer must state the following in his report (or in a note which must accompany that report):

(1) in the case of a valuation made by a person other than himself, that it appeared to himself reasonable to arrange for it to be made or to accept a valuation so made,

(2) whoever made the valuation, that the method of valuation was reasonable in all the circumstances,

(3) that it appears to the valuer that there has been no material change in the value of the consideration since the valuation, and

(4) that, on the basis of the valuation, the value of the consideration, together with any cash by which the nominal value of the shares or any premium payable on them is to be paid up, is not less than so much of the aggregate of the nominal value and the whole of any such premium as is treated as paid up by the consideration and any such cash.

[s108(6)]

Where only part of the consideration is valued

22.13 Where only part of the consideration to be received by the company is to be applied in paying up the shares (or any premium on the shares), the report must cover that part of the consideration which is to be so applied and:

(1) the valuer must carry out, or arrange for, such other valuations as will enable him to determine that proportion, and

(2) his report must state what valuations have been made for this purpose, and also the reason for, and method and date of, any such valuation, as well as any other matters which may be relevant to that determination.

[s108(7)]

Assistance by officers of the company

22.14 A person carrying out a valuation or making a report is entitled to require from the officers of the company such information and explanation as he considers necessary for that purpose [s110(1)].

22.15 A person who knowingly or recklessly makes to such a person a statement (orally or in writing) which is misleading, false or deceptive in a material particular, is liable to imprisonment or a fine, or both [s110(2),(3)].

CHAPTER 23

Financial assistance for the acquisition of own shares

General prohibition

23.01 The Act contains the following provisions relating to the giving by a company of financial assistance for an acquisition of its own or its holding company's shares. The rules cover the giving of such assistance by limited companies as well as by unlimited companies.

23.02 Where a person is acquiring or is proposing to acquire shares in a company, it is unlawful for the company or any of its subsidiaries to give any financial assistance directly or indirectly for the purpose of that acquisition, before or at the same time as the acquisition takes place [s151(1)]. Furthermore, where a person has acquired shares in a company and any liability has been incurred by that or any other person, for the purpose of that acquisition, it is unlawful for the company or any of its subsidiaries to give financial assistance directly or indirectly for the purpose of reducing or discharging the liability so incurred [s151(2), 152(3)].

23.03 If a company contravenes these provisions it is liable to a fine and every officer of the company who is in default is liable to a fine or imprisonment or both [s151(3)].

Definition of financial assistance

23.04 Financial assistance is widely defined to cover the following:

(1) financial assistance given by way of gift,

(2) financial assistance given by way of guarantee, security or indemnity, other than an indemnity in respect of the indemnifier's own neglect or default, or by way of release or waiver,

161

(3) financial assistance given by way of a loan or any other agreement under which any of the obligations of the person giving the assistance are to be fulfilled at a time when in accordance with the agreement any obligation of another party to the agreement remains unfulfilled, or by way of the novation of, or the assignment of rights arising under a loan or such other agreement, or

(4) any other financial assistance given by a company the net assets of which are thereby reduced to a material extent or by a company which has no net assets.

[s152(1)(a)]

23.05 For the purpose of (4) above, "net assets" means the aggregate of the company's assets less the aggregate of its liabilities including provisions for liabilities and charges [s152(2)].

23.06 It is considered that (4) above effectively excludes from the scope of the prohibition the payment by a company of minor costs associated with an acquisition of its own shares.

23.07 The definition is very broad, albeit somewhat circuitous (financial assistance means financial assistance), and covers the provision of finance in almost any manner or form, whether directly or indirectly, for the purposes specified in paragraph 23.02 above. There are, however, some important exceptions and exemptions (particularly for private companies) and these are described in the paragraphs which follow.

Transactions not prohibited

23.08 The following exceptions apply to both public and private companies.

Where assistance only incidental

23.09 A company may give financial assistance for the purpose of an acquisition of shares in itself or its holding company if:

(1) the company's principal purpose in giving that assistance is not to give it for the purpose of any such acquisition, or the giving of the assistance for that purpose is only an incidental part of some larger purpose of the company, and

(2) the financial assistance is given in good faith in the interests of the company giving the assistance.

[s153(1)]

23.10 Similarly, where a person has already acquired shares in a company, the company or a subsidiary of the company may give financial assistance if:

(1) its principal purpose in giving that assistance is not to reduce or discharge any liability incurred by any person for the purpose of the acquisition, or the reduction or discharge of any such liability is only an incidental part of some larger purpose of the company giving the assistance, and

(2) the assistance is given in good faith in the interests of the company giving the assistance.

[s153(2)]

23.11 These exemptions are intended to remove from the scope of the prohibition, a transaction which has the incidental consequence, but not the main purpose, of providing financial assistance for the acquisition of the company's shares. An example might be where, for normal commercial reasons, a group of companies needs to increase its general level of borrowings after the acquisition of a new company and the new company assists in obtaining or securing the new borrowings.

Money-lending companies

23.12 Where the lending of monies is part of the ordinary business of the company, it is not prohibited from lending money in the ordinary course of its business [s153(4)(a)]. There are, however, restrictions on advances to directors (see Chapters 27, 28 and 31) and on what may be done by a public company (see para 23.16 below).

Employees' share scheme

23.13 A company is not prohibited from providing money for the acquisition, in accordance with an employees' share scheme, of fully paid shares in the company or its holding company [s153(4)(b), 743]. There is a restriction on what may be done by a public company (see para 23.16 below).

23.14 It is possible that directors who are also employees may benefit under this exemption but, where a loan is involved (as opposed to an outright gift), care should be taken to ensure that the rules governing advances to directors are not contravened (see Chapters 27, 28 and 31).

Loans to employees (other than directors)

23.15 A company is not prohibited from making loans to persons (other than directors) employed in good faith by the company to enable them to acquire fully paid shares in the company or its holding company to be held by them by way of beneficial ownership [s153(4)(c)].

23.16 This exception and the two previous exceptions (paras 23.12 and 23.13) are subject to a special restriction for public companies. A public company may take advantage of these exceptions only if the company has net assets which are not thereby reduced (for example, if the finance is provided in the form of a recoverable loan) or, to the extent that its net assets are reduced, if the financial assistance is provided out of its distributable profits [s154(1),(2)].

Further exceptions

23.17 Further transactions which are not prohibited are:

(1) a distribution of a company's assets by way of dividend lawfully made, or a distribution made in the course of the company's winding up,

(2) the allotment of bonus shares,

(3) a reduction of capital confirmed by order of the court,

(4) a redemption or purchase of the company's own shares made in accordance with the Act,

(5) anything done in pursuance of an order of the court under section 425 (power of company to compromise with creditors and members),

(6) anything done under an arrangement made under sections 582 and 601 (liquidator accepting shares as consideration for sale of company property; arrangements binding on creditors).

[s153(3)]

Relaxation of restrictions for private companies

23.18 In addition to those set out earlier in this chapter, the Act contains special provisions which allow a private company to give financial assistance to a third party for the acquisition of its own shares (or those of its holding company), subject to appropriate safeguards for members and creditors. This would, for example, allow a private company to finance a "management buyout".

23.19 The conditions under which a private company may give financial assistance for the acquisition of shares in the company or, if it is a subsidiary of another private company, in that other company are set out in sections 155 to 158 of the Act [s155(1)]. A company may give financial assistance only if the company has net assets which are not thereby reduced or, to the extent that they are reduced, if the assistance is provided out of distributable profits [s154(2), 155(2)]. A subsidiary may not give financial assistance for the acquisition of shares in a company which is its holding company if, between the two companies, there is an intermediate holding company which is a public company [s155(3)].

Special resolution

23.20 Unless the company proposing to give the financial assistance is a wholly-owned subsidiary, the giving of assistance must be approved by special resolution of the company in general meeting [s155(4)]. A copy of the special resolution must be forwarded to the registrar of companies within fifteen days after it is passed [s380(1)].

23.21 Where the financial assistance is to be given by a company in respect of an acquisition of shares in its holding company, that holding company and any intermediate holding company between those two companies must (except for any company which is a wholly-owned subsidiary) also approve the assistance by passing a special resolution [s155(5)].

23.22 The special resolution must be passed on the date the directors make their statutory declaration or within the week following, but the resolution will not be effective:

(1) unless the statutory declaration of the directors and the report of the auditors are available for inspection by members of the company at the meeting at which the resolution is passed, or

(2) if, on application, the resolution is cancelled by the court.

[s157(1),(4)]

23.23 A prescribed minimum of the company's shareholders (broadly, those holding ten per cent of any class of its shares) may apply to court for the cancellation of the resolution [s157(2),(3)].

Statutory declaration by all the directors

23.24 The directors of the company proposing to give the financial assistance and, where the assistance is to be in respect of an acquisition of shares in its holding company, the directors of that holding company and of any intermediate holding company between those two companies, are required, before the financial assistance is given, to make a statutory declaration in the prescribed form (form number 155(6)a or, for the holding company, form 155(6)b) [s155(6)]. The declaration must contain the prescribed particulars of the assistance to be given and of the business of the company and identify the person to whom the assistance is to be given [s156(1)]. The declaration must state that the directors have formed the opinion, as regards the company's initial situation immediately following the date on which the assistance is proposed to be given, that there will be no ground on which the company could then be found to be unable to pay its debts, and either:

(1) if it is intended to commence the winding up of the company within twelve months of that date, that the company will be able to pay its debts in full within twelve months of the commencement of the winding up, or

(2) in any other case, that the company will be able to pay its debts as they fall due during the year immediately following that date.

[s156(2)]

23.25 In forming their opinion, the directors must take into account the same liabilities (including the company's contingent and prospective liabilities) as would be relevant, in a winding up by the court, to the question whether the company is unable to pay its debts [s156(3), 517, 518]. From the use of the term "take into account", it is not clear in the initial test of solvency to what extent contingent and prospective liabilities should be aggregated with other known liabilities. Some authorities state that this means that all contingent and prospective liabilities must be introduced at face value into total liabilities, while others contend that the words "take into account" mean that the contingent and prospective liabilities have to be considered with regard to the likelihood, or otherwise, of their ever becoming payable, and included as appropriate.

23.26 The Law Society's Standing Committee on Company Law is reported* as being of the opinion that the contingent and prospective liabilities have to be considered with regard to the likelihood of their becoming payable. This is clearly a matter on which companies will wish to seek legal advice on the application of the law to their particular circumstances.

23.27 A director who makes a statutory declaration without having reasonable grounds for the opinion expressed is liable to imprisonment or a fine, or both [s156(7)].

Report by the auditors

23.28 The statutory declaration must have annexed to it a report by the company's auditors (addressed to the directors) stating that they have enquired into the company's state of affairs and are not aware of anything

---

* Law Society's Gazette, 28th July 1982 at page 968.

to indicate that the opinion expressed by the directors in their declaration (that is, as to the ability of the company to pay its debts), is unreasonable in all the circumstances [s156(4)].

Delivery to the registrar of companies

23.29 The statutory declaration of the directors and the report of the auditors must be delivered to the registrar of companies, together with a copy of any related special resolution passed by the company (as described earlier) within fifteen days of the passing of the resolution or, where no such resolution is required to be passed, within fifteen days of the making of the declaration [s156(5), 380(1)]. Failure to comply with this requirement carries penalties [s156(6)].

Time for giving financial assistance

23.30 Financial assistance may *not* be given:

(1) before the expiry of four weeks from the date on which the last relevant authorising special resolution was passed unless, in respect of each special resolution, every member of the company who is entitled to vote at its general meetings voted in favour of the resolution,

(2) where an application for the cancellation of any such resolution is made, before the final determination of the application, unless the court otherwise orders, and

(3) later than eight weeks after the date on which the earliest of the relevant statutory declarations by the directors of the company or its holding company was made, unless the court, on application, otherwise orders.

[s158(1) to (4)]

CHAPTER 24

Redemption and purchase of own shares

24.01 The Act contains provisions allowing companies to purchase or redeem their own shares. In particular, subject to appropriate safeguards, private companies may purchase or redeem their shares out of capital. The provisions allowing companies to purchase their own shares were included in the 1981 Act and came into force on 15th June 1982.

24.02 The principal advantages of allowing a company to purchase its own shares were considered by Professor Gower in a Green Paper* published in June 1980. Several of the advantages stated, including that of facilitating the retention of family control, apply mainly to private companies. In such cases, it provides a degree of potential marketability for the company's shares, because a shareholder has the company itself available as a possible buyer for a shareholding.

24.03 Reasons why companies may wish to purchase their own shares include the following:

(1) To buy out a dissentient shareholder.

(2) To retain family control.

(3) To encourage investment by a third party in an unlisted company where a contract to purchase the shares at a future date is part of the agreement to invest. This is of particular relevance in the case of a management buy-out funded by external financiers.

(4) To allow shares issued under an employees' share scheme to be purchased when employees leave the company's employment. The facility to repurchase shares has also been used as a selling point to encourage investors in companies eligible under the Business Expansion Scheme.

(5) To provide a means of using surplus cash advantageously.

---

* The purchase by a company of its own shares – a consultative document – Cmnd 7944.

Redeemable shares

24.04 If authorised by its articles, a limited liability company may issue shares of any class which are to be redeemed or are liable to be redeemed at the option of the company or the shareholder [s159(1)]. This provision was first included in the 1981 Act. Under earlier legislation, only preference shares could be redeemable. Any redeemable preference shares in issue on 15th June 1982 may still be redeemed but under the provisions of the 1985 Act [s180(1)].

24.05 The following conditions and those set out in paras 24.08 and 24.09 below, must be fulfilled in relation to the issue and redemption of redeemable shares:

(1) Redeemable shares may be issued only if the company has in issue shares which are not redeemable [s159(2)].

(2) The shares may not be redeemed unless they are fully paid [s159(3)].

(3) The terms of redemption must provide for payment on redemption [s159(3)].

(4) Shares redeemed must be treated as cancelled on redemption, but the redemption is not taken as reducing the amount of the company's authorised share capital [s160(4)].

24.06 The redemption of shares may be effected on such terms and in such manner as may be provided for in the company's articles (provided the provisions of the Act are complied with) [s160(3)].

24.07 Where a company is about to redeem any shares, it shall have power to issue shares up to the nominal amount of the shares to be redeemed as if those shares had never been issued [s160(5)]. This facilitates redemption out of the proceeds of a fresh issue of shares if that issue would otherwise take the company over the limit of its authorised share capital.

Financing of the redemption

24.08 Except for private companies which are able to take advantage of the facility to redeem shares out of capital (see para 24.38), the shares may be redeemed only out of the company's distributable profits or out of the proceeds of a fresh issue of shares made for the purposes of the redemption [s160(1)].

24.09 Any premium payable on redemption must be paid out of distributable profits of the company [s160(1)], subject to the following exceptions:

(1) The premium payable on redemption of redeemable preference shares issued before 15th June 1982 may be paid out of the share premium account [s180(2)].

169

(2) Where the shares are to be redeemed out of the proceeds of a fresh issue of shares, and the shares to be redeemed were originally issued at a premium, any premium payable on their redemption may be paid out of the proceeds of that fresh issue, up to an amount which is the lesser of:
(a) the aggregate of the premium received by the company on the issue of the shares being redeemed, and
(b) the current balance on the company's share premium account (including any amounts transferred to that account in respect of premiums on the fresh issue of shares).

[s160(2)]

24.10 It is evident that exception (2) applies irrespective of when the redeemable shares were issued and whether they are ordinary or preference shares.

Example:

A company has shares with a nominal value of £1,000 (originally issued at a premium of £200), which are to be redeemed at a cost of £1,500, financed by a new issue of 1,000 shares at £1.30 per share. The balance on the share premium account (before the new issue) is £400. The balance sheets of the company before and after the redemption and issue will be:

Before	£	After	£
Share capital	1,000	Share capital	1,000
Share premium	400	Share premium	500
Distributable reserves	500	Distributable reserves	200
	1,900		1,700

and the accounting entries will be:

	£	£
Issue of shares		
DR cash	1,300	
CR share capital		1,000
CR share premium		300
	1,300	1,300
Redemption of shares		
DR share capital	1,000	
DR share premium	200	
DR distributable		
reserves	300	
CR cash		1,500
	1,500	1,500

Purchase of own shares

Power to purchase own shares

24.11 If authorised by its articles, a limited liability company (whether public or private) may purchase its own shares (including any redeemable shares) [s162(1)]. The conditions set out in sections 159 to 161 of the Act (described earlier in this chapter) apply also to the purchase by a company of its own shares except that the terms and manner of purchase need not be determined by the articles [s162(2)]. Thus, in particular, shares may not be purchased unless they are fully paid and must be treated as cancelled on purchase. The rules set out in paragraphs 24.08 and 24.09 apply to the financing of the purchase except for the first exception in para 24.09. The provisions allowing a private company to make a payment out of capital in restricted circumstances are described in para 24.38.

24.12 A company may not purchase any of its shares unless, after the purchase, there would be at least one member of the company holding non-redeemable shares [s162(3)].

24.13 The requirements for the authorisation of purchases of own shares depend on whether the transaction is an "off-market purchase" or a "market purchase".

Definition of off-market purchase

24.14 An off-market purchase of shares is one where:

(1) the shares are not purchased on a recognised stock exchange (that is, The Stock Exchange), or

(2) the shares are purchased on a recognised stock exchange but are not subject to a "marketing arrangement" on that stock exchange.

[s163(1)]

24.15 Shares are subject to a marketing arrangement on a stock exchange if either:
(a) they are listed on that stock exchange, or
(b) the company has been afforded facilities for dealings in those shares to take place on that stock exchange without prior permission for individual transactions from the authority governing that stock exchange and without limit as to the time during which those facilities are to be available.

[s163(2)]

24.16 An off-market purchase would thus not include a purchase made on the Unlisted Securities Market.

Authority for off-market purchase

24.17 A company (public or private) may make an off-market purchase of its own shares only in pursuance of a contract of purchase approved in advance or under a contingent purchase contract (see para 24.22) [s164(1)]. In either case the terms of the proposed contract of purchase must be authorised in advance by a special resolution [s164(2), 165(2)]. The authority may be varied, revoked or renewed by special resolution [s164(3)]. A copy of a special resolution must be forwarded to the registrar of companies within fifteen days after it is passed [s380(1)].

24.18 In the case of a public company the resolution must specify a date on which the authority is to expire. In a resolution conferring or renewing authority, that date must not be later than eighteen months after the date on which that resolution is passed [s164(4)].

24.19 A special resolution to confer, vary, revoke or renew authority is not effective if any member holding shares to which the resolution relates exercises the voting rights carried by any of those shares in voting on the resolution and the resolution would not have been passed if he had not done so. Notwithstanding anything in a company's articles, any member of the company may demand a poll on such a special resolution [s164(5)].

24.20 Any such resolution is not effective unless a copy of the proposed contract (if it is in writing) or (if not) a written memorandum of its terms is available for inspection by members of the company, both:

(1) at the company's registered office for not less than fifteen days ending with the date of the meeting at which the resolution is passed, and

(2) at the meeting itself.

The names of the members holding shares to which the contract relates must also be stated [s164(6)].

24.21 A company may agree to a variation of an existing contract of purchase only if the variation is authorised in advance by special resolution. The provisions of section 164(3) to (6) (paras 24.17 to 24.20) apply in relation to the variation except that, in addition to the proposed variation, a copy of the original contract (or, as the case may require, a memorandum of its terms) and any previous variations must be available for inspection by members (see para 24.20) before and at the meeting at which the proposed variation is to be voted upon [s164(7)].

Redemption and purchase of own shares **24.27**

Authority for a contingent purchase contract

24.22 A contingent purchase contract by a company for the purchase of its shares is, in effect, an option under which the company may become entitled or obliged to purchase those shares [s165(1)].

24.23 A contingent purchase contract must be authorised in advance by special resolution. The provisions of section 164(3) to (7) (authority for an off-market purchase – paras 24.17 to 24.21) apply also to a contingent purchase contract and its terms [s165(2)].

Definition of a market purchase

24.24 A market purchase is defined as being a purchase made on a recognised stock exchange (that is, The Stock Exchange), other than a purchase which is an off-market purchase (see para 24.14) [s163(3)]. A market purchase would thus include one made on the Unlisted Securities Market but would exclude purchases under Rule 163 or other off-market arrangements.

Authority for a market purchase

24.25 A company may make a market purchase of its own shares if the purchase is approved in advance by an ordinary resolution of the company in general meeting [s166(1)]. The authorising resolution may be conditional or unconditional and may confer general authority or may be limited to the purchase of shares of any particular class or description [s166(2)]. The authority may be varied, revoked or renewed by ordinary resolution [s166(4)].

24.26 The authority must:

(1) specify the maximum number of shares authorised to be acquired,

(2) determine both maximum and minimum prices which may be paid for those shares, and

(3) specify a date on which the authority is to expire which, in a resolution to confer or renew authority, must not be more than eighteen months after the passing of the resolution.

[s166(3),(4)]

24.27 If permitted by the terms of the authority, a company may purchase its own shares after the time limit has expired where the contract of purchase was concluded before the authority expired [s166(5)].

24.28 The authorising resolution may determine the maximum and minimum prices to be paid for the shares by specifying a particular sum, or by providing a basis or formula for calculating the price without reference to any person's discretion or opinion [s166(6)].

24.29 Copies of each resolution conferring, varying, revoking or renewing authority for a market purchase of own shares must be sent to the registrar of companies within fifteen days of the passing of the resolution [s166(7)].

Disclosures

24.30 Where a company has purchased its own shares, the Act requires the company to make a return, in the prescribed form (form 169), to the registrar of companies within 28 days of the shares being delivered to the company. The return must state, with respect to each class of shares purchased, the number and nominal value of those shares and the date on which they were delivered to the company [s169(1)]. A public company must also state the aggregate amount paid by the company for the shares and, for each class, the maximum and minimum prices paid [s169(2)].

24.31 Provided the 28 day time limit is met, particulars of shares delivered to the company on different dates and under different contracts may be included in a single, aggregated return [s169(3)].

24.32 Where a company enters into any contract for an off-market purchase, a contingent purchase contract or a contract for a market purchase, it must keep, at its registered office, a copy of the contract or, where the contract is not in writing, a memorandum of its terms, for ten years from the date on which the purchase of all the shares is completed or the contract otherwise determines [s169(4)]. This applies also to any variation of a contract for as long as it applies to the contract itself [s169(9)].

24.33 Every copy of a contract or memorandum thereof (or variation thereof) which is required to be kept must be available during business hours (for at least two hours every day) for inspection without charge by any member of the company and, if the company is a public company, by any other person [s169(5)]. There are penalties for failure to comply with the foregoing requirements [s169(6),(7)]. Where an inspection is refused, the court may, by order, compel an immediate inspection [s169(8)].

24.34 Comprehensive disclosure is also required to be made in the directors' report (see para 9.03(10)), or in the accounts of banks, insurance and exempt shipping companies where they are prepared in accordance with Schedule 9 of the Act (see Chapter 13).

Assignment or release of a company's rights to purchase its own shares

24.35 The rights of a company under a contract for an off-market purchase, a contingent purchase contract or a contract for a market purchase of its own shares are not capable of being assigned [s167(1)]. However, a company may, subject to prior approval by special resolution, release its rights under a contract for an off-market purchase or a contingent purchase contract. The requirements of section 164(3) to (7) (see paras 24.17 to 24.21) apply to the approval of a proposed release agreement in the same way as they apply to a proposed variation of an existing contract [s167(2)].

Payments apart from purchase price to be made out of distributable profits

24.36 In addition to any payment of the purchase price which has to be made out of distributable profits, any payment made by a company in consideration:

(1) of acquiring a right to purchase its own shares (that is, a contingent purchase contract),

(2) for a variation of an existing contract for an off-market purchase or a contingent purchase contract, or

(3) for a release from any of its obligations with respect to the purchase of any of its shares,

must be made out of distributable profits [s168(1)].

24.37 If this requirement is not satisfied, any related purchase of its shares under an option or a variation in an option or purchase contract would be unlawful and any release from an obligation would be void [s 168(2)].

Redemption or purchase of own shares out of capital by a private company

24.38 In addition to the general power to redeem or purchase shares out of distributable profits or the proceeds of a fresh issue of shares, a private company is also allowed to make a payment out of capital for the redemption or purchase, subject to the conditions described below. This payment out of capital is referred to as the "permissible capital payment" and may be made to the extent that the purchase or redemption price exceeds the sum of the available profits of the company and the proceeds of any fresh issue of shares made for that purpose. This relaxation of the rules which took effect in 1982 is having only a limited application in practice because distributable profits must first be utilised in full; also, the directors are required to make a declaration of solvency.

24.39 If authorised by its articles, a private company may make a payment (referred to below as a "payment out of capital") for the redemption or purchase of its own shares, otherwise than out of distributable profits of the company or the proceeds of a fresh issue of shares [s171(1),(2)]. Payment may be made out of capital to the extent that the price of redemption or purchase exceeds the sum of the "available profits" of the company and the proceeds of any fresh issue of shares made for the purpose of the redemption or purchase. This amount is referred to in the Act as the "permissible capital payment" [s171(3)].

"Available profits"

24.40 A company's "available profits" are its distributable profits determined in accordance with the provisions of the Act [s172(1)]. The amount of a company's distributable profits is to be determined by reference to accounts prepared as at any date within the three months ending with the date on which the directors' statutory declaration is made (see para 24.41) [s172(2),(6)]. The accounts must be such as to enable a reasonable judgement to be made [s172(3)]. Allowance must be made for distributions lawfully made subsequent to the date of the accounts and, for this purpose, "distribution" includes the following:

(1) financial assistance lawfully given out of distributable profits,

(2) any payment lawfully made out of distributable profits in respect of the purchase of own shares, and

(3) any payment under section 168(1) (see para 24.36) lawfully made by the company.

[s172(4),(5)]

Statutory declaration by all the directors

24.41 All the directors must make a statutory declaration in the prescribed form (form 173) specifying the amount of the permissible capital payment for the shares in question and stating that, having made full enquiry into the affairs and prospects of the company, they have formed the opinion:

(1) as regards the company's initial situation immediately following the date on which the payment out of capital is proposed to be made, that there will be no grounds on which the company could then be found to be unable to pay its debts, and

(2) as regards the company's prospects for the year immediately following that date, that having regard to their intentions with respect to the management of the company's business during that year and to the amount and character of the financial resources which will, in their view, be available to the company during that year, the company will

be able to continue to carry on business as a going concern (and will accordingly be able to pay its debts as they fall due) thoughout that year.

[s173(3),(5)]

24.42 In forming their opinion in (1) above, the directors must take into account the same liabilities (including contingent and prospective liabilities) as would be relevant, in a winding up by the court, to the question whether the company is unable to pay its debts [s173(4),517,518]. From the use of the term "take into account", it is not clear in the initial test of solvency to what extent contingent and prospective liabilities should be aggregated with other known liabilities. Some authorities state that this means that all contingent and prospective liabilities must be introduced at face value into total liabilities, while others contend that the words "take into account" mean that the contingent and prospective liabilities have to be considered with regard to the likelihood, or otherwise, of their ever becoming payable, and included as appropriate.

24.43 The Law Society's Standing Committee on Company Law is reported* as being of the opinion that the contingent and prospective liabilities have to be considered with regard to the likelihood of their becoming payable. This is clearly a matter on which companies will wish to seek legal advice on the application of the law to their particular circumstances.

24.44 The second part of the declaration is concerned with the timing and availability of funds in the ensuing year.

24.45 A director who makes a declaration without having reasonable grounds for the opinion expressed in the declaration is liable to imprisonment or a fine, or both [s173(6)].

Report by the auditors on the statutory declaration

24.46 The statutory declaration by the directors must have annexed to it a report addressed to the directors by the company's auditors stating that:

(1) they have enquired into the company's state of affairs, and

(2) in their opinion, the amount specified in the directors' statutory declaration as being the permissible capital payment for the shares in question has been properly determined in accordance with sections 171 and 172 of the Act, and

---

* Law Society's Gazette, 28th July 1982 at page 968.

(3) they are not aware of anything to indicate that the opinion expressed by the directors in their statutory declaration, as to any of the matters specified in para 24.41 above, is unreasonable in all the circumstances.

[s173(5)]

Special resolution approving payment out of capital/timing of payment

24.47 A payment out of capital must be approved by special resolution of the company in general meeting [s173(1),(2)].

24.48 The resolution for the payment out of capital must be passed on or within the week immediately following the date on which the directors make their statutory declaration, and the payment out of capital must be made no earlier than five weeks nor more than seven weeks after the date of the resolution for the payment [s174(1)]. A copy of the special resolution must be forwarded to the registrar of companies within fifteen days after it is passed [s380(1)].

24.49 A special resolution approving a payment out of capital will not be effective if any member holding shares to which the resolution relates, exercises the voting rights carried by any of those shares in voting on the resolution and the resolution would not have been passed if he had not done so [s174(2),(3),(5)].

24.50 Notwithstanding anything in a company's articles, any member of the company may demand a poll on a special resolution to approve a payment out of capital [s174(3)].

24.51 The resolution is ineffective unless the directors' statutory declaration and report of the auditors are available for inspection by the members at the meeting at which the resolution is passed [s174(4)].

Publicity for payment out of capital

24.52 The Act requires a payment out of capital to be publicised in the manner set out in the following paragraphs.

24.53 Within the week immediately following the passing of a resolution for payment out of capital, the company must publish in the "Gazette" a notice:

(1) stating that the company has approved a payment out of capital for the redemption or purchase (or both) of its own shares,

(2) specifying the amount of the permissible capital payment for the shares and the date of the resolution for the payment,

(3) stating that the statutory declaration of the directors and the report of the auditors to the directors are available for inspection at the company's registered office, and

(4) stating that any creditor of the company may, within five weeks of the resolution, apply to the court under section 176 of the Act for an order prohibiting the payment.

[s175(1)]

For a company registered in England and Wales, the "Gazette" means the London Gazette and, for a company registered in Scotland, it means the Edinburgh Gazette [s744].

24.54 A company is also required, within the same time limit, to place a similar notice in "an appropriate national newspaper" or, alternatively, to send a copy of such a notice to each of its creditors [s175(2)]. "An appropriate national newspaper" is one which circulates throughout England and Wales (for a company registered in England and Wales) or one which circulates throughout Scotland (for a company registered in Scotland) [s175(3)].

24.55 The company must deliver to the registrar of companies a copy of the statutory declaration of the directors and the report of the auditors, not later than the "first notice date"; that is, the earlier of (a) the date of publication of the notice in the Gazette, and (b) publication of the notice in a national newspaper or the giving of the notice to the company's creditors [s175(4),(5)].

24.56 The statutory declaration and report of the auditors must be kept at the company's registered office for the period beginning with the first notice date and ending five weeks after the passing of the resolution for payment out of capital and be open to inspection, without charge, by any member or creditor during business hours on any day during that period [s175(6)]. If the company refuses to allow an inspection, the court may compel an immediate inspection, and may impose a fine on the company and every officer in default [s175(7),(8)].

Objections by members or creditors

24.57 Where a private company passes a special resolution approving a payment out of capital for the redemption or purchase of any of its own shares, any member of the company (other than one who consented to or voted in favour of the resolution) and any creditor of the company may, within five weeks of the passing of the resolution, apply to the court for the cancellation of the resolution [s176(1)]. Those persons entitled to make such an application to the court may appoint, in writing, one or more of their number to act on their behalf [s176(2)].

24.58 Where an application is made, the company must:

(1) forthwith give notice, in the prescribed form [form 176], of that fact to the registrar of companies, and

(2) within fifteen days of the making of any court order, or such longer period as the court may direct, deliver an office copy of the order to the registrar.

[s176(3)]

24.59 The court may adjourn the proceedings in order that a satisfactory arrangement can be made for the purchase of the interests of dissentient members or for the protection of dissentient creditors and may give such directions and make such orders as it considers necessary for that purpose [s177(1)].

24.60 At the end of the hearing, the court is required to make an order on such terms and conditions as it thinks fit, either confirming or cancelling the resolution for payment out of capital. If it confirms the resolution, it may, in particular, alter or extend any date or time limit specified in the resolution or by the Act [s177(2)]. The court has this power for obvious reasons, in particular where any of the time limits have passed while the hearing was taking place.

24.61 The order of the court may also provide for the purchase by the company of the shares of any of its members and for the reduction accordingly of the company's capital, and may make such alterations in the company's memorandum and articles as may be required in consequence of that provision [s177(3),(4),(5)].

Liability of past directors and shareholders

24.62 Where the winding up of a company commences within one year of the making of a payment out of capital (referred to in the Act as the "relevant payment") for the redemption or purchase of any of its own shares, and its funds are insufficient for the payment of its debts and liabilities and the costs of the winding up, the following persons are liable to contribute to the assets of the company:

(1) the person from whom the shares were redeemed or purchased, and

(2) the directors who signed the statutory declaration, except for a director who shows that he had reasonable grounds for forming the opinion set out in the declaration.

[s504(1),(2)]

24.63 A person from whom any of the shares were redeemed or purchased is liable to contribute an amount not exceeding that part of the relevant payment which relates to his shares. The directors (in (2) above) are jointly and severally liable with that person [s504(3)].

24.64 Any person who has made a contribution required by section 504 may apply to the court for an order to recover from any other person jointly and severally liable with him, such an amount as the court thinks just and equitable [s504(4)].

24.65 A person who is liable to make a contribution under section 504 may petition the court for the winding up of the company [s519(3)].

The capital redemption reserve

24.66 Where shares are redeemed or purchased, an amount must be transferred from distributable profits to a non-distributable reserve called "the capital redemption reserve", in the circumstances and to the extent described in the following paragraphs. The purpose of this requirement is to ensure that capital is maintained where a company purchases or redeems its own shares, except to the extent that a private company is permitted to make payments out of capital.

General rules

24.67 Where a company redeems or purchases any of its own shares wholly out of profits, an amount equal to the nominal value of those shares must be transferred to the capital redemption reserve [s170(1)].

24.68 Where the redemption or purchase is made wholly out of the proceeds of a fresh issue of shares, or is made partly out of profits and partly out of the proceeds of a fresh issue, and the aggregate amount of the proceeds is less than the aggregate nominal value of the shares redeemed or purchased, the amount of the difference must be transferred to the capital redemption reserve [s170(2)].

24.69 The capital redemption reserve is treated as being equivalent to paid up share capital but may be applied in paying up unissued shares of the company to be allotted to its existing members as fully paid bonus shares [s170(4)].

24.70 These requirements are illustrated in the example which follows:

Transfer to capital redemption reserve on redemption or purchase of own shares			
	X	Y	Z
Nominal value of shares redeemed or purchased	£1,000	£1,000	£1,000
Redemption or purchase price	£1,000	£1,100	£900*
Redemption or purchase made out of:			
(1) Profits available for distribution	£1,000	£850+	–
(2) Proceeds of a fresh issue of shares	–	£250	£900
Amount to be transferred to capital redemption reserve:	£1,000	£750	£100

*that is, at a discount of £100.
+Except as noted in para 24.09, any premium payable would be charged directly to distributable profits.

24.71 Where the aggregate of the amount of the "permissible capital payment" for any shares redeemed or purchased and the amount of the proceeds of any fresh issue of shares is less than the nominal amount of the shares redeemed or purchased, the amount of the difference must be transferred to the capital redemption reserve [s171(4),(6)].

24.72 Conversely, where the aggregate of the amount of the permissible capital payment and the amount of the proceeds of any fresh issue of shares, exceeds the nominal amount of the shares redeemed or purchased:

(1) the amount of any capital redemption reserve, share premium account or fully paid share capital of the company, and

(2) any unrealised profits standing to the credit of the company's revaluation reserve,

may be reduced by a sum not exceeding that excess [s171(5),(6)].

24.73 An effect of using unrealised profits for this purpose is that if and when the profits become realised, they will not be available for distribution as they will already have been utilised.

24.74 For an illustration of the effect where a private company redeems or purchases its own shares out of capital and of the accounting effects of the above rules generally, see Appendix 2.

Failure to redeem or purchase own shares

24.75 Where a company fails to redeem on the due date redeemable shares which were issued on or after 15 June 1982, and where, on or after that date, a company fails to purchase its own shares after agreeing a contract of purchase, the following provisions apply [s178(1)].

24.76 The company is not liable in damages in respect of any failure on its part to redeem or purchase any of its own shares [s178(2)]. However, this is without prejudice to any right of the shareholder other than his right to sue for damages; in other words, the shareholder has the right to sue for specific performance [s178(3)].

24.77 If a shareholder sues for specific performance, the court is not permitted to grant such an order if the company shows that it is unable to meet the cost of redeeming or purchasing the shares out of distributable profits [s178(3)].

24.78 If the company is wound up and at the commencement of the winding up any of the relevant shares have not been redeemed or purchased, the terms of the redemption or purchase may be enforced against the company except:

(1) if the terms provided for the redemption or purchase to take place at a date later than that of the commencement of the winding up, or

(2) if during the period beginning with the date on which the redemption or purchase was to have taken place and ending with the commencement of the winding up, the company could not at any time have lawfully made a distribution equal in value to the price at which the shares were to have been redeemed or purchased.

[s178(4),(5)]

24.79 Where, in a winding up, a redemption or purchase can be enforced against a company, all other debts and liabilities of the company (other than any due to members in their character as such) and any amounts due on shares which have a priority over the shares to be redeemed or purchased, shall be paid in priority to the purchase or redemption price [s178(6)].

Alteration of provisions by statutory instrument

24.80 The Secretary of State is given wide powers to modify the provisions in relation to the redemption or purchase by a company of its own shares [s179].

Taxation aspects

24.81 The taxation implications of a redemption or purchase of own shares also require careful consideration, but are outside the scope of this book. Companies should consult their professional advisers.

Stock Exchange requirements

24.82 The Stock Exchange requirements are incorporated in "Admission of Securities to Listing" (the "Yellow Book"), and are set out in the paragraphs which follow. All references are to Section 5, Chapter 2 of Admission of Securities to Listing unless otherwise stated.

Notification to The Stock Exchange of authority to purchase own shares

24.83 Whenever the board of a listed or USM company decides to submit to the company's shareholders a proposal for the company to be authorised to purchase its own shares, immediate notification to The Stock Exchange is required. This notification should include an indication as to whether the proposal relates to specific purchases or to a general authorisation to make purchases (para 16(d)).

Circulars to shareholders

24.84 The circular sent to the company's shareholders, seeking their authority for the purchase of the company's own shares, should be treated as a Class 1 circular for stock exchange purposes where the exercise in full of the authority sought would result in the purchase of fifteen per cent or more of the share capital. In that case, the circular should be in accordance with chapter 1 of section 6 and the working capital statement required should be based on the assumption that the authority sought is used in full at the maximum price allowed. This assumption should also be stated. Where the authority being sought relates to specific proposals, the names of the shareholders who will be parties to the proposed contract and all the material terms of the proposal must be stated in the circular (para 31.4).

24.85 Where the board is seeking a general authority to purchase the company's own shares in the market, the circular should state the board's intentions with regard to the authority to be thus conferred. The shareholders should be notified if the company proposes to "stand in the market" for a fixed period of time or until a specified number of shares have been acquired on the market (para 31.4).

24.86 A purchase on the market by way of a "put through" from a person with whom the company has a Class 4 relationship, normally a director or substantial shareholder, should be treated in accordance with the customary procedures for Class 4 transactions and specific approval of the shareholders sought under Section 6, Chapter 1, para 6.1 (para 31.4).

24.87 Where such a purchase is made by an off-market purchase, the terms would in any case be subject to prior authorisation as required by the Act.

24.88 Immediate notification of the outcome of the shareholders' meeting should be made to The Stock Exchange and four copies of the relevant resolutions forwarded as soon as possible thereafter (para 16(d)).

Convertible securities, warrants and options to subscribe for ordinary shares

24.89 Where there are in issue convertible securities, warrants or options to subscribe for equity capital, The Stock Exchange requires a separate class meeting of the holders to be held. Their approval by extraordinary resolution must be obtained before the company enters into any purchase contract or exercises a general authority to make market purchases. This approval is required irrespective of whether the trust deed or issue terms contain provisions regarding adjustments to be made on the purchase by a company of its own shares (para 31.4).

24.90 The circular containing the notice of meeting must set out clearly the anticipated effect on the conversion or subscription expectations of the holders, in terms of the attributable assets and earnings of the company, as if the company were to exercise the proposed authority in full. Additionally, any special adjustments which the company may be proposing should be set out and the above information restated on the revised basis (para 31.4).

Purchase of five per cent or more

24.91 Purchases within a period of twelve months of a significant amount of the company's share capital, defined as five per cent or more, should be made either by way of a tender offer or a partial offer to all shareholders, proportionate to each shareholder's overall holding (paras 4 and 31.4).

24.92 The tender offer should be made on The Stock Exchange at a stated maximum price and notice of the offer should be given by means of an advertisement in two national newspapers at least seven days before the offer closes (para 31.4).

Model code for securities transactions by directors

24.93 The model code for directors is regarded by The Stock Exchange as being applicable to purchases by a company of its own shares. Accordingly, the company should not purchase shares at any time when the directors would not be free to deal in shares on their own account. The principal periods when directors should not deal in the company's shares are for the two months before the announcement of preliminary annual results and half-yearly results (para 45).

24.94 The legislation in the Company Securities (Insider Dealing) Act 1985 (which was first included in the 1980 Act) relating to insider dealing may also be relevant in these circumstances. These provisions are outside the scope of this book.

Notification of purchases to The Stock Exchange

24.95 Notification of all purchases by a company of its own shares must be made to The Stock Exchange by midday on the following dealing day. The notification should include the number of shares purchased and the purchase price per share or, where shares are purchased at more than one price, the highest and lowest prices paid (para 17).

Particulars to be included in the directors' report

24.96 The directors' report attached to the company's annual accounts should contain the following information in addition to that required by the Act:
(a) particulars of any authorities or approvals given to the board to purchase the company's own shares which existed (that is, were outstanding) at the end of the financial year,
(b) the names of the sellers in the case of all purchases made, or proposed to be made, either otherwise than through the market or by tender or partial offer to all shareholders, and
(c) equivalent information to that required by what is now Sch 7 Part II of the Act in relation to any purchase of its own shares, options or contracts for purchase entered into since the end of the financial year (para 21(p)).

CHAPTER 25

Company names and business names

25.01 The Companies Act 1985 and the Business Names Act 1985 include a system for regulating company names and the names under which companies, individuals and partnerships may carry on business. These provisions were introduced by the 1981 Act and replaced regulations under the Registration of Business Names Act 1916 which was repealed by that Act. The regulations set out in the Companies Act 1985 are described first.

Company names

Name as stated in the memorandum

25.02 The name of a public company must end with the words "public limited company" or the permitted abbreviation "p.l.c." (or the Welsh equivalents if the memorandum states that the company's registered office is to be in Wales) [s25(1), 27(4)]. In the case of any other limited liability company, the last word must be "limited" or "ltd" (or the Welsh equivalents) except where the company is exempt from having the word "limited" as part of its name (see para 25.14) [s25(2), 27(4)].

Prohibition on registration of certain names

25.03 A company may not be registered under the Companies Act 1985, by a name:

(1) which includes, otherwise than at the end of the name, any of the following words or their permitted abbreviations: "limited", "unlimited" or "public limited company" (or their Welsh equivalents),

(2) which is the same as a name appearing in the index of names kept by the registrar of companies (see para 25.07),

(3) the use of which by the company would, in the opinion of the Secretary of State, constitute a criminal offence, or

(4) which, in the opinion of the Secretary of State, is offensive.

[s26(1)]

25.04 Except with the approval of the Secretary of State, a company may not be registered under the Act by a name which:

(1) in the opinion of the Secretary of State would be likely to give the impression that the company is connected in any way with Her Majesty's government or with any local authority, or

(2) includes any word or expression for the time being specified in regulations made under section 29 of the Act (Words and expressions requiring approval).

[s26(2)]

25.05 A regulation (SI 1981 No. 1685) published under the authority of the 1981 Act listed the words requiring approval (see paras 25.35 and 25.36).

25.06 In determining whether one name is the same as another, the following are to be disregarded:

(1) the definite article where it is the first word of the name,

(2) the following (or any abbreviations thereof) where they appear at the end of the name: "company", "and company", "company limited", "and company limited", "limited", "unlimited", "public limited company" or their Welsh equivalents, and

(3) type and case of letters, accents, spaces between letters and punctuation marks.

"And" and "&" are taken to be the same.

[s26(3)]

Index of names

25.07 The registrar of companies is required to keep an index of the names of the following bodies:

(1) companies within the meaning of the Act (that is, companies formed and registered under the 1985 Act or earlier Companies Acts – [s735(1)]),

(2) oversea companies (that is, companies incorporated outside Great Britain which have established a place of business in Great Britain and which have registered under Part XXIII of the 1985 Act),

(3) incorporated and unincorporated bodies which are subject to section 718 of the 1985 Act (unregistered companies),

(4) limited partnerships registered under the Limited Partnerships Act 1907,

(5) companies within the meaning of the Companies Act (Northern Ireland) 1960,

(6) companies incorporated outside Northern Ireland and which have registered under section 356 of the Companies Act (Northern Ireland) 1960, and which have a place of business there, and

(7) societies registered under the Industrial and Provident Societies Act 1965 (or the 1969 Act of Northern Ireland).

[s714(1)]

25.08 The Secretary of State may, by statutory instrument, add to or delete from the above list any class of body, whether incorporated or unincorporated [s714(2)].

Change of name

25.09 A company may, by special resolution, change its name and the change will be effective from the date on which the altered certificate of incorporation is issued. The new name which the company chooses must comply with the provisions of section 26 of the Act (Prohibition on registration of certain names) as discussed above [s28(1),(6)].

25.10 Where a company has been registered by a name which is the same as or, in the opinion of the Secretary of State, too like a name appearing (or which should have appeared) at the time in the index of names, the Secretary of State may, within twelve months, direct the company to change its name within such period as he may specify [s28(2),(4)].

25.11 Where it appears to the Secretary of State that a company has given misleading information in connection with its registration by a particular name or has given undertakings or assurances for that purpose which have not been fulfilled, the Secretary of State may, within five years of its registration with that name, direct the company to change its name within such period as he may specify [s28(3),(4)]. This provision is designed to prevent the continuance of company names gained by deception.

25.12 Where a company changes its name, the registrar of companies must issue it with an altered certificate of incorporation [s28(6)].

25.13 Where a company changes its name under the above provisions, the change will not affect any of its rights or obligations, or render defective any legal proceedings [s28(7)].

Companies exempt from requirement to use the word "limited"

25.14 A company will be exempt from the requirement to use the word "limited" in its name and will also be exempt from the requirements of the Act to publish its name and to send lists of its members to the registrar of companies, if it is a company:

(1) which is a private company limited by guarantee, or

(2) which on 25th February 1982 was a private company limited by shares with a name which does not include the word "limited" by virtue of a licence granted under section 19 of the 1948 Act,

[s30(1),(2),(7)]

and which complies with the following requirements:

(a) that the objects of the company are (or, for a company about to be registered, are to be) the promotion of commerce, act, science, education, religion, charity or any profession and anything incidental or conducive to any of those objects, and

(b) that the memorandum or articles of the company:
    (i) require any profits or other income of the company to be applied in promoting its objects,
    (ii) prohibit the payment of dividends to its members, and
    (iii) require all the assets which would otherwise be available to its members generally, to be transferred on its winding-up either to another body with objects similar to its own, or to another body the objects of which are the promotion of charity and anything incidental or conducive thereto, whether or not the other body is a member of the company.

[s30(3)]

25.15 The registrar of companies may accept a statutory declaration in the relevant form (form numbers 30(5)(a), 30(5)(b), 30(5)(c)) as evidence that the company complies with the above requirements, and the registrar may also refuse to register a company by a name which does not include the word "limited" unless he receives such a declaration [s30(4),(5)].

25.16 A company which is exempt under section 30 and the name of which does not include "limited", may not alter its memorandum or articles so that they are in conflict with the requirements of paragraph 25.14 (a) and (b) above [s31(1)].

25.17 If it appears to the Secretary of State that a company which has taken advantage of the above provisions has carried on any business other than the promotion of any of the objects mentioned in paragraph 25.14(a) above, or has applied any of its profits or other income otherwise than in promoting such objects or has paid a dividend to any of its members, he may direct the company to change its name by a directors' resolution so that it ends with "limited". A copy of the directors' resolution must be sent to the registrar of companies within fifteen days of its being passed [s31(2), 380(1)]. A company which has received such a direction may not thereafter be registered by a name which does not include the word "limited", without the approval of the Secretary of State [s31(3)].

25.18 The Act sets out additional provisions relating to companies registered under Part XXII of the Act (Companies not formed under the companies legislation but authorised to register) [s687].

Power to require company to abandon misleading name

25.19 The Secretary of State may direct a company to change its registered name if he considers that it gives an indication of the company's activities which is so misleading as to be likely to cause harm to the public [s32(1)]. Unless within three weeks the company applies to the court to have the direction set aside, the direction must be complied with within six weeks or any longer period which the Secretary of State may allow [s32(2),(3)]. There is a penalty for contravention of these provisions [s32(4)].

Public/private status

25.20 The Act contains the following provisions to ensure that the public/private company designations are used correctly.

25.21 Only a public company is permitted to carry on any trade, profession or business under a name which includes, as its last part, the words "public limited company", or "p.l.c." (or the Welsh equivalents) [s27(3),(4), 33(1)], and a public company may not use a name which may reasonably be expected to give the impression that it is a private company, in circumstances in which the fact that it is a public company is likely to be material to any person [s33(2)]. This should cover, inter alia, the use by a public company of a name (for example, a trade name) which conceals its public status in circumstances where knowledge of that status would be a material factor in connection with any proposed contract [for example, if a public company attempts to enter into a contract before the issue of its certificate to commence business].

25.22 Furthermore, it is also an offence for any person to trade or carry on business under a name of which "limited" (or the Welsh equivalent), or any contraction or imitation thereof is the last word, unless that person is incorporated with limited liability [s34].

Business names

25.23 The rules governing the names under which persons may carry on business in Great Britain are set out in the Business Names Act 1985.

Control of business names

25.24 The Business Names Act 1985 applies to any person who has a place of business in Great Britain and who carries on business in Great Britain under a name which:

(1) in a partnership, does not consist of the surnames of all partners who are individuals and the corporate names of all partners who are bodies corporate, without any addition other than a permitted addition (see para 25.25 below);

(2) as an individual, does not consist of his surname without any addition other than a permitted addition;

(3) as a company which is capable of being wound up under the Companies Act 1985, does not consist of its corporate name without any addition other than a permitted addition.

[BN Act s1(1)]

25.25 The permitted additions are the addition only of forenames or initials or an indication that the business is carried on in succession to a former owner of the business [BN Act s1(2)].

25.26 Except as noted below, a person to whom the Business Names Act applies may not, without the written approval of the Secretary of State, carry on business in Great Britain under a name which:

(1) would be likely to give the impression that the business is connected with Her Majesty's government or with any local authority, or

(2) includes any word or expression specified in regulations made under that Act.

[BN Act s2(1), 3]

25.27 A regulation (SI 1981 No. 1685) published under the authority of the Companies Act 1981 listed the words requiring approval (see paras 25.35 and 25.37).

25.28 The provisions of paragraph 25.26 do not apply to the carrying on of a business by any person who carried on that business immediately before 26th February 1982 and who continues to carry it on under the name which immediately before that date was its "lawful business name" (as defined) [BN Act s2(3)]. Also, where a business is transferred on or after

26th February 1982, the provisions do not apply for the twelve months after the transfer where the business is continued under the name which was its lawful business name [BN Act s2(2)]. A lawful business name is a name under which the business was carried on without contravening the Business Names Act 1985 or The Registration of Business Names Act 1916 (repealed in 1982) [BN Act s8(1)].

Disclosure of names of persons using business names

25.29 Any person to whom the Business Names Act 1985 applies is required:

(1) except as noted in para 25.31 below, to state in legible characters on all its business letters, written orders for goods and services to be supplied to the business, invoices, receipts and demands for payment of debts arising in the course of business, the following:
  (a) the name of each partner, if the business is a partnership,
  (b) the name of the individual carrying on business as a sole trader,
  (c) its corporate name where the business is carried on by a company, and
  (d) in relation to each person named, an address within Great Britain at which service of any document relating in any way to the business will be effective, and

(2) in any premises where the business is carried on and to which the customers of the business or suppliers of any goods or services to the business have access, to display in a prominent position, so that it may easily be read by its customers or suppliers, a notice containing those names and addresses. The Secretary of State may prescribe the form in which the notices are to be displayed.

[BN Act s4(1),(5)]

25.30 Any person to whom this Act applies must give the names and addresses immediately (in writing) to any person who, in the course of business with that person, asks for them [BN Act s4(2)].

25.31 The requirement to disclose names and addresses on business stationery does not apply in relation to any document issued by a partnership or more than twenty persons which maintains, as its principal place of business, a list of the names of all the partners if:

(1) none of the names of the partners appears in the document otherwise than in the text or as a signatory, and

(2) the document states the address of the partnership's principal place of business and that the list of the partners' names is open to inspection at that place.

[BN Act s4(3)]

25.32 Where a partnership maintains a list of partners' names, any person may inspect the list during office hours [BN Act s4(4)]. Any partner who, without reasonable cause, refuses an inspection or permits an inspection to be refused, is guilty of an offence [BN Act s4(7)]. It is also an offence to contravene the provisions set out in paras 25.29 and 25.30 [BN Act s4(6)].

25.33 The above provisions for the disclosure of names and addresses apply only where the business is carried on under a name as described in para 25.24 above. For example, if a partnership trades under a name which consists of the names of all its partners (for example, Smith and Brown), no further information regarding the names and addresses of the partners will be required to be given under this section.

25.34 The Act provides civil remedies for a breach of section 4 [BN Act s5].

Words and expressions requiring prior approval

25.35 The Secretary of State for Trade may, by regulations, specify words or expressions which require his approval before they may be used in a company's corporate name or in a business name and, in relation to any such word or expression, specify a government department or other body as the "relevant" body from whom approval must be obtained [s29(1), BN Act s3(1)]. A regulation [SI 1981 No. 1685] published under the authority of the Companies Act 1981 listed the words (many of which relate to medical and financial services) requiring prior approval.

25.36 Where a company proposes to have as, or as part of, its corporate name, any such word or expression, a written request must be made to the relevant body to indicate whether (and if so why) it has any objection to the proposal. A statement that such a request has been made and a copy of any response received from the relevant body must be filed with the registrar of companies [s29(2),(3)].

25.37 A broadly similar procedure has to be followed where a person to whom the Business Names Act applies (see para 25.24) proposes to carry on business under a name which is or includes any such word or expression [BN Act s3(2)].

Regulations

25.38 Regulations under the Business Names Act are to be made by statutory instrument and may contain such transitional provisions and savings as the Secretary of State thinks appropriate and may make different provision for different cases or classes of case [BN Act s6(1)].

CHAPTER 26

Company identification

26.01 The Act requires a company to display its name at every place of business and also to give prescribed particulars on its business stationery. The requirements relating to the display by oversea companies of their corporate name, country of incorporation and other particulars are set out in paragraph 14.08.

Display of name at every place of business

26.02 Every company must paint or affix its (registered) name on the outside of every office or place in which its business is carried on, in a conspicuous position and in letters easily legible [s348(1)].

Company stationery

Name

26.03 A company's name must be stated in the following business documents:

(1) in all business letters of the company,

(2) in all notices and other official publications,

(3) in all bills of exchange, promissory notes, endorsements, cheques and orders for money or goods purporting to be signed by or on behalf of the company, and

(4) in all its invoices, receipts and letters of credit.

[s349(1)]

26.04 A company's name must also be engraved in legible characters on its company seal [s350(1)].

l l l l l l l l l l l

Other particulars

26.05 The following particulars must be stated in all business letters and order forms of the company:

(1) the company's place of registration and the number with which it is registered,

(2) the address of its registered office,

(3) if the company is an investment company (see para 20.40), the fact that it is an investment company, and

(4) in the case of a limited company exempt from the obligation to use the word "limited" as part of its name, the fact that it is a limited company.

[s351(1)]

Except for those registered before 23rd November 1916, a company may not state the name of any of its directors (otherwise than in the text or as a signatory) on any of the company's business letters, unless the full name (or surname and initials of Christian names) of every individual and corporate director is given [s305(1),(2),(4)].

26.06 Any reference to a company's share capital which is made on the stationery used for its business letters, or on its order forms, must be to its paid-up share capital [s351(2)].

26.07 Where a company's name includes the Welsh equivalent of "public limited company" or "limited" as its last part, the fact that the company is a public limited company or, as the case may be, a limited company must be stated in English:

(1) in all prospectuses, bill-heads, letter paper, notices and other official publications of the company, and

(2) in a notice conspicuously displayed in every place in which the company's business is carried on.

[s351(3),(4)]

Penalties

26.08 The Act provides for penalties for contravention of the requirements set out above [s305(3), 348(2), 349(2),(3),(4), 350(2), 351(5)].

CHAPTER 27

Prohibition on loans and other advances to directors

Introduction

27.01 The Act includes comprehensive provisions, which contain a general prohibition on loans and related guarantees, and which distinguish between "relevant" companies (that is, companies which are a p.l.c. or a member of a group containing a p.l.c.) and others. The prohibition is extended for relevant companies to cover other forms of credit and also transactions with persons who are defined as being "connected" with a director. There are specified exceptions to the prohibitions (in particular, for money-lending companies – see Chapter 31), and provisions designed to prevent companies from avoiding the prohibitions by entering into indirect arrangements.

27.02 A company's memorandum or articles of association may be more restrictive than the legislation. In addition, directors should be aware of their general fiduciary duties towards a company.

Director

27.03 A "director" is defined as including any person occupying the position of director, by whatever name called [s741(1)]. Thus it is the position held by a person and the functions he carries out (rather than his title) which would normally determine whether he is a director.

Shadow director

27.04 The Act also refers to a "shadow director" who is defined as a person in accordance with whose directions or instructions the directors are accustomed to act. However, a person is not deemed to be a shadow director by reason only that the directors act on advice given by him in a professional capacity (for example, as a lawyer) [s741(2)].

27.05 For the purpose of sections 330 to 346 of the Act (described in this chapter and those which follow), a shadow director is treated as a director [s330(5)].

Prohibition on loans

27.06 Subject to the specific exceptions which are described in Chapter 28, no company may make a loan, or enter into any guarantee or provide any security in connection with a loan made by any person, to a director of the company or of its holding company [s330(1),(2)]. It follows that a holding company is not prohibited from lending money to a person who is a director of its subsidiary company but who is not also a director of the holding company or of a superior holding company. It would not, however, be lawful for the subsidiary to guarantee the loan or reimburse the holding company.

27.07 The term "loan" is not defined in the Act, but in a recent case (*Champagne Perrier-Jouet SA v H. H. Finch Ltd [1982] 1 WLR 1359; [1982] 3 AER 713*) concerning the legality of a transaction in the context of the 1948 Act, the judge stated that "the correct meaning of 'loan' was that to be found in the Shorter English Dictionary: 'a sum of money lent for a time to be returned in money or money's worth'". There seems to be no reason why this definition should not be used in practice also for the purposes of the 1985 Act.

27.08 The Act does not state whether payment of remuneration for services which have yet to be performed (although made under the authority of a contract of service), or drawings made in anticipation of remuneration which has not been finally determined (for example, bonuses), constitute loans; in view of contrary opinions which exist, caution should be exercised.

27.09 Not all amounts due by a director will fall within the ambit of the Act. In some cases the amount may be in respect of an advance for bona fide company expenditure which is neither prohibited nor disclosable (see para 28.09).

27.10 Where an amount due from a director is written off, particularly where the debt is forgiven, consideration should be given as to whether the amount written off falls to be disclosed within directors' remuneration (see Chapter 7). Where a debt is written off but not forgiven it would still subsist (that is, remain unsettled or otherwise undischarged) and, therefore, if the amount was originally a loan or similar transaction, it would remain disclosable as such for every accounting period in which it still subsists.

Prohibition on other forms of credit

27.11 It is clear that if there was a prohibition only on "straightforward" loans, all manner of indirect loans and other forms of credit could lawfully be made, thus largely avoiding the prohibition on loans. For this reason, the provisions were extended for relevant companies (that is, p.l.c.s and companies in a group containing a p.l.c. – see para 27.14) to cover:

(1) "quasi-loans" (broadly, a payment of, or an undertaking to pay, an amount on behalf of another person which is to be refunded by that person: that is, an indirect loan) [s330(3), 331(3),(4)],

(2) "credit transactions" (broadly, a transaction with deferred payment) [s330(4), 331(7)], as well as

(3) loans, quasi-loans and credit transactions for directors' "connected persons" [s330(3),(4)],

in each case including related guarantees, securities and "indirect arrangements" [s330(3),(4),(6),(7)]. These are described in more detail in paras 27.26 to 27.31 below.

27.12 Non-relevant companies may therefore enter into quasi-loans and credit transactions with their directors and transactions (including loans) with connected persons, provided the transactions do not contravene the company's memorandum or articles, and provided also that the directors do not act in contravention of their general fiduciary duty to the company.

27.13 Subject to specified exceptions, all loans, quasi-loans and credit transactions with directors and their connected persons, whether lawful or not, are required to be disclosed in company accounts (see Chapter 29).

Relevant company

27.14 A relevant company is any company which:
(a) is a public company, or
(b) is a subsidiary of a public company, or
(c) is a subsidiary of a company which has as another subsidiary a public company, or
(d) has a subsidiary which is a public company.

[s331(6)]

"Company" means a company formed and registered under the Companies Act 1985 or an earlier Companies Act [s735(1)]. The expression therefore does not embrace bodies corporate incorporated outside Great Britain and thus the inclusion of such a body corporate (even if public under its own national law) in a group would not of itself result in the British members of that group being regarded as relevant companies.

Connected person

27.15 Persons who are regarded as connected with a director comprise, broadly, spouse and minor children (including stepchildren), companies in which the director has a twenty per cent or greater interest, and business partners. The statutory definition is given in the next paragraph and is explained in those which follow.

27.16 The following persons are defined as being connected with a director:

(1) a member of the director's family (that is, spouse, and the following persons if they are under 18: child, stepchild or illegitimate child);

(2) except where the context otherwise requires, a body corporate with which the director is associated (described further in paragraphs 27.18 to 27.25 below);

(3) a person acting in his capacity as trustee (other than as trustee under an employees' share scheme or a pension scheme) of a trust, the beneficiaries of which include or may include the director or any member of the director's family (as defined in (1) above) or a body corporate with which the director is associated;

(4) a person acting in his capacity as partner of the director or of any other connected person in (1) to (3) above;

(5) a Scottish firm in which:
    (a) that director is a partner,
    (b) a partner is a person who, by virtue of paragraphs (1), (2) or (3) above, is connected with that director, or
    (c) a partner is a Scottish firm in which that director is a partner or in which there is a partner who, by virtue of (1), (2) or (3) above, is connected with that director;
unless that person is also a director of the company [s346(2),(3)].

Family

27.17 It is clear from the above definition that other close members of a director's family, for example parents or brothers and sisters, are not regarded as connected persons.

Associated body corporate

27.18 "A body corporate with which the director is associated" is one in which the director and his connected persons are together:

(1) "interested" in *at least* twenty per cent of the nominal value of its equity share capital, or

(2) are entitled to exercise or control the exercise of *more than* twenty per cent of the voting power at any general meeting.

[s346(4)]

27.19 A director of a company is deemed to control a body corporate if, but only if:

(1) he or any person connected with him is interested in any part of the equity share capital of that body or is entitled to exercise or control the exercise of any part of the voting power at any general meeting of that body, *and*

(2) that director, the persons connected with him *and the other directors of that company*, together, are interested in more than one-half of that share capital or are entitled to exercise or control the exercise of more than one-half of that voting power.

[s346(5)]

27.20 References in the two preceding paragraphs to the exercise of voting power being controlled by a director include voting power the exercise of which is controlled by a body corporate which is controlled by that director [s346(8)].

27.21 For the purpose only of determining whether a body corporate is associated with a director, another body corporate with which the director is associated is not regarded as a connected person, except where that body corporate is a partner of the director or a trustee of a trust the beneficiaries of which include, or may include, the director or a member of the director's family (see para 27.16) [s346(6)].

27.22 The rules for determining whether a person is "interested" in the shares of a company are found in Schedule 13 of the Act (see Chapter 8) [s346(7)] and include "any interest of any kind whatsoever"; as well as direct holdings, this would include indirect interests arising through beneficial trust interests or through an intermediate company.

27.23 The rules for determining whether a person is associated with a body corporate are illustrated in the following paragraphs. As noted earlier, this association can arise through an interest in shares or through

201

control of voting power. For simplicity, a body corporate (that is, an entity incorporated in Great Britain or elsewhere) is referred to as a company.

Association through an interest in shares
27.24

(1) A person (together with most of his connected persons – that is, normally his immediate family and business partners – see para 27.21) must be "interested" in twenty per cent or more of the equity share capital of a company before that company is regarded as being associated (and hence connected) with that person.

(2) An "interest" in the shares of a company can arise through a direct holding of shares in that company or through an indirect holding (perhaps via an intermediate company) or a combination of direct and indirect holdings.

(3) There is a limit placed on the inclusion of indirect holdings via another (intermediate) company which are taken into account in determining whether a person's interest in the shares of a company is over the twenty per cent threshold referred to above. For example, where A Ltd holds shares in B Ltd, Mr X would be deemed to be interested in A Ltd's holdings in B Ltd, only where either of the following two conditions are met:
  (a) Mr X is able to exercise or control the exercise of more than 50% of the voting power at general meetings of A Ltd, *or*
  (b) the directors of A Ltd are accustomed to act in accordance with Mr X's directions or instructions.

[s346(7) Sch 13 para 4]

(4) Once the conditions in (3) are met, Mr X would be deemed to be interested in (all of, not a proportion of) whatever shares in other companies A Ltd is itself interested. This holding would then be added to any other interests that Mr X (or his connected persons) may have. For example (assuming there are no other connections or interests):

(i)

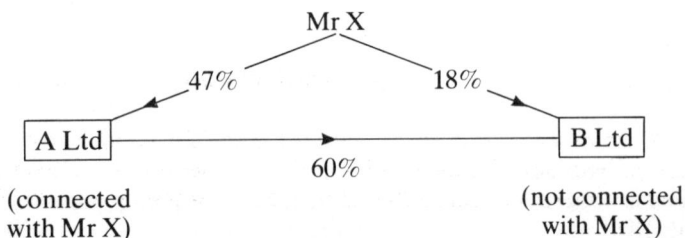

Mr X

47%   18%

A Ltd   60%   B Ltd

(connected with Mr X)   (not connected with Mr X)

(ii)

Mr X

52%   18%

A Ltd ──────────►──────────── B Ltd

2%

(connected
with Mr X)

(connected
with Mr X)

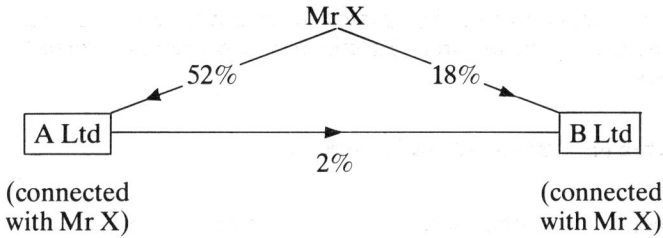

Thus in (i) despite Mr X having an *effective* holding in B Ltd of 46.2% (18% + 47% of 60%), B Ltd would *not* be connected with Mr X, whereas in (ii) with an *effective* holding of only 19.04% (18% + 52% of 2%) B Ltd would be connected with Mr X. Therefore, if Mr X was a director of C p.l.c. (which is not related to A Ltd or B Ltd) any loans by C p.l.c. to B Ltd or other transactions between C p.l.c. and B Ltd would be regarded in example (ii) as a loan to or transaction with a person connected with Mr X for the purposes of both the prohibitions and the disclosure rules as they affect C p.l.c.

Association through control of voting power

27.25 A person's being entitled to exercise or control the exercise of voting power in a company could arise from the voting power attaching to shares which that person holds directly in the company or as a result of his holding shares in an intermediate company.

This may be illustrated by the following examples:

(i)

Mr X   Other shareholders
100% of 'A' shares   100% of 'B' shares

A Ltd

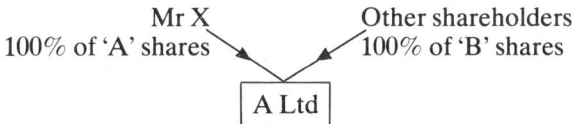

The nominal value of the issued equity shares of A Ltd is as follows:

'A' shares   10,000 of £1 each

'B' shares   375,000 of £1 each

Each 'A' share carries 10 votes, whereas each 'B' share carries 1 vote. Therefore by being able to exercise 100,000 votes out of a maximum of 475,000 votes (that is, more than 20%), Mr X is associated with A Ltd [s346(4)(b)].

(ii)

Mr X

↓ 51% of voting power

A Ltd

↓ 21% of voting power

B Ltd

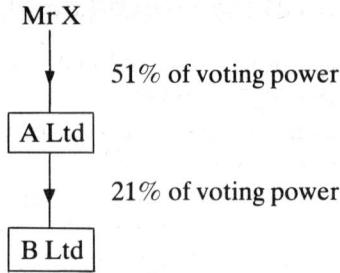

Mr X controls A Ltd because he is interested in part of its equity share capital and (in this example) is entitled to exercise more than one-half of its voting power [s346(5)]. Because Mr X controls A Ltd, he is regarded as controlling A Ltd's exercise of its voting power in B Ltd, and because this exceeds 20% of the potential voting power at B Ltd's general meetings, B Ltd is regarded as being associated with Mr X [s346(4)(b), (8)].

(iii) In determining whether a director of a reporting company controls another company, the interests of the other directors of the reporting company in the shares in and the control of the voting power of that other company have to be aggregated with those of the director in question and those of most of his connected persons (that is, normally his immediate family and business partners – see para 27.21) [s346(5),(6)].

Mr X, Mr Y and Mr Z (but not Mrs Z) are all directors of H Ltd (the reporting company). The following particulars are relevant in determining whether A Ltd is "controlled" by any or all of the directors of H Ltd. All shares are equity shares and carry equal voting rights.

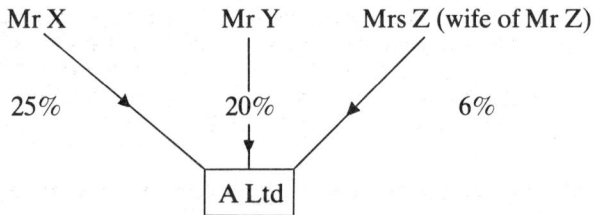

Mr X   Mr Y   Mrs Z (wife of Mr Z)

25%   20%   6%

A Ltd

Only Mr Z would be regarded as controlling A Ltd. That is because in determining whether Mr X or Mr Y control A Ltd, the interests in shares and voting power held by a person who is "connected" with *another* director (of the reporting company – H Ltd) are not included. However, had Mr Z held the shares himself, all three (X, Y and Z) would have been regarded as controlling A Ltd [s346(5)].

Extension of the prohibition for relevant companies

27.26 In addition to the prohibition on loans to directors, a *relevant company* (see para 27.14) may not:

(1) make a loan to a person connected with a director of the company or of its holding company [s330(3)],

(2) make a "quasi-loan" to a director of the company or of its holding company, or to a person connected with such a director [s330(3)],

(3) enter into a "credit transaction" as creditor for (that is, on behalf of) such a director or connected person [s330(4)],

(4) enter into a guarantee or provide any security in connection with a loan, quasi-loan or credit transaction made by any other person for such a director or connected person [s330(3),(4)].

Quasi-loan

27.27 A "quasi-loan" is a transaction under which the "creditor" (for example, the company) pays, or agrees to pay, an amount for the "borrower" (for example, a director):

(1) on terms that the borrower (or a person on his behalf) will reimburse the company, or

(2) which results in a liability on the borrower to reimburse the creditor.

[s331(3)]

Examples:

(i) Where a director uses a company credit card to defray his personal expenditure and subsequently reimburses the company, the quasi-loan would normally arise when the director signs the charge form.

(ii) The provision by a company of a travel season ticket where the director reimburses the company by a deduction from his salary would also constitute a quasi-loan; if the cost of the ticket was advanced by the company to the director who then himself obtained the ticket, the transaction would be a loan and may be lawful depending on the amount involved (see in particular 28.07 below).

27.28 Any arrangement whereby a company incurs expenditure to be covered by a deduction from salary is likely to be a quasi-loan and thus care should be taken where a director of a relevant company uses the company's purchasing facilities for his private purposes. Where the quasi-loan is likely to exceed either of the permitted exception limits (that is, where the transaction is not repayable within two months or where the amount of the transaction together with the outstanding amount of previous quasi-loans exceeds £1,000 – see 28.08 below), the director should first put the company in funds to avoid a quasi-loan arising.

Credit transaction

27.29 A "credit transaction" is a transaction under which one party (for example, the company):

(1) supplies goods or sells land under a hire purchase agreement or conditional sale agreement,

(2) leases or hires any land or goods in return for periodical payments, or

(3) otherwise disposes of land or supplies goods or services on the understanding that payment, whether in a lump sum or instalments or by way of periodical payments or otherwise, is to be deferred.

[s331(7)]

"Services" means anything other than goods or land [s331(8)].

27.30 A credit transaction may, very broadly, be expressed as a transaction under which payment in full does not take place either before or at the time the transaction is entered into. Transactions entered into on normal trade terms (including, for example, settlement within 30 days) would thus normally be credit transactions within the meaning of the Act. The Act specifically places no limit on the amount which may be outstanding in respect of credit transactions which are entered into on arm's length terms and in the ordinary course of a company's business (see 28.08 below) [s335(2)]. For each director of a relevant company, there is a limit of £5,000 on credit transactions not in the ordinary course of business [s335(1)]. For all companies (whether relevant companies or not) disclosure is required where the outstanding amount of credit transactions (whether or not on normal trade terms) for a director exceeds £5,000 at any time during the accounting period [s232, Sch 6 para 11(1),(2)].

27.31 The definition of a credit transaction includes a transaction "under which one party . . . leases or hires any land or goods in return for periodical payments". It is not clear whether a right to occupy premises in return for periodical payments would fall within the definition, if that right was not in the form of a lease.

Indirect arrangements

27.32 The regulations are extended for *all* companies to cover "indirect arrangements", which may otherwise have enabled a company to avoid the restrictions described earlier in this chapter. These indirect arrangements fall into two categories:

(1) A company may not arrange for the assignment to it or the assumption by it of any rights, obligations or liabilities under a transaction which, had it been entered into by the company, would have been in contravention of the Act [s330(6)].

Example:

Mr A, a director of X Ltd, takes out a building society loan of £50,000 to purchase his house. X Ltd subsequently takes over the loan and repays the building society. This would be unlawful for a company which is not a recognised bank or other money-lending company, and may also be unlawful for such companies – see Chapter 31.

---

(2) A company may also not take part in any arrangement whereby:
   (a) another person enters into a transaction which, had it been entered into by the company, would have been in contravention of the Act, *and*
   (b) that other person, in pursuance of the arrangement, has obtained or is to obtain any *benefit* from the company or any other member of the group.

[s330(7)]

Examples:

(i) Where a third party has made loans to the directors of a company in return for the placing by that company of substantial business (or deposits) with that third party, the business (or deposits) placed would constitute a "benefit" to the third party. This would constitute an indirect arrangement for loans and would be unlawful if the loans could not lawfully have been made by the company itself.

(ii) X Ltd makes loans to the directors of Y Ltd in return for loans made by Y Ltd to the directors of X Ltd. Such a "back to back" arrangement may constitute an unlawful arrangement for X Ltd if the grant by X Ltd of loans to the directors of Y Ltd is regarded as providing Y Ltd with a "benefit". The position of Y Ltd would be construed accordingly.

(iii) Mr J, who is a director of X p.l.c., takes a lease of premises from and pays rent to A Ltd (of which he is not a director) in return for X p.l.c. placing business with A Ltd. This arrangement would constitute an indirect credit transaction by X p.l.c. This indirect credit transaction would be unlawful for X p.l.c. only if it would have been unlawful had it been entered into directly between X p.l.c. and Mr J. The exceptions to the general prohibition on credit transactions by relevant companies are set out in 28.08 below.

Effective date

27.33 The above prohibitions and the exceptions thereto apply only to transactions and arrangements entered into on or after 22 December 1980 [the date the corresponding provisions of the 1980 Act came into force] although the disclosure provisions are wider ranging and require that transactions which were entered into before that date and which subsist (that is, remain unsettled or otherwise undischarged) thereafter must be disclosed in the accounts for the periods during which they still subsist.

27.34 The prohibitions do not act retrospectively and therefore any transaction lawfully entered into before a person becomes a director is not rendered unlawful on that person's appointment to the board of directors.

Effect of contravention

27.35 Where a company enters into any transaction or arrangement in contravention of section 330 (that is, after allowing for any of the exceptions described in Chapters 28 and 31) the transaction or arrangement is voidable at the instance of the company unless:

(1) restitution of the money or other asset which is the subject matter is not possible or the company has been indemnified (see 27.36 below) for any loss or damage suffered by it, or

(2) any person (other than the person for whom the transaction or arrangement was made), without actual notice of the contravention, has acquired rights bona fide for value which would be affected by avoidance of the transaction or arrangement.

[s341(1)]

27.36 Furthermore, whether or not the transaction or arrangement has been avoided, the director and, where applicable, the connected person who was a party to the transaction or arrangement, as well as any other director of the company who authorised it, are liable:

(1) to account to the company for any gain made as a result of the transaction or arrangement, and

(2) to indemnify the company for any resulting loss or damage.

This is without prejudice to any liability imposed otherwise than by this provision [s341(2),(3)].

27.37 However, where the transaction or arrangement was entered into with a person connected with a director, that director will not be liable where he shows that he took all reasonable steps to ensure compliance with the provisions [s341(4)]. Connected persons and other authorising directors will not be liable where they show that, at the time the transaction or arrangement was entered into, they were unaware of the contravention [s341(5)].

27.38 The Act also provides criminal penalties for a breach of section 330 [s342].

Law governing transactions

27.39 It is immaterial for the operation of the prohibitions, the exceptions and the disclosure requirements, whether the law governing a transaction or arrangement is that of the UK, or part of it, or some other system of law [s347]. Accordingly, a British company cannot avoid the provisions by making a transaction or arrangement subject to foreign law.

CHAPTER 28

Permitted transactions with directors

28.01 There are a number of exceptions from the prohibitions on loans and similar transactions. Transactions which fall within the exceptions are, however, generally, still disclosable (see Chapter 29).

28.02 Under the exceptions, transactions are, generally, permitted up to an amount referred to as the "aggregate of the relevant amounts". In broad terms, this comprises the aggregate amount to be advanced under the particular exception to the director by the company or any of its subsidiaries, plus the amount outstanding from any earlier transaction made under the same exception.

28.03 The amounts outstanding under earlier transactions (made under the same exception) with connected persons must also be included in the calculation, where a relevant company enters into a transaction under one of the exceptions.

28.04 Where a proposed transaction falls outside the criteria for a particular exception, it may be possible to restructure it (particularly in the case of loans and quasi-loans) so that it falls within one of the other exceptions.

28.05 A company's memorandum or articles of association may, however, be more restrictive than the Act and may, therefore, not permit a transaction which is not prohibited by the Act.

Exceptions from the rules on prohibited transactions

28.06 The exceptions from the prohibitions are set out in the paragraphs which follow.

Loans

28.07 Any company (whether a relevant company or not) may make a loan to a director of the company or of its holding company if the aggregate of the relevant amounts (that is, amounts outstanding under this exception from that director – see 28.18 below) does not exceed £2,500 [s334].

This exception does *not* extend:

(1) to connected persons (and thus does not allow a relevant company to make a loan to a person connected with a director), or

(2) to guarantees of, or security provided in connection with, loans made by third persons.

Quasi-loans and credit transactions

28.08 A relevant company is not prohibited from:

(1) Making a quasi-loan to one of its directors or to a director of its holding company, if:
   (a) the company is to be reimbursed within two months, *and*
   (b) the amount of the quasi-loan together with the aggregate amount of earlier quasi-loans still outstanding to the company and its subsidiaries (and fellow subsidiaries where the proposed quasi-loan is to be made for a director of the company's holding company) does not exceed £1,000.

   [s332(1),(2)]

   This exception does *not* extend to quasi-loans for connected persons, or to guarantees of or security provided in connection with quasi-loans made by third parties.

(2) Entering into a credit transaction for a director or connected person:
   (a) where the aggregate of the relevant amounts does not exceed £5,000, *or*
   (b) where the company enters into the transaction in the ordinary course of its business and its value is no greater and the terms no more favourable than would be offered by the company to someone of the same financial standing but unconnected with the company.

   [s335(1),(2)]

   This exception appears to extend to guarantees of credit transactions entered into by third parties.

211

Thus, there is no statutory limitation on the amount of credit transactions with directors and connected persons which a relevant company may enter into, provided it does so in the ordinary course of its business *and* on arm's length terms. Transactions in excess of £5,000 on favourable terms would not be permitted.

The Act does not prohibit a company which is not a relevant company from entering into quasi-loans and credit transactions.

Business expenditure (including floats and advances)

28.09 Where a company makes available money and travellers cheques (or similar facilities) to a director for bona fide business trips or to settle other company expenditure, the director is generally regarded as holding the funds on behalf of the company and acting as agent when meeting company expenditure out of those funds. Similarly, the use of a company credit card solely to defray business expenditure would not constitute a quasi-loan, as there is no obligation on the director to re-imburse the company. Such arrangements should be outside the scope of section 330 and should therefore not contravene that section nor require disclosure in the accounts.

28.10 When the 1980 Act received the Royal Assent, the Department of Trade issued, as part of a press notice dated 2nd May 1980, a background note (which has no legal force) which stated:

"payments or advances made for the purpose of defraying expenses incurred by directors acting as agents for the company are not, of course, caught by any of these provisions, as such payments do not call for reimbursement by the director and therefore do not amount to a provision of credit".

28.11 There is, however, a statutory exception for advances for business expenditure and this is described in the following paragraphs. The exception relates to transactions and arrangements which would otherwise be prohibited under section 330 and does not affect those which do not come within the scope of that section (see para 28.09).

28.12 A relevant or non-relevant company may provide any of its own directors (but not a director of its holding company) with funds to meet expenditure incurred or to be incurred by him for the purposes of the company or to enable him properly to perform his duties as an officer of the company or to enable a director to avoid incurring such expenditure [s337(1),(2)]. Prior approval by the company in general meeting is required or, alternatively, the funds may be provided on condition that if approval of the company is not given at or before the next AGM, the loan will be repaid or any other liability discharged, within six months of the AGM [s337(3)]. The purpose of the expenditure, the amount of the funds to be provided by the company and the extent of the company's liability must be disclosed at any general meeting at which such approval is given [s337(4)]. A relevant company may enter into a transaction under this exception only if the aggregate of the relevant amounts (broadly, the value of the proposed transaction and the outstanding amount of any previous transaction under this exception) does not exceed £10,000 for the same director [s337(3)]. There is no statutory limit for a director of a non-relevant company.

28.13 This exception would cover loans and indirect arrangements for loans and, for relevant companies, would extend to quasi-loans, credit transactions and related indirect arrangements. An example of a transaction which would come within this exception would be a bridging loan by a company to a director (of up to £10,000 for a director of a relevant company), where the director is required by the company to move house for business purposes.

Intra-group transactions

28.14 The exceptions for intra-group transactions are as follows:

(1) A company is not prohibited from entering into a loan, quasi-loan, or credit transaction for its holding company, or from guaranteeing or providing any security in connection with a loan, quasi-loan or credit transaction made by any other person for its holding company [s336].

(2) Where a relevant company is a member of a group, that company is not prohibited from:
   (a) making a loan or quasi-loan to another member of that group, or
   (b) entering into a guarantee or providing any security in connection with a loan or a quasi-loan made by any person to another member of that group,
   by reason only that a director of one member of the group is associated with another member of the group (see para 27.18) [s333].

28.15 In other words, a company which is a member of a group may make a loan or quasi-loan to another member of that group notwithstanding that the company receiving the loan is regarded as being a body corporate with which a director of the (lending) company (or its holding company) is associated, and hence connected with him.

Money-lending companies

28.16 There are additional specific exceptions for recognised banks and other money-lending companies, which are described in Chapter 31.

Financial assistance for the acquisition of own shares

28.17 Section 155 of the Act permits a private company in defined circumstances to provide financial assistance for the acquisition of its own shares (see Chapter 23). It has been suggested that an effect of this is to allow an (implied) additional exception to the prohibitions on granting loans to directors by permitting private companies to make loans to assist directors in acquiring the company's shares. There would appear to be little to support this interpretation. However, a private company which is not a relevant company may be able to structure the financial assistance in the form of a quasi-loan which, for such companies, is not prohibited under the Act. The exceptions for money-lending companies should also be borne in mind (see Chapter 31).

Determination of the value of a transaction

Relevant amounts

28.18 Under the exceptions, transactions are often permitted up to an amount referred to as the "aggregate of the relevant amounts".

28.19 The "aggregate of the relevant amounts" in relation to a transaction or arrangement which is proposed to be made under one of the exceptions is the aggregate of:

(1) the "value" of the proposed transaction or arrangement,

(2) the "value" of any existing "indirect arrangement" (see 27.32) which was entered into by virtue of the same exception, and

(3) the "amount outstanding" under a previous permitted transaction made under the same exception.

[s339(2)]

"Value" is defined in para 28.23 and "amount outstanding" means the "value" of the transaction less any amount by which that value has been reduced [s339(6)].

28.20 Transactions and arrangements to be taken into account for this purpose are those entered into by the company and any of its subsidiaries and, where a director of its holding company is concerned, by the holding company and any of its subsidiaries [s339(2)].

Example:

X Ltd has two subsidiaries Y Ltd and Z Ltd, neither of which is a subsidiary of the other. In considering whether Y Ltd may make a loan to Mr D, a director of X Ltd (who is not also a director of Y Ltd), there has to be taken into consideration amounts already advanced to Mr D by X Ltd, Y Ltd and Z Ltd.

28.21 In calculating the amount outstanding under a previous transaction made under the same exception, there must be brought into account the amounts outstanding from the director as well as, in the case of relevant companies, his connected persons (except for loans to directors under the £2,500 exemption which is not available to connected persons) [s339(1) to (3)]. Transactions made for connected persons by non-relevant companies are ignored because they would not have been made by virtue of one of the exceptions. It follows that it would not be possible for a relevant company effectively to increase the permitted limits for transactions by entering into transactions first with directors and then with their connected persons (or vice versa).

28.22 The following transactions would not have to be aggregated as they would not have been made by virtue of one of the exceptions:

(1) illegal transactions,

(2) those which were entered into before 22nd December 1980 (the day the provisions came into force), although subsequent "indirect arrangements" in relation to such transactions would have to be taken into account, and

(3) those which are not subject to the prohibitions (for example, quasi-loans by non-relevant companies).

Definition of value

28.23 The "value" of a transaction or arrangement is defined as follows:

(1) For a loan: the principal of the loan.

(2) For a quasi-loan: the amount, or maximum amount, which the borrower is liable to reimburse the creditor.

(3) For a guarantee or security: the amount guaranteed or secured.

(4) For an "indirect arrangement": the value (ascertained in accordance with these rules) of the transaction to which the arrangement relates, less any amount by which the liabilities (under the arrangement or transaction) of the person for whom the transaction was made, have been reduced (that is, the net outstanding value). The effect of this is that if a transaction had a gross value of £20,000 and £5,000 had been paid off, only £15,000 would be taken into the calculation.

(5) In any other case (which would include credit transactions): the arm's length price of the goods, land and services.

[s340(1)to(6)]

28.24 Where, for any reason, the value of a transaction or arrangement is not capable of being expressed as a specific sum of money, its value is deemed to be in excess of £50,000 [s340(7)]. The inability to determine the value of a transaction or arrangement could thus result in its automatically falling outside the permitted limits of some of the exceptions.

28.25 It follows that, for these purposes, the amount stated in a contract is not necessarily its "value", particularly where that stated amount is less than the arm's length price.

28.26 An effect of having to attribute an arm's length value to transactions is that a company may not indirectly avoid the monetary limits specified in the Act by agreeing to an artificially lower price, which would also have the effect of giving a "benefit" to the recipient of the asset, which may possibly be disclosable as part of his emoluments (see para 7.15).

Power to increase financial limits

28.27 The Secretary of State has the power to increase, but not to decrease, by statutory instrument the maximum amounts which may be advanced under the exceptions described in this chapter and Chapter 31 (money-lending companies), as well as the thresholds for approval of substantial property transactions (Chapter 32) [s345].

CHAPTER 29

Disclosure of transactions with directors

29.01 The Act requires disclosure in company accounts of prescribed particulars relating to loans, quasi-loans and credit transactions, whether or not the transactions were prohibited by the Act, and distinguishes between the disclosure of transactions involving directors and those involving other officers, which are covered in Chapter 30. Disclosure is also required of transactions and arrangements in which a director had, directly or indirectly, a "material interest".

Requirement to disclose

29.02 The circumstances in which disclosure is required and the particulars requiring disclosure are set out in Schedule 6 of the Act [s232(1),(2)]. The provisions apply in respect of shadow directors as well as directors [s232(3)]. References in this chapter to directors should therefore be read as including shadow directors.

29.03 The disclosures must be made by a holding company in the notes to its group accounts and by any other company in the notes to its individual accounts [s232(1),(2),(3)]. Where a holding company does not prepare group accounts for a financial year by virtue of section 229(2) or (3) of the Act, for example in the case of a wholly-owned intermediate holding company, it must still give, in its individual accounts, the information which it would otherwise have been required to give in its group accounts [s232(4)].

29.04 The disclosure requirements apply in respect of transactions or arrangements with directors who have held that office *at any time* during the financial year [Sch 6 paras 1,2]. The Act requires particulars of individual transactions or arrangements to be disclosed separately and thus there is, generally, little scope for aggregation unless a series of transactions is covered by one arrangement.

29.05 *Disclosure of transactions with directors*

29.05 Subject to specified exceptions (see paragraphs 29.25 to 29.37), disclosure must be made in respect of:

(1) any transaction or arrangement of a kind described in section 330 (that is, loans, quasi-loans, credit transactions and "indirect arrangements"),

(2) agreements to enter into such transactions, and

(3) any other transaction or arrangement in which a director had directly or indirectly a material interest.

[Sch 6 paras 1,2]

Thus, (1) and (2) require the disclosure of an agreement to enter into these types of transactions, as well as the transactions themselves.

29.06 The transactions, arrangements and agreements which are required to be disclosed by all companies (that is, both relevant and non-relevant) are those entered into by the company or by a subsidiary of the company:

(1) for a person who at any time during the financial year was a director of the company or a director of its holding company, or

(2) for a person who was connected with such a director.

[Sch 6 paras 1,2]

29.07 The Act obviously does not attempt to list the types of transactions in which a director could be regarded as having a material interest. Examples could include those falling under section 320 (substantial property transactions involving directors) and also consultancy contracts with a director's private firm. The matter is considered further in 29.15 to 29.22 below.

29.08 The disclosure provisions apply whether or not:

(1) The transaction or arrangement was prohibited by section 330 [Sch 6 para 6(a)]. Thus, *permitted* loans, quasi-loans etc., are nevertheless disclosable, as are quasi-loans and credit transactions entered into by those companies which are not relevant companies, because they are transactions "of a kind described in section 330", even though not unlawful under that section. Furthermore, the fact that a transaction is entered into by a foreign subsidiary does not exempt the British parent from the disclosure requirements.

(2) The person for whom the transaction or arrangement was made was a director or connected person at the time it was made [Sch 6 para 6(b)]. Thus, a loan made to a person who subsequently became a director would require disclosure if any part of the loan was outstanding in the year of his appointment to the board.

(3) A subsidiary was such at the time it entered into a transaction or arrangement [Sch 6 para 6(c)].

Examples:

(i) Y Ltd, which is a subsidiary of X Ltd, lends £2,000 to Mr J who is a director of both X Ltd and Y Ltd. Disclosure must be made in the accounts of both X Ltd and Y Ltd.

(ii) X Ltd lends £2,000 to Mr P, who is not a director of X Ltd but who is a director of both A Ltd, which is X Ltd's holding company, and of Z Ltd, which is a subsidiary of A Ltd but which is neither a subsidiary nor holding company of X Ltd. Disclosure must be made in both X Ltd's and A Ltd's accounts but need not be given in Z Ltd's accounts.

(iii) X Ltd lends £3,000 to Mr J, who is a director of its subsidiary Y Ltd but not a director of X Ltd. This need not be disclosed, unless Mr J is an officer of X Ltd (see Chapter 30).

29.09 For any company which is, or is the holding company of, a recognised bank, the above rules do not apply to transactions specified in para 29.05(1) and (2) above (that is, loans, quasi-loans, credit transactions and indirect arrangements) *to which that recognised bank is a party*. Chapter 31 describes the special rules which apply in such cases [s232(5), Sch 6 para 4]. This exception does not, however, apply to transactions or arrangements in which directors have a material interest, particulars of which must still be disclosed in the accounts.

Particulars to be given

Loans, quasi-loans, credit transactions and indirect arrangements

29.10 The particulars which are required to be given in respect of each disclosable transaction, arrangement or agreement are as follows:

In all cases

(1) A statement of the fact that the transaction, arrangement or agreement was made or subsisted during the financial year [Sch 6 para 9(2)(a)].

(2) The name of the director and, where applicable, the connected person for whom it was made [Sch 6 para 9(2)(b)].

(3) Its principal terms (see 29.13 below) [Sch 6 para 9(1)].

(4) The additional disclosures, as appropriate, set out below.

Additional disclosures

(5) For a loan, agreement for a loan, or an indirect loan under section 330(6) or (7) (see 27.32 above):

   (a) the amount of the liability, in respect of principal and interest, at the beginning and end of the financial year and the maximum amount of that liability at any time during that year,

   (b) the amount of any interest due but unpaid, and

   (c) any provision in the accounts for non-recovery of all or part of the loan or any interest thereon.

[Sch 6 para 9(2)(d)]

(6) For a guarantee or security for a loan or indirect guarantee or security under section 330(6):

   (a) the amount for which the company or a subsidiary was liable under the guarantee or in respect of the security, both at the beginning and end of the financial year,

   (b) the maximum amount for which the company or a subsidiary may become so liable, and

   (c) any amount paid or liability incurred by the company or a subsidiary in fulfilling the guarantee or discharging the security, including any loss incurred by reason of the enforcement of the guarantee or security.

[Sch 6 para 9(2)(e)]

(7) For quasi-loans, credit transactions and related arrangements or agreements (including indirect arrangements for such transactions), the "value" (as defined, see 28.23 above) of the transaction or arrangement or, where applicable, the "value" of the transaction or arrangement to which the agreement relates [Sch 6 para 9(2)(f)].

29.11 There is thus no requirement to disclose the amount outstanding for quasi-loans and credit transactions; the "gross" amount remains disclosable for as long as the transaction subsists, although companies may wish to disclose also the amount outstanding.

Material interests in transactions or arrangements

29.12 There are required to be disclosed:

(1) The principal terms (see 29.13 below) [Sch 6 para 9(1)].

(2) A statement of the fact that the transaction, arrangement or agreement was made or subsisted during the financial year [Sch 6 para 9(2)(a)].

(3) The name of the director and, where applicable, the connected person for whom it was made [Sch 6 para 9(2)(b)].

(4) The name of the director with the material interest and the nature of that interest [Sch 6 para 9(2)(c)].

(5) The "value" (as defined, see 28.23 above) of the transaction or arrangement or, where applicable, the "value" of the transaction or arrangement to which the agreement relates [Sch 6 para 9(2)(f)].

Principal terms

29.13 The "principal terms" of a transaction are not defined in the Act. The extent of the disclosure required will therefore depend on the circumstances of each individual case, but the principal terms would typically include, but are not limited to, those relating to:

(1) the advance and repayment of any money,

(2) the purchase price of and payment for any non-cash asset,

(3) any payment of interest, and

(4) any guarantee or security given.

Corresponding amounts

29.14 Schedule 6 does not state whether corresponding amounts have to be disclosed but, in the absence of any other provision requiring their disclosure, it is considered that this is not required. Schedule 4 (which, however, does not cover special category accounts – see Chapter 13) generally requires disclosure of corresponding amounts for all items shown in the notes to the accounts, except for transactions involving directors and other officers [Sch 4 para 58(3)(b)].

Material interests in contracts

29.15 As noted in 29.05 above, the accounts are required to disclose particulars of transactions or arrangements with the company or a subsidiary in which a director (but not a connected person) of the company or of its holding company had, directly or indirectly, a "material interest".

29.16 Any transaction or arrangement between a company and a director of the company or of its holding company or a person connected with such a director is to be treated as one in which the director is interested [Sch 6 para 3(1)]. Such an interest is not "material" if the majority of the other directors of the company for which the accounts are being prepared are bona fide of that opinion. If the directors have not considered the matter there is no presumption either way as to materiality [Sch 6 para 3(2)]. In practice, the directors' consideration of the matter should be evidenced by a board minute. For contracts and arrangements of a relatively low value, there is, however, a disclosure de minimis of up to £5,000, depending on the size of the company. This is described in 29.26(2) below.

29.17 The concept of what constitutes a material interest for these purposes has given rise to problems of interpretation. It is evident that it is the director's interest which has to be "material" before disclosure is required, but the Act does not give any guidance as to how material is to be interpreted. Divergent views have developed as to the meaning of material. One view is that material should be interpreted as meaning the type of interest which would be "relevant" information for shareholders and other users of the accounts (that is, the "relevant" view); another is that material means that the director has a "substantial" interest in the transaction. These views are described in more detail below.

The relevant view

29.18 In this case, "material" is interpreted as meaning relevant for the purpose for which the information is given. Under Schedule 6 of the Act, this purpose is presumably to inform shareholders about the activities of their directors, so that the shareholders are in a better position to exercise their powers as shareholders. In other words, the accounts should disclose particulars of those transactions which might be of interest to or influence the decisions of the shareholders or other users of the accounts.

The substantial view

29.19 In this case, "material" is interpreted as meaning that the director has a "substantial" interest in the transaction or arrangement. If, for example, a director bought a bar of chocolate in the staff canteen and then proceeded to eat all of it, his interest in the purchase would be regarded as substantial and therefore material. If the director ate only a quarter of the bar of chocolate and gave away the rest it might be argued that his interest was not substantial and hence was not material. The problem which arises under this approach is the level at which an interest becomes material; any level set by a company would be arbitrary and would obviously vary from company to company. The substantial approach could result in a small interest in a large contract being undisclosed; for example, if a director received a 2½ per cent commission (of £100,000) on a £4 million contract placed by the company. Under the *relevant approach*, particulars of such a transaction would almost certainly need to be disclosed.

29.20 Whichever view prevails, it is thought that the size of a transaction in relation to the director's personal finances would not be of primary importance.

29.21 In view of this uncertainty and pending clarification by further legislation or by the courts, it may be advisable to disclose particulars of transactions in cases of doubt and where it is considered that shareholders and other users of the accounts should be informed of such transactions.

29.22 The Department of Trade is aware of the concern over the volume of disclosure which may be necessary in order to comply with Schedule 6 para (1)(c) and (2)(c) [formerly s54(1)(c) and (2)(c) of the 1980 Act] and, in September 1981, circulated a discussion paper to interested parties with whom it normally consults on company law matters. In this paper, the Department drew attention to the drafting of the section which refers to any other transaction or *arrangement* and suggested that where it can be demonstrated that a number of transactions have been entered into in pursuance of a single arrangement, individual amounts do not require disclosure but may be aggregated. This may be the case, for example, where a company has a continuing arrangement for the supply of goods or services, for instance where a director is a partner in a firm of solicitors which regularly acts as legal advisers to the company. The exemption from disclosure for transactions or arrangements in the ordinary course of business may also be of assistance (see para 29.29).

Closely controlled groups

29.23 The requirement to disclose particulars of individual transactions and arrangements could result in a substantial addition to the notes to the accounts where there are a number of transactions between companies which have a significant degree of common control and ownership, because that could result in those companies falling within the definition of a connected person (see paragraphs 27.18 to 27.25 above). Common control and ownership could arise, for example, where a director of one company owns, or has a substantial stake in, another company, neither of which holds shares in the other; as a result, they may have a close trading relationship where, for example, one company maufactures goods which are sold to third parties by the other company. A further example would be a vertical group where a director of a holding company controls more than one-half of the voting power at its general meetings. The subsidiaries of that holding company would be regarded as connected persons because the director would, himself, be deemed to be "interested" in the shares in the subsidiaries by virtue of his control of the holding company (see paras 8.14 and 27.19 above).

29.24 This problem has been partially alleviated by the exceptions described in paras 29.31 and 29.35 below.

Exceptions from disclosure

General

29.25 The disclosure provisions do not apply to the following transactions, arrangements and agreements:

(1) Those between one company and another in which a director of the former or of its subsidiary or holding company is interested only by virtue of being a director of the other company [Sch 6 para 5(a)].

(2) Those which were not entered into during the financial year and which did not subsist at any time during that period – that is, those which were settled or otherwise discharged in earlier years [Sch 6 para 5(c)].

(3) A contract *of* service between a company and one of its directors or a director of its holding company, or between a director of a company and any of its subsidiaries [Sch 6 para 5(b)]. The inspection by members of such contracts, at the company's registered office or elsewhere as permitted, is regulated by section 318 of the Act. The Stock Exchange requires listed companies to make directors' service contracts available for inspection at the AGM and to include in the directors' report a statement of the unexpired period of any service contract of any director proposed for re-election at the forthcoming AGM [Admission of Securities to Listing, Section 5, chapter 2, paragraph 43].

There is a distinction between a contract *of* service, where a director is employed by a company, and a contract *for* services, where a director is an independent contractor; there is *no* disclosure exception for the latter. An example of a contract *for* services would be a consultancy agreement.

De minimis

29.26 There is no de minimis exception for loans and quasi-loans but disclosure in the accounts is not required for credit transactions (and related arrangements) and "material interest" transactions in the following cases:

(1) For the following types of transactions and arrangements made by a company or by a subsidiary of the company for a person who was a director of the company or of its holding company or who was connected with such a director, where (taken together) their aggregate outstanding (arm's length) value did not at any time during the financial year exceed £5,000.
(a) credit transactions,
(b) guarantees or security for credit transactions,

(c) "indirect arrangements" for credit transactions, and

(d) agreements to enter into credit transactions.

[Sch 6 para 11(1),(2)]

(2) For any transaction or arrangement with a company or any of its subsidiaries in which a director of the company or of its holding company had a material interest if:

    (a) the value of each transaction or arrangement in which that director had (directly or indirectly) a material interest and which was made during the financial year with the company or any of its subsidiaries, *and*

    (b) the value of each such transaction or arrangement made in an earlier financial year, less the amount, if any, by which the liabilities of the person for whom the transaction or arrangement was made have been reduced (that is, the value outstanding),

did not at any time in the financial year exceed, in aggregate, £1,000 or, if more, did not exceed the lesser of £5,000 and 1% of the value of the company's net assets as at the end of the financial year.

[Sch 6 para 12]

29.27 The Secretary of State has the power to increase the above monetary limits [s345, Sch 6 para 13].

"Material interest" transactions and arrangements

29.28 The Act provides two further exceptions in relation to transactions or arrangements in which a director has a material interest.

29.29 Firstly, disclosure is not required if:

(1) each party to the transaction or arrangement which is a member of the same group of companies as the company entered into the transaction or arrangement in the ordinary course of business, and

(2) the terms of the transaction or arrangement are not less favourable to any such party than it would be reasonable to expect if the interest in the transaction or arrangement had not been that of a director of the company or of its holding company.

[Sch 6 para 7]

29.30 Although the explanatory note to the statutory instrument [S.I. 1984 No. 1860] which first brought these exceptions into force does not state that the reporting company must be a member of a group in order to fall within the exception, it appears to be a condition of the exception that the reporting company must be a member of a group.

29.31 Secondly, disclosure is not required if:

(1) the company is a member of a group of companies, and

(2) either the company is a wholly-owned subsidiary or no body corporate (other than the company or a subsidiary of the company) which is a member of the group of companies which includes the company's ultimate holding company was a party to the transaction or arrangement, and

(3) the director in question was at some time during the financial year associated with the company, and

(4) the material interest of the director in question in the transaction or arrangement would not have arisen if he had not been associated with the company at any time during the financial year.

[Sch 6 para 8]

29.32 The wording of this exception is obscure. A number of doubts have been expressed as to the effectiveness of the exception in providing relief from the disclosure requirements, not least because it appears to be based on the belief that it is the director's association with the reporting company which gives rise to a disclosable interest. If A Ltd enters into a transaction with B Ltd, when considering whether any disclosure is required in A Ltd's accounts, it is the director's association with B Ltd which is relevant for this purpose (if this were not the case, every single transaction which A Ltd enters into might be a candidate for disclosure). This view is also supported by the Act which states that "a transaction or arrangement between a company [the reporting company] and a director of it or of its holding company, or a person connected with such a director, is to be treated (if it would not otherwise be so) as a transaction, arrangement or agreement in which that director is interested" [Sch 6 para 3].

29.33 The stated purpose* of this (second) exception is to exempt from disclosure "any transaction between members of a group of companies which would have been disclosable only because of a director's being associated with the contracting companies, provided no minority interests in the reporting company are affected", thereby seeking to alleviate the problem referred to in para 29.23 above.

Intra-group loans and quasi-loans

29.34 There is an exemption from disclosure of the particulars set out in para 29.10(5),(6) and (7) above in relation to loans and quasi-loans between wholly-owned members of the same group of companies. This

---

* Explanatory note to SI 1984 No. 1860, which first brought the exception into force.

exception is also designed to deal with the position where there is a closely owned group which results in the members of that group being regarded as "connected" with the major shareholder(s) in the parent (see para 29.23).

29.35 The exception is as follows: The particulars required by para 29.10(5),(6) and (7) above do not have to be disclosed in the case of a loan or quasi-loan made or agreed to be made by a company to or for a body corporate which is:

(1) a body corporate of which that company is a wholly-owned subsidiary, or

(2) a wholly-owned subsidiary of a body corporate of which that company is a wholly-owned subsidiary, or

(3) a wholly-owned subsidiary of that company,

if particulars of that loan, quasi-loan or agreement for it would not have been required to be included in that company's annual accounts if the first-mentioned body corporate had not been associated with a director of that company at any time during the relevant period [Sch 6 para 10].

29.36 In such cases, disclosure is restricted to a statement that the transaction or arrangement was made or subsisted during the financial year, the name of the director and of the connected company, and the principal terms of the transaction or arrangement.

29.37 Notably, the exception does not extend to credit transactions or to transactions with a body corporate which is associated with a director of the reporting company's holding company.

Contract of service

29.38 There is uncertainty as to what extent, if any, the exception set out in 29.25(3) above (exemption from disclosure for directors' contracts of service) allows for an exemption from disclosure for transactions or arrangements which are included in a director's contract of service. It is not uncommon for a contract of service to provide, as part of a director's terms of service, that he shall have the right to occupy a company house or other accommodation. If no payment is involved, it could be argued that particulars may not require disclosure in the accounts. Where the contract of service merely entitles the director to a further agreement which is to be entered into subsequently, that further agreement would be disclosable in the company's accounts, either as a credit transaction if a periodical rental is payable (however small that rental may be), or as an arrangement in which the director has a material interest. Although particulars of a director's contract of service do not have to be disclosed in the accounts, it is difficult to argue that this exemption extends to a credit transaction or an agreement for a loan or any other section 330 transaction which, for whatever reason, is included in the same document as the director's terms of service. In view of this uncertainty, it may be advisable for companies to disclose in their accounts particulars of such arrangements which are included in a director's contract of service.

29.39 The inclusion of a transaction, for example a loan, in a contract of service does not, of course, make it lawful where it would not otherwise have been lawful.

Duty of auditors

29.40 Where any accounts do not comply with the disclosure requirements of Schedule 6 (set out above), the auditors must include in their audit report a statement giving the required particulars so far as they are reasonably able to do so [s237(5)].

General duty of disclosure to a company

29.41 A person who is in any way, whether directly or indirectly, interested in a proposed contract, arrangement or agreement with a company of which he is a director, is required to declare the nature of that interest at the meeting of the directors of the company at which the proposal is first considered [s317(1),(2),(5)].

29.42 Transactions and arrangements of a kind described in section 330 of the Act (that is, loans, quasi-loans, credit transactions, related guarantees and indirect arrangements) made by a company for a director of the company or a person connected with a director, are specifically brought within the ambit of the above notification requirements [s317(6)].

29.43 A director may give a general notice that he is a member of a specified company or firm, or that a specified person is "connected" with him, and that he is to be regarded as being interested in any contract which may be made with that company, firm or person [s317(3)].

29.44 These provisions apply also to a shadow director except that he must declare his interest by a written notice to the directors, and not at a meeting of the directors [s317(8)].

CHAPTER 30

Disclosure of transactions with officers other than directors

30.01 Except for transactions entered into by recognised banks, companies are required to disclose the outstanding amounts of loans and similar transactions made by the company or by a subsidiary to or on behalf of officers (other than directors) of the company. "Officers" includes a director, manager, or secretary. The meaning of the term "manager" and the inclusion of other persons as officers of a company, for example the company's auditor, is considered in 30.09 and 30.10 below.

Requirement to disclose

30.02 The notes to the group accounts or (if the company has no subsidiaries or does not otherwise prepare group accounts) the notes to the individual accounts are required to disclose, for *each* of the following three categories of transaction, the aggregate amounts outstanding at the end of the financial year and the number of officers for whom they were made [s233(1),(2),(4),(5), Sch 6 para 16(1)].

30.03 This disclosure is required in respect of the following types of transactions, arrangements and agreements for persons who at any time during the financial year were officers of the company (but not directors):

(1) loans,

(2) quasi-loans, and

(3) credit transactions,

in each case including related guarantees, securities and "indirect arrangements" of the kind described in 27.32 above [s233(1),(2), Sch 6 para 15].

30.04 "Amount outstanding" means the amount of the outstanding liabilities of the person for whom the transaction, arrangement or agreement was made or, in the case of a guarantee or security, the amount guaranteed or secured [Sch 6 para 17]. Disclosure of individual transactions or amounts outstanding is not required. The disclosure provisions do not apply to transactions with persons who are connected with officers.

30.05 Disclosure is not required in relation to an officer where the aggregate amount outstanding, at the end of the financial year, by that officer under all three categories of transaction taken together does not exceed £2,500 [Sch 6 para 16(2)]. The Secretary of State has the power to increase this limit [Sch 6 para 16(3)].

30.06 The provisions do not apply in relation to any transaction made by a company which is a recognised bank under the Banking Act 1979, for any of its officers or for any of the officers of its holding company [s233(3), 744]. This exemption does not extend to transactions by money-lending companies which are not recognised banks. It follows that the holding company of a recognised bank is not required to take account of transactions made by that bank for officers of the holding company.

30.07 Schedule 6 does not state whether corresponding amounts have to be disclosed but, in the absence of any other provision requiring their disclosure, it is considered that this is not required. Schedule 4 (which, however, does not cover special category accounts – see Chapter 13) generally requires disclosure of corresponding amounts for all items shown in the notes to the accounts, except for transactions involving directors and other officers [Sch 4 para 58(3)(b)].

Duty of auditors

30.08 Where any accounts do not comply with the above disclosure requirements, the auditors must include in their audit report a statement giving the required particulars so far as they are reasonably able to do so [s237(5)].

Manager

30.09 The term "officer" is defined as including a "manager" [s744]. "Manager" is not defined in the Companies Acts but has been interpreted in case law; the factual background in particular cases appears to have had a significant effect on its interpretation. For practical purposes it is accepted that not everyone whose job description is "manager", or which includes the term "manager", is a manager for the purposes of the

Companies Act. On the hand, in order to be regarded as a manager, it is not necessary that a person be a manager of the whole of the company's affairs, provided that the person has a substantial supervisory role and regularly makes what might be described as policy decisions or managerial decisions on behalf of the company and is not simply a person whose functions are limited to implementing the instructions of a superior. This view would be in line with the decision in *Re a Company* *[1980] 2 WLR 241* which was decided in the context of the Companies Acts, where Lord Justice Shaw stated that:

> "The expression 'manager' should not be too narrowly construed. It is not to be equated with a managing or other director or a general manager. As I see it, any person who in the affairs of a company exercises a supervisory control which reflects the general policy of the company for the time being or which is related to the general administration of the company is in the sphere of management".

The decision in *Re a Company* is a broader construction than that in the earlier case of *Registrar of Restrictive Trading Agreements* v. *W. H. Smith and Sons Limited* *[1969] 1 WLR 1460*, in which, for the *purposes of* section 15(3) (power to interrogate on oath) of the *Restrictive Trade Practices Act 1956*, it was decided that a "manager" was someone who was "concerned with the management of the affairs of the company as a whole and did not include a branch manager". Because *Re a Company* was decided in the context of the Companies Acts, it would seem that the interpretation in that case is to be preferred for this purpose.

Auditors as officers

30.10 There is little doubt that an auditor is an officer of a company for the purposes of the foregoing provisions of the 1985 Act; in which case, the amounts outstanding in respect of loans, quasi-loans and credit transactions with a company's auditors should be included as part of the aggregate disclosures of transactions for officers. Auditors should also be aware of their appropriate professional body's ethical rules relating to transactions with clients.

30.11 The disclosure exemption in relation to transactions made by a recognised bank for an officer of the company or of its holding company, and the £2,500 de minimis should, in practice, reduce the potential disclosure in relation to auditors.

CHAPTER 31

Directors' transactions with banks and money-lending companies

31.01 Chapters 27 and 28 describe the rules which prohibit loans and similar transactions with directors and the general exceptions thereto. In addition to the exceptions described in Chapter 28, the Act allows further exceptions for loans and quasi-loans made on normal commercial terms, and for subsidised home loans. No limit is placed on the amount which may be advanced on normal commercial terms by recognised banks, or by other money-lending companies which are not relevant companies. Recognised banks and other money-lending companies may also advance up to a total amount outstanding of £50,000 per director for housing loans on favourable terms. For other money-lending companies which are relevant companies, there is a combined limit of £50,000 per director for transactions in the ordinary course of business and subsidised home loans taken together; for those which are not relevant companies, the limit on the amount which may be advanced as a favourable housing loan is reduced by the outstanding amount of any loans on normal commercial terms.

31.02 There are also special provisions for the disclosure of transactions with directors which were entered into by recognised banks, but not for those entered into by other money-lending companies to which the normal rules apply.

Definitions

Money-lending company

31.03 "Money-lending company" means a company, the ordinary business of which includes the making of loans or quasi-loans or the giving of guarantees in connection with loans or quasi-loans [s338(2)]. Recognised banks fall within this definition.

Recognised bank

31.04 "Recognised bank" means a company which is recognised as a bank for the purposes of the Banking Act 1979 [s744]. It would therefore *not* include a licensed institution within the meaning of that Act.

Money-lending exception

31.05 A money-lending company is not prohibited by section 330 (see Chapter 27) from:

(1) making a loan or quasi-loan to any person, or

(2) entering into a guarantee in connection with any other loan or quasi-loan.

[s338(1)]

The expression "guarantee" includes an indemnity [s331(2)]. It follows that the exception does not extend to credit transactions or to the provision of security. This overall money-lending exception comprises transactions on normal commercial terms and (in defined cases) housing loans on favourable terms.

31.06 The conditions under which advantage may be taken of this exception and its application to recognised banks and to other money-lending companies are set out in the paragraphs which follow. The memorandum or articles of association of a company may, of course, prohibit transactions which are not prohibited by the Act.

Exception for recognised banks

Loans and quasi-loans on normal commercial terms

31.07 No limit is placed on the amount of loans, quasi-loans and guarantees in respect of loans and quasi-loans which a recognised bank may enter into for a director (or connected person), provided the following conditions are satisfied:

(1) the loan, quasi-loan or guarantee is entered into in the ordinary course of the company's business, and

(2) the amount of the loan or quasi-loan or the amount guaranteed is not greater and the terms thereof are not more favourable to that person than is reasonable to expect the company to have offered to, or in respect of, a person of the same financial standing but not connected with the company.

[s338(1),(3),(4)]

Housing loans on favourable terms

31.08 Additionally, provided it does so in the ordinary course of its business, a recognised bank may make a loan to one of its directors or to a director of its holding company, for the purchase or improvement of his only or main residence, or in substitution of a loan by any person for this purpose. In either case, such loans must ordinarily be made by the recognised bank to its *employees* on terms no less favourable than those on which the transaction for the director is to be made, *and* the "aggregate of the relevant amounts" (broadly all such amounts outstanding but see 28.19 above and 31.09 below) must not exceed £50,000 for the same director [s338(1),(6)]. This exception does *not* extend to guarantees or the provision of security or to quasi-loans and transactions with persons connected with a director, although for a company which is not a relevant company the Act does not prohibit quasi-loans or transactions with persons who are connected with directors. It is thus important that, in appropriate cases, a transaction should take the form of a loan in order to gain exemption.

31.09 In determining the "aggregate of the relevant amounts" for the purpose of the housing loans exception described in the preceding paragraph, there must be taken into account only the amount of the proposed loan and the amount outstanding from any previous loan to that director which was made under that exception [s339(4)]. Thus, in the case of a recognised bank, loans on normal commercial terms, even though used for housing purposes, are not aggregated in determining whether a housing loan on favourable terms is lawful.

Exception for money-lending companies (other than recognised banks)

31.10 For a money-lending company which is not a recognised bank, the operation of the money-lending exception (see para 31.05) which comprises transactions on normal commercial terms and housing loans on favourable terms is set out in the paragraphs which follow.

Loans and quasi-loans on normal commercial terms

31.11 A company is not prohibited from making a loan or quasi-loan or from entering into a guarantee in connection with a loan or quasi-loan, provided it does so on normal commercial terms (see para 31.07 above) [s338(1),(3)]. Transactions with connected persons would thus also be covered by this exception. A relevant company may enter into a transaction only if the "aggregate of the relevant amounts" (see paras 28.19, 31.14 and 31.17) does not exceed £50,000 [s338(4)].

31.12 The exception in respect of quasi-loans and transactions with connected persons is of practical significance only to relevant companies because it is only for such companies that they are restricted.

Housing loans on favourable terms

31.13 A housing loan on favourable terms may be made to a director of the company or of its holding company on the same basis and conditions as set out in para 31.08. No company may make a loan under this exception if the aggregate of the relevant amounts exceeds £50,000 [s338(1),(6)]. Such loans fall within the same basic money-lending exception as those made on normal commercial terms and the interaction of the two on the permitted limits is described in the following paragraph.

31.14 This aggregation process works in the following manner:

(1) If the company is a relevant company, amounts advanced under this exception, when taken *together with* amounts outstanding from previous transactions made under the money-lending exception (that is, loans and quasi-loans on normal commercial terms and housing loans on favourable terms) to the director and connected persons (but see 31.17 below) must not exceed £50,000 per director.

(2) For a company which is *not* a relevant company, the amount of any loans which may be made to a director under this exception is £50,000, *less* any amounts outstanding from that director in respect of earlier loans made under the housing exception as well as loans on normal commercial terms (any amount outstanding from quasi-loans or from connected persons would not be taken into account because they would not have been made by virtue of the money-lending exception).

31.15 It follows that for a money-lending company which is *not* a relevant company to take maximum advantage of the provisions, housing loans on favourable terms should be made before loans on normal commercial terms because, although for such companies there is no limit on loans on normal commercial terms, they would nevertheless have been made by virtue of the money-lending exception and amounts outstanding would reduce the potential amount which may be advanced as a subsidised housing loan on favourable terms.

31.16 The Secretary of State has the power to increase the above limits [s345(1)].

Director's control of a company

31.17 For the purpose only of the above calculation of the aggregate of the relevant amounts, a company which a director does *not* "control" (see

27.19) is regarded as *not* being connected with that director [s338(5)]. It appears that the intention of this provision is for there to be no limit placed on the amount which may be advanced on normal commercial terms by money-lending companies to a company which a director does not control and, furthermore, that outstanding loans and quasi-loans to the company are not to be taken into account in determining whether other transactions are lawful.

Disclosure in accounts

31.18 Except in the case of a company which is, or is the holding company of, a recognised bank, the normal accounts disclosure requirements apply (see Chapter 29).

31.19 A reporting company which is, or is the holding company of, a recognised bank is exempt from the disclosure requirements of Sch 6 paras 1 and 2 in relation to loans, quasi-loans, credit transactions and "indirect arrangements" for directors of the reporting company or of its holding company and their connected persons, to which the *recognised bank is a party* [s232(5), Sch 6 para 4]. The normal rules apply to transactions or arrangements in which a director has a material interest, as well as to any transactions to which the recognised bank is not a party.

31.20 Details of individual transactions are not required but, instead, aggregate amounts outstanding must be given. The notes to the individual accounts or, where the company is required to prepare group accounts, to the group accounts must contain a statement of the aggregate amounts outstanding at the end of the financial year and the number of persons for whom they were made, for each of the following types of transaction:

(1) loans,

(2) quasi-loans, and

(3) credit transactions,

in each case including guarantees, security provided and "indirect arrangements" as set out in section 330, made by the company if it is a recognised bank and by any subsidiary which is a recognised bank, for directors of the company preparing the accounts and their connected persons. Disclosure is *not* required in relation to persons who are not directors of the reporting company but who are directors of the reporting company's holding company [s234(1),(2),(3), Sch 6 paras 18,19]. It follows that where a recognised bank enters into transactions with persons who are directors only of its holding company, they are not disclosable in the accounts of that recognised bank or of any intermediate holding company of which those persons are also not directors.

31.21 In the application of these provisions to loans and quasi-loans made for a person connected with a director, a company which a director (or shadow director) does not control (see para 27.19) is not regarded as connected with him [Sch 6 para 20].

31.22 Corresponding amounts for the previous financial year are not required to be disclosed.

31.23 The above rules apply in respect of shadow directors as well as directors [s234(2)].

Duty of auditors

31.24 Where any accounts do not comply with the disclosure requirements set out above, the auditors must include in their audit report a statement giving the required particulars so far as they are reasonably able to do so [s237(5)].

Register of transactions

31.25 A company which is, or is the holding company of, a recognised bank is required to maintain a register containing a copy of each transaction, arrangement or agreement of which particulars would, but for their exemption from Sch 6 para 1 and 2 (see 31.19 above), be required to be disclosed in the notes to their accounts, or group accounts, for the current financial year and for each of the preceding ten financial years. This requirement relates to all transactions, arrangements and agreements which subsisted at any time during each financial year in question and not merely to those with an amount outstanding at the end of that year [s343(1),(2)]. Where a transaction, arrangement or agreement is not in writing, the register must contain a written memorandum setting out its terms [s343(3)].

31.26 Particulars of transactions are not required to be entered into the register where they were entered into and settled before 22 December 1980 (the date on which the corresponding provisions of the 1980 Act came into force) as such transactions would not, in any event, have been subject to the disclosure requirements of Sch 6 paras 1 and 2.

Special statement

31.27 Such companies are required also to make available for inspection by their members at the company's AGM and, for a period of at least fifteen days ending with the date of the AGM, a statement containing the particulars which, but for the exemption (see 31.19 above), would have been disclosable in their accounts for the last complete financial year preceding the meeting [s343(4),(5)]. This requirement does not apply to a recognised bank which is a wholly-owned subsidiary of a company incorporated in the UK [s344(2)].

Exemption

31.28 The above requirements (in relation to the inclusion of entries in the register and the disclosure of particulars in the special statement for a particular financial year) do not apply to transactions, arrangements or agreements made or subsisting during the financial year for a director or connected person, where the aggregate of their "values" (see para 28.23) *for that person*, less the amount (if any) by which the value of those transactions, arrangements and agreements has been reduced, did not at any time during that financial year exceed £1,000 [s344(1)].

Example:

The value of transactions subsisting during 1985 for Mr A (a director of X p.l.c.) was £900 and for Mrs A (a connected person) was £500. Particulars of these transactions do not have to be recorded in the register or be disclosed in the special statement for 1985. If the value of transactions for Mr A was £1,500, particulars thereof would have to be recorded and disclosed but the exception for Mrs A's transactions would remain.

Report by the auditors

31.29 The company's auditors are required to examine the annual statement before it is made available to members and to report to the members stating whether, in their opinion, the statement contains the required particulars and, if in their opinion it does not, to include the particulars in their report in so far as they are reasonably able to do so. The report of the auditors must be annexed to the statement before it is made available to members [s343(6),(7)].

CHAPTER 32

Substantial property transactions by directors

32.01 Subject to specified exceptions, where any company (whether a relevant company or not) proposes to enter into an arrangement for the acquisition of substantial non-cash assets from (or their transfer to) a director of the company or of its holding company or a person who is connected with such a director, prior approval of the shareholders is generally required. Substantial non-cash assets are those the value of which is £1,000 or more and which also exceeds the lesser of £50,000 and ten per cent of the company's net assets.

32.02 Prior consultation (including a circular to shareholders) and approval in general meeting is required by The Stock Exchange for "Class 4" transactions with directors by listed companies and similarly for USM companies (see paragraphs 32.19 to 32.22 below).

Approval of transactions

32.03 Subject to the exceptions set out in paragraph 32.12, a "company" may not enter into an "arrangement":

(1) whereby a person who is a director of the company or of its holding company, or is connected with such a director, acquires or is to acquire from the company one or more non-cash assets of the requisite value, or

(2) whereby the company acquires or is to acquire one or more non-cash assets of the requisite value from such a director or connected person,

unless the arrangement is first approved by an ordinary resolution of the company in general meeting and, if the director or connected person is a director of the holding company or a person connected with such a director, by an ordinary resolution of the holding company in general meeting [s320(1)]. By requiring approval only where the arrangement is entered into by a "company" (meaning a British company), it follows that

239

where a proposed transaction is to be entered into by a foreign subsidiary of a British company, the Act does not require approval by the foreign subsidiary or its British parent. There is also a specific exception covering this matter (see para 32.12(4)).

32.04 A non-cash asset is of the requisite value if it has a "value" which is not less that £1,000 and which also exceeds the lesser of £50,000 and 10% of the company's net assets [s320(2)]. The Secretary of State has the power to increase the £1,000 and £50,000 thresholds [s345].

32.05 The amount of the company's net assets is to be determined by reference to the company's individual accounts for its most recent financial year for which accounts have been laid before its members. Where there are no such accounts, the company's net assets are taken to be equal to the amount of its called-up share capital [s320(2)].

32.06 For the purpose of the statutory provisions described in this chapter, a "shadow director" (see para 27.04) is regarded as a director [s320(3)].

32.07 The term "non-cash asset" means any property or interest in property other than cash ("cash" includes foreign currency) [s739(1)]. It is thus very widely drawn and would, for example, cover not only property in the sense of land and buildings but also shares and other securities.

32.08 "Acquisition of non-cash asset" includes (but is not limited to) the creation or extinction of an interest in, or a right over, any property; it also includes the discharge of any person's liability, other than a liability for a liquidated sum [s739(2)]. It follows that the grant of a lease to or a right to occupy premises by a director would be the acquisition by the director of a non-cash asset.

32.09 The term "arrangement" has been used deliberately to make the provisions far reaching and is not necessarily restricted to arrangements which are enforceable in law. It is immaterial for the operation of the provisions whether the law governing the arrangement is that of the UK (or part of it) or some other system of law [s347]. Accordingly, a British company cannot escape the provisions by making an arrangement subject to foreign law.

32.10 Although not explicitly stated, it is considered that the provisions would apply to indirect arrangements which have a common intention from the outset that the company is to acquire a non-cash asset from a director (or vice versa). Thus, the provisions could not be avoided by deliberately routeing the transaction via an intermediary.

32.11 The inclusion in a director's contract of service of a clause enabling the director to acquire a non-cash asset from the company (for example, where a director is granted an option to purchase a company house which he occupies) would not relieve the company from the obligation to seek prior shareholder approval where it would otherwise be required by the Act.

Exceptions

32.12 Approval is not required in the following cases:

(1) By the shareholders of a wholly-owned subsidiary of another body corporate (wherever incorporated) [s321(1)].

(2) If:
   (a) the non-cash asset is to be acquired:
      – by a holding company from any of its wholly-owned subsidsidiaries (or vice versa), or
      – by one wholly-owned subsidiary of a holding company from another wholly-owned subsidiary of that same holding company, or
   (b) the arrangement is entered into by a company which is being wound up unless the winding up is a members' voluntary winding up.
   [s321(2)]

(3) For any arrangement whereby a person is to acquire an asset from a company of which he is a member, if the arrangement is made in his character as a member [s321(3)]. This might, for example, apply to a distribution in kind.

(4) By any body corporate unless it is a company (meaning a company formed and registered under the 1985 Act or the earlier Companies Acts) or a body which has registered under section 680 of the Act [s321(1)].

Effect of contravention

32.13 An arrangement entered into by a company in contravention of the provisions of section 320 (set out earlier) and any transaction entered into in pursuance of the arrangement (whether by the company or any other person) is voidable at the instance of the company unless one or more of the following conditions is satisfied:

(1) restitution of any money or other asset which is the subject matter is not possible, or the company has been indemnified (see below) by any other person for any loss or damage suffered by it, or

(2) any person (not a party to the transaction or arrangement) without actual notice of the contravention has acquired rights bona fide for value which would be affected by its avoidance, or

(3) the arrangement is, within a reasonable period (which is not defined), affirmed by the company in general meeting, and (where required) by the holding company in general meeting.

[s322(2)]

Furthermore, whether or not the arrangement has been avoided, the director and, where applicable, the connected person who was a party to the arrangement, as well as any other directors of the company who authorised it, are liable:

(1) to account to the company for any gain they made directly or indirectly from the arrangement or transaction, and

(2) to indemnify the company for any resulting loss or damage.

This is without prejudice to any liability imposed otherwise than by this provision [s322(3),(4)].

32.14 Where the arrangement was entered into with a person connected with a director, that director will not be liable where he shows that he took all reasonable steps to ensure compliance with the provisions [s322(5)]. Connected persons and other authorising directors will not be liable where they show that they were unaware of the contravention [s322(6)].

32.15 Chapter 29 sets out the requirements for the disclosure of transactions with directors.

General duty of disclosure to company

32.16 A person who is in any way, whether directly or indirectly, interested in a proposed contract, arrangement or agreement with a company of which he is a director, is required to declare the nature of that interest at the meeting of the directors of the company at which the proposal is first considered [s317(1),(2),(4)]. Transactions covered by this requirement would include substantial property transactions for which prior shareholder approval is required.

32.17 A director may give a general notice that he is a member of a specified company or firm, or that a specified person is "connected" with him, and that he is to be regarded as being interested in any contract which may be made with that company, firm or person [s317(3)].

32.18 These provisions apply also to a shadow director except that he must declare his interest by a written notice to the directors, and not at a meeting of the directors [s317(8)].

Stock Exchange regulations

32.19 As well as complying with the statutory provisions set out above, where a listed company, or one of its subsidiaries, proposes to enter into what is described as a "Class 4 transaction" (broadly, those which involve a present or past director, or a present or past substantial shareholder) the Quotations Department of The Stock Exchange and, where appropriate, the Panel on Take-overs and Mergers, must be consulted as soon as possible *prior* to any contract being entered into or take-over offer being made or accepted. The Committee on Quotations of The Stock Exchange will normally require that a circular be sent to shareholders and that the transaction be subject to the consent of the company in general meeting. The Committee may also require that the interested party abstains from voting and that a statement to this effect is included in the circular. There are similar provisions for companies the securities of which are traded on the Unlisted Securities Market.

32.20 There is no materiality threshold stated in "Admission of Securities to Listing", the "Yellow Book" issued by The Stock Exchange, and The Stock Exchange should therefore be consulted in the first instance. In practice, however, it is unlikely that The Stock Exchange would require a Class 4 circular for transactions of a very low amount.

32.21 A Class 4 transaction is defined in Section 6 chapter 1, paragraph 6.1 of the Yellow Book as one which falls within any of the following categories:

(1) An acquisition or disposal of assets by the company or any one of its subsidiaries from or to, or from or to an "associate" (as defined in para 32.22) of, a director or substantial shareholder.

(2) A transaction under which the company or any one of its subsidiaries is to take an interest in a company, any part of the equity share capital of which has been or is to be, acquired, whether by subscription or otherwise, by, or by an associate of, a director.

(3) A transaction, a principal purpose or effect of which is the granting of credit (including the lending of money) by the company or any one of its subsidiaries to, or to an associate of, a director or substantial shareholder, excluding a granting of credit upon normal commercial terms in the ordinary and usual course of business.

(4) A take-over offer by the company or any one of its subsidiaries, any acceptance of which, to its knowledge after making all reasonable enquiries, could result in a significant acquisition from, or from an associate of, a director or substantial shareholder.

[It is possible for the requisite consent of the company in general meeting to be sought after the offer has been made, provided that the offer is expressed as being conditional on such consent being obtained and provided this is permitted under the Rules of the City Code on Take-overs and Mergers.]

(5) The company or any one of its subsidiaries accepting a take-over offer which to its knowledge, after making all reasonable enquiries, would thereby result in a significant disposal to, or to an associate of, a director or substantial shareholder.

32.22 The definition of "associate" for the purpose of Class 4 transactions is similar to the statutory definition of "connected persons". In relation to a director, "associates" comprise:

(1) spouse and children under 18 ("the director's family"),

(2) the trustees (as such) of any trust of which the director or any of the director's family is a beneficiary or discretionary object, and

(3) any company in the equity capital of which the director and the director's family are directly or indirectly interested so as to control thirty per cent or more of the voting power at general meetings or control the composition of a majority of the board of directors (Section 6, chapter 1, paragraph 1.2).

CHAPTER 33

Directors' contracts of employment

33.01 A public or private company is prohibited from granting to a director (or shadow director) a right of employment for a period exceeding five years, where the company is not free to terminate the employment by unconditional notice, without first obtaining the approval of the company in general meeting.

Directors' contracts of employment exceeding five years

33.02 A company may not, without prior approval, enter into any agreement whereby a director's employment with the company (or where he is a director of a holding company, with that holding company or with its subsidiaries), is to continue or may be continued otherwise than at the instance of the company for a period exceeding five years, if the company is not free to terminate the employment by notice, unconditionally [s319(1)]. The foregoing and the matters set out in paragraphs 33.03 to 33.09 apply also to "shadow directors" (see para 27.04) [s319(7)].

33.03 It follows that a company is not prohibited from entering into an agreement for a period exceeding five years if the company has an unconditional right of termination, or if it obtains the requisite approval.

33.04 Approval must be given in general meeting by the company proposing to enter into the contract and, where the person is a director of its holding company, also by that company in general meeting [s319(3)]. It is thus not permissible for a subsidiary to enter into such an agreement with a director of its holding company without approval being given by both the shareholders of the subsidiary (except where it is wholly-owned – see para 33.08) and of the holding company.

33.05 A written memorandum setting out the proposed agreement must be available for inspection by the members at the company's registered office for at least the fifteen days ending with the date of the meeting at which the agreement is to be approved and at the meeting itself [s319(5)].

33.06 "Employment" is defined as including "employment under a contract *for* services" [s319(7)]. It would therefore include a "consultancy" agreement; this interpretation is further supported by the use in the general prohibition of the word "agreement" (instead of "contract of employment") which is intended to prevent the provisions being avoided by a company entering into a service or consultancy contract with a director's own firm.

33.07 Where any additional agreement is entered into more than six months before the expiry of an earlier agreement (which is subject to the restrictions on its termination as outlined above), for the purpose of establishing whether the further agreement is one requiring approval under the provisions outlined above, the unexpired period of the original agreement is added to the period of the later agreement [s319(2)]. This prevents the company from avoiding the provisions by entering into a series of agreements. It should, however, be permissible to keep a five year contract "topped up", without prior shareholder approval, by entering into a subsequent agreement to extend the period of the earlier agreement by the period already expired, provided the unexpired period of that earlier agreement (including any previous extensions) and the proposed extension does not exceed five years.

33.08 Approval by the shareholders is not required in the case of a company which is a wholly-owned subsidiary of any body corporate, wherever incorporated [s319(4)].

33.09 Where an agreement incorporates a term in contravention of this section, the term (but not the whole agreement) is void and the agreement is deemed to contain a term entitling the company to terminate the agreement by giving reasonable notice [s319(6)].

Removal of a director from office

33.10 A company may by ordinary resolution remove a director before the expiration of his period of office (as director), notwithstanding anything in its articles or in any agreement between it and him. Special notice of such a resolution is required [s303(1),(2)].

33.11 Removal from office under section 303 of the Act does not deprive a director of compensation or damages payable to him in respect of the termination of his appointment as director or of any appointment terminating with that as director [s303(5)].

APPENDIX 1

Summary of accounting disclosures required by The Stock Exchange for listed companies

"Admission of Securities to Listing" (the "Yellow Book" issued by The Stock Exchange) contains a number of requirements which relate to the annual reports of listed companies. Some of the matters are also required by law or by SSAP. Companies which have only debt securities or fixed income shares listed are exempt from some of the requirements (Chapter 1). The Yellow Book requirements are summarised below.

All references below are to paragraphs in Section 5, Chapter 2 of the Yellow Book.

A. General

1. The company must issue an annual report and accounts within six months of the end of the financial period to which they relate. If the accounts do not give a true and fair view of the state of affairs and profit and loss of the company or group, more detailed and/or additional information must be provided. If the company has subsidiaries, the accounts must be in consolidated form. The company's own accounts must be published if they contain significant additional information (para 20).

B. Directors' report

1. Explanation, if applicable, of any material differences between actual results and any published forecast (para 21(b)).

2. Statement by the directors of the reasons for any significant departure from applicable standard accounting practices (that is, SSAPs and IASs) (para 21(a)).

247

3. Statement of the unexpired period of any service contract of any director proposed for re-election at the forthcoming AGM, or negative statement if appropriate (para 43(c)).

4. Statement as at the end of the year of the interests of each director in the capital of any member of the group as recorded in the register of directors' interests, together with any options in respect of such capital. Beneficial and non-beneficial interests are to be distinguished. There must also be a note of any changes in the interests or options between the end of the financial year and a date not more than one month prior to the date of the notice of the annual general meeting; if there is no such change, that fact must be disclosed (para 21(h)).

5. In the case of a UK company, a statement must be given, as at a date not more than one month prior to the date of notice of the annual general meeting, showing the names and holdings of shareholders (other than directors) holding 5% or more of any class of shares having full voting rights. Negative statement required if there is no such interest (para 21(i)).

6. In the case of a UK company, particulars of any shareholders' authority existing at the end of the year for the purchase by the company of its own shares. In the case of such purchases made otherwise than through the market or by tender or partial offer to all shareholders, disclose also the names of the sellers of such shares purchased, or proposed to be purchased, by the company during the year. In the case of purchases, or options or contracts to make such purchases, entered into since the end of the year, equivalent information to that required by Schedule 7 Part II of the 1985 Act (see para 9.03(10)) must be given (para 21(p)).

7. In the case of a UK company, a statement as to whether or not, so far as the directors are aware, the close company provisions apply and whether there has been any change in that respect since the end of the financial year (para 21(j)).

8. Particulars in the accounts of a listed subsidiary of the participation by a parent company in any vendor consideration placing made during the year (para 22).

9. Explanation of any business, other than routine business at an AGM, to be considered by shareholders at or on the same day as the annual general meeting (para 32)

C. Profit and loss account

1. Geographical analysis by continent of turnover of company or group. If 50% or more of overseas operations relates to one continent, a

further analysis (for example, by country within that continent) is required. If the contribution, from a specific area, to profit or loss is "abnormal" in nature, an appropriate statement should be made. "Abnormal" is defined as substantially out of line with the normal ratio of profit to turnover (para 21(c)).

2. Details of any arrangement under which a director has waived or agreed to waive any emoluments (including future emoluments) (para 21(n)).

3. Details of any arrangement under which a shareholder has waived or agreed to waive any dividends (para 21(o)).

D. Balance sheet

1. For (a) bank loans and overdrafts and (b) other borrowings state the aggregate amounts repayable:
   (1) in one year or less or on demand,
   (2) between one and two years,
   (3) between two and five years, and
   (4) in five years or more.
   (para 21(f))

E. Notes to the accounts

1. Particulars of any contract of significance subsisting during or at the end of the financial year in which a director is or was materially interested. If there has been no such contract, a statement of this fact (para 21(k)).

2. Particulars of any contract of significance between the company or one of its subsidiaries and a corporate substantial shareholder (para 21(l)).

A "contract of significance" is one which represents in amount or value a sum equal to 1% or more of:
(a) in the case of a capital transaction or a transaction of which the principal purpose is the granting of credit, the net assets of the company, or
(b) in other cases, the total purchases, sales, payments or receipts, as the case may be, of the company.

"Corporate substantial shareholder" means any body corporate entitled to exercise or control the exercise of 30% or more of the voting power at general meetings of the company or one which is in a position to control the composition of a majority of the board of directors of the company.

3. Particulars of any contract for the provision of services to the company or any of its subsidiaries by a corporate substantial shareholder. Exceptionally, such a contract need not be disclosed if the principal business of the shareholder is the provision of such services and it is not a contract of significance (para 21(m)).

4. Statement of the amount of interest capitalised during the year, with an indication of the amount and treatment of any related tax relief (para 21(g)).

5. In respect of each company (not being a subsidiary) in which the group interest in its equity capital is 20% or more:
   (a) principal country of operation,
   (b) particulars of issued capital and debt securities, and
   (c) the percentage of each class of debt securities attributable to the company's interest (direct or indirect).
   (para 21(e))

6. Principal country of operation in which each important subsidiary operates (para 21(d)).

Examples of the accounting treatment of the purchase and redemption of own shares

Example 1 – Redemption or purchase at a premium, wholly out of profits

Where a company redeems or purchases shares wholly out of profits, an amount equal to the nominal value of the shares being redeemed or purchased must be transferred to the capital redemption reserve.

	£
Nominal value of shares redeemed/purchased	1,000
Redemption/purchase price	1,100
Distributable profits	3,000

The accounting entries upon redemption will be:

	£	£
(a) DR Share capital	1,000	
DR Distributable reserves	100	
CR Cash		1,100
(b) DR Distributable reserves	1,000	
CR Capital redemption reserve		1,000

The balance sheet before and after the redemption or purchase may be summarised as follows:

Appendix 2   *Examples of the accounting for purchase of own shares*

Before	£	*After*	£
Share capital	5,000	Share capital	4,000
		Capital redemption reserve	1,000
			5,000
Distributable reserves	3,000	Distributable reserves	1,900
Other reserves	1,000	Other reserves	1,000
	9,000		7,900
Net assets	9,000	Net assets	7,900

Example 2 – Redemption or purchase at a discount out of profits and the proceeds of a fresh issue

Where the purchase or redemption is made wholly out of the proceeds of a fresh issue of shares, or partly out of the proceeds of a fresh issue and partly out of distributable profits, and the aggregate amount of the proceeds of the fresh issue is less than the aggregate nominal value of the shares purchased or redeemed, the difference must be transferred to the capital redemption reserve.

	£
Nominal value of shares redeemed/purchased	1,000
Redemption/purchase price (that is, at a discount)	900
Proceeds of a fresh issue made at par	650
Distributable profits	250
	900

The accounting entries will be

	£	£
(a) DR Share capital	1,000	
CR Cash		900
CR Capital redemption reserve		100
(b) DR Cash	650	
CR Share capital		650
(c) DR Distributable reserves	250	
CR Capital redemption reserve		250

252

The total amount credited to the capital redemption reserve (£350) is the difference between the nominal value of the shares redeemed/purchased (£1,000) and the proceeds of the new issue (£650).

The balance sheet before and after the redemption or purchase may be summarised as follows:

Before	£	*After*	£
Share capital	5,000	Share capital	4,650
		Capital redemption reserve	350
			5,000
Distributable reserves	3,000	Distributable reserves	2,750
Other reserves	1,000	Other reserves	1,000
	9,000		8,750
Net assets	9,000	Net assets	8,750

Example 3 – Redemption/purchase of shares by a private company at a discount and partly out of capital

Where the aggregate of the proceeds of the fresh issue and the permissible capital payment is less than the aggregate nominal value of the shares being redeemed/purchased, the amount of the difference must be transferred to capital redemption reserve.

	£
Nominal value of shares redeemed/purchased	1,000
Redemption/purchase price	900

Redemption/purchase price made up as follows:	£
Distributable profits	200
Proceeds of a fresh issue made at par	600
Permissible capital payment	100
	900

Appendix 2 *Examples of the accounting for purchase of own shares*

The accounting entries will be:

		£	£
(a)	DR Share capital	1,000	
	CR Cash		900
	CR Capital redemption reserve		100
		1,000	1,000
(b)	DR Cash	600	
	CR Share capital		600
(c)	DR Distributable reserves	200	
	CR Capital redemption reserve		200

The total transfer to capital redemption reserve (£300) is the difference between the nominal value of the shares redeemed/purchased (£1,000) and the sum of the permissible capital payment (£100) and the proceeds of the fresh issue (£600).

Share capital is reduced by £400 and the transfer to the capital redemption reserve of only £300 has resulted in a payment out of capital of £100.

The balance sheet before and after the redemption or purchase may be summarised as follows:

Before	£	*After*	£
Share capital	5,000	Share capital	4,600
		Capital redemption reserve	300
			4,900
Distributable reserves	200	Distributable reserves	–
Other reserves	1,000	Other reserves	1,000
	6,200		5,900
Net assets	6,200	Net assets	5,900

254

Example 4 – Redemption/purchase of shares by a private company at a premium and partly out of capital

Where the aggregate of the proceeds of the fresh issue and the permissible capital payment exceeds the nominal value of the shares being redeemed or purchased, the amount of any capital redemption reserve, share premium account, fully paid share capital or any unrealised reserves may be reduced by the amount of the excess.

	£
Nominal value of shares redeemed/purchased (originally issued at par)	1,000
Redemption/purchase price	1,100

Redemption/purchase price made up as follows:	£
Distributable profits	50
Proceeds of a fresh issue made at par	850
Permissible capital payment	200
	1,100

The current balance on the company's share premium account is £400.

The accounting entries will be:

	£	£
(a) DR Cash	850	
CR Share capital		850
(b) DR Share capital	1,000	
DR Distributable profits	50	
DR Share premium	50	
CR Cash		1,100
	1,100	1,100

The share capital has been reduced by £150 and the share premium by £50, resulting in a payment out of capital of £200. If the company had no share premium account, the £50 by which the share premium was reduced could have been charged to the capital redemption reserve (if any), or even to fully paid share capital, presumably for presentation purposes being shown as a deduction from share capital.

Appendix 2 *Examples of the accounting for purchase of own shares*

The balance sheet before and after the redemption or purchase may be summarised as follows:

Before	£	*After*	£
Share capital	5,000	Share capital	4,850
Share premium	400	Share premium	350
	5,400		5,200
Distributable reserves	50	Distributable reserves	–
	5,450		5,200
Net assets	5,450	Net assets	5,200

APPENDIX 3

Prescribed formats for company accounts

Balance sheet – format 1

A. **Called up share capital not paid**

B. **Fixed assets**
I **Intangible assets**
  1. Development costs
  2. Concessions, patents, licences, trade marks and similar rights and assets
  3. Goodwill
  4. Payments on account
II **Tangible assets**
  1. Land and buildings
  2. Plant and machinery
  3. Fixtures, fittings, tools and equipment
  4. Payments on account and assets in course of construction
III **Investments**
  1. Shares in group companies
  2. Loans to group companies
  3. Shares in related companies
  4. Loans to related companies
  5. Other investments other than loans
  6. Other loans
  7. Own shares

C. **Current assets**
I **Stocks**
  1. Raw materials and consumables
  2. Work in progress
  3. Finished goods and goods for resale
  4. Payments on account
II **Debtors**
  1. Trade debtors

  2. Amounts owed by group companies
  3. Amounts owed by related companies
  4. Other debtors
  5. Called up share capital not paid
  6. Prepayments and accrued income
III **Investments**
  1. Shares in group companies
  2. Own shares
  3. Other investments
IV **Cash at bank and in hand**

D. **Prepayments and accrued income**

E. **Creditors: amounts falling due within one year**
  1. Debenture loans
  2. Bank loans and overdrafts
  3. Payments received on account
  4. Trade creditors
  5. Bills of exchange payable
  6. Amounts owed to group companies
  7. Amounts owed to related companies
  8. Other creditors including taxation and social security
  9. Accruals and deferred income

F. **Net current assets (liabilities)**

G. **Total assets less current liabilities**

H. **Creditors: amounts falling due after more than one year**
  1. Debenture loans
  2. Bank loans and overdrafts
  3. Payments received on account
  4. Trade creditors
  5. Bills of exchange payable
  6. Amounts owed to group companies
  7. Amounts owed to related companies
  8. Other creditors including taxation and social security
  9. Accruals and deferred income

I. **Provisions for liabilities and charges**
  1. Pensions and similar obligations
  2. Taxation, including deferred taxation
  3. Other provisions

J. **Accruals and deferred income**

K. **Capital and reserves**
I **Called up share capital**
II **Share premium account**
III **Revaluation reserve**
IV **Other reserves**
   1. Capital redemption reserve
   2. Reserve for own shares
   3. Reserves provided for by the articles of association
   4. Other reserves
V **Profit and loss account**

Profit and loss account – formats 1 and 2

Format 1

1. Turnover
2. Cost of sales
3. Gross profit or loss
4. Distribution costs
5. Administrative expenses
6. Other operating income
7. Income from shares in group companies
8. Income from shares in related companies
9. Income from other fixed asset investments
10. Other interest receivable and similar income
11. Amounts written off investments
12. Interest payable and similar charges
13. Tax on profit or loss on ordinary activities
14. Profit or loss on ordinary activities after taxation
15. Extraordinary income
16. Extraordinary charges
17. Extraordinary profit or loss
18. Tax on extraordinary profit or loss
19. Other taxes not shown under the above items
20. Profit or loss for the financial year

Format 2

---

1. Turnover
2. Change in stocks of finished goods and in work in progress
3. Own work capitalised
4. Other operating income
5. *(a)* Raw materials and consumables
   (b) Other external charges
6. Staff costs:
   (a) wages and salaries
   (b) social security costs
   (c) other pension costs
7. *(a)* Depreciation and other amounts written off tangible and intangible fixed assets
   (b) Exceptional amounts written off current assets
8. Other operating charges
9. Income from shares in group companies
10. Income from shares in related companies
11. Income from other fixed asset investments
12. Other interest receivable and similar income
13. Amounts written off investments
14. Interest payable and similar charges
15. Tax on profit or loss on ordinary activities
16. Profit or loss on ordinary activities after taxation
17. Extraordinary income
18. Extraordinary charges
19. Extraordinary profit or loss
20. Tax on extraordinary profit or loss
21. Other taxes not shown under the above items
22. Profit or loss for the financial year

Index

Index

Arrears of fixed cumulative
dividends 6.19

Articles of association
restrictions on directors'
transactions 28.05,31.06

Associate, meaning of for stock
exchange purposes 32.22

Associated companies 11.05-11.09
(see also "Related companies")

Auditors
appointment of 15.01-15.03,
15.10,15.11
company meetings,
attendance at 15.06,15.07,
15.27-15.31
duty to disclose directors' and
higher paid employees'
remuneration 7.48
duty to disclose directors'
transactions 15.45,29.40,31.24
duty to disclose officers'
transactions 30.08
false statements to 15.35
officers, as 15.17,30.10,30.11
powers of 15.32-15.34
qualification of 15.13-15.21
removal of 15.08-15.12
remuneration of 6.23(7),15.04,15.05
resignation of 15.22-15.31
safeguarding position of 15.10-15.12

Auditors' report
on accounts 15.36-15.49
on accounts of special category
companies 15.46-15.49
on directors' transactions
with recognised banks 31.29
on financial assistance for acquisition
of own shares 23.28,23.29
on inconsistency of directors' reports
with accounts 15.41
on modified accounts 12.19,12.21,
12.22,15.36
on purchase of own shares 24.46,
24.51,24.53,24.55,24.56
on reregistration of private company
as public 21.07,21.10-21.16
on shares issued by a public
company for a non-cash
consideration 22.01-22.15

Balance sheet (see also "Group
accounts")
approval by the
directors 3.02-3.05,12.32
formats prescribed for 4.06-4.11
modification for small companies
and groups 12.17,12.18
preparation, requirement for
2.12,2.18
supplementary information
charges on assets 6.20
commitments 6.20,6.21
contingent liabilities 6.20
debentures 6.06
fixed assets 6.07
foreign currency translation
6.40,12.18
indebtedness 6.15-6.19
investments 6.08-6.10
pension commitments 6.20
reserves and provisions 6.11-6.14
share capital 6.05
special category
accounts, in 13.05-13.06
taxation 6.14
true and fair view 2.15,2.17,2.29,
5.05-5.07,13.04,13.08

Banking companies (see also
"Money-lending company",
"Recognised bank", "Special
category companies")
recognised bank,
meaning of 13.02,31.04
special provisions for transactions
with directors 31.01-31.29

Bank loans and overdrafts 6.23

Base stock 5.42

Benefits in kind
disclosure of 7.11,7.15

Body corporate, meaning of 12.03

Body corporate associated with
a director, meaning of 27.18-27.25

Bonus shares 22.02,24.69

Business expenditure
exception to prohibition of loans and
similar transactions 28.09-28.13

Business names
approval of 25.26-25.28,25.35,25.37
control of 25.23-25.28,25.35-25.38
disclosure of 25.29-25.34

Index

266

Index